Body and Soul

Body and Soul

The Transcendence of Materialism

Kelly Nicholson

WestviewPress

A Division of HarperCollins*Publishers*

For Maria

Copyright © 1997 by Westview Press, A Division of HarperCollins Publishers, Inc.

Published in 1997 in the United States of America by Westview Press, 5500 Central Avenue, Boulder, Colorado 80301-2877, and in the United Kingdom by Westview Press, 12 Hid's Copse Road, Cumnor Hill, Oxford OX2 9JJ

Library of Congress Cataloging-in-Publication Data
Nicholson, Kelly.
   Body and soul : the transcendence of materialism / Kelly
Nicholson.
      p.   cm.
   Includes bibliographical references and index.
   ISBN 0-8133-3256-7 — ISBN 0-8133-3257-5 (pbk.)
   1. Materialism—Controversial literature.   2. Philosophy of mind.
3. Consciousness.   4. Ethics.   5. Religion—Philosophy.
6. Philosophical anthropology.   I. Title.
B825.N53   1997
146´.3—dc21   96-37524
                                                                          CIP

The paper used in this publication meets the requirements of the American National Standard for Permanence of Paper for Printed Library Materials Z39.48-1984.

10   9   8   7   6   5   4   3   2   1

Contents

Introduction

There are certain questions that lie at the very heart of our existence. Who are we, and what is this life in which we find ourselves engaged? Is reality just what we find here before our eyes, or is it something more? What does it mean to say that one course of action is truly better than some other? And where are we headed, when all is said and done?

These are some of the basic questions of philosophy. They are also thought to be questions very deep and difficult. Have they any resolution? Certainly many thinkers have believed that they do, for many books that purport to answer them have been written. Yet throughout the history of philosophy those writers have arrived at many different and contradictory answers, and the present age shows no indication that agreement is any nearer. We seem to be as divided over these issues as ever before.

Consider, as one example, our attitude toward ourselves. At times we seem to think of human beings as being material creatures. In this frame of mind, we think of ourselves as being organisms, as being the blood kin of other creatures that have issued, once upon a time, from the sediment; we are things, we imagine, that are composed of cells and molecules, forged by processes of nature, and the result, for all we know, of sheer cosmic happenstance. We imagine likewise that we can be studied and comprehended as integral parts of a universe whose basic nature is material. We tend, in this vein, to equate reality with materiality: What is real, what is fact, is what can be absorbed by the outward senses.

It is thought by many that in this day and age "science" leaves no room for belief in a reality of any other kind. To think that there is something real, yet undetectable by the senses, they suppose, is fanciful, unrealistic, a compromise of intellectual integrity. The good and hard-minded attitude, by contrast, is one that sees reality as material and sees human beings and their enterprises as being no more than fleeting cosmic accident. This attitude receives its classical expression in an essay written some years ago by Bertrand Russell. A person with that attitude, according to Russell, thinks he is the product

> of causes which had no prevision of the end they were achieving; that his origin, his growth, his hopes and fears, his loves and his beliefs, are but the outcome of accidental collocations of atoms; that no fire, no heroism, no intensity of thought and feeling, can preserve an individual life beyond the grave; that all the labors of the ages, all the devotion, all the inspiration, all the noonday brightness of human genius, are destined to extinction in the vast death of the solar

system, and that the whole temple of man's achievement must inevitably be buried beneath the debris of a universe in ruins—all these things, if not quite beyond dispute, are yet so nearly certain that no philosophy which rejects them can hope to stand.[1]

Only, writes Russell, within this logical scaffolding, on the firm foundation of this unyielding despair, can our philosophical habitation now be built.

But again, and down through the ages, there is expressed another view of life quite different from this one. It is a view from which outward and material reality is but one aspect of a reality greater and more profound. From ancient times, we find in various places a voice giving cry to it. There is the poet who tells us:

> Though inland far we be,
> Our souls have sight of that immortal sea
> Which brought us hither.[2]

There is the seeker of mystic union who asks: "What do you seek here, since this world is not your resting place? Your true home is in Heaven; therefore remember that all the things of this world are transitory. All things are passing, and yourself with them. See that you do not cling to them, lest you become entangled with them."[3]

Or we can cite the verdict of the classical Indian *Upanishads,* which is that "above the senses is the mind. Above the mind is the intellect. Above the intellect is the ego. Above the ego is the unmanifested seed, the Primal cause. And verily beyond the unmanifested seed is the Self, the unconditioned, knowing whom one attains to freedom and achieves immortality."[4]

Or again, the Spanish scholar Miguel de Unamuno, who insists:

> The feeling of the vanity of the passing world kindles love in us, the only thing that triumphs over the vain and the transitory, the only thing that fills life and eternalizes it. . . . And love, above all when it struggles against destiny, overwhelms us with the feeling of the vanity of this world of appearances and gives us a glimpse of another world, in which destiny is overcome and liberty is law.[5]

The world's literature abounds in such claims. In literature we find expressed, in varying ways and from different cultural vantage points, the idea that we are more than what the materialist view would make of us. We hear it said that reality is more than what our ordinary senses may disclose. Contained within our experience, thinks Wordsworth, are intimations of eternity. Our real nature, say the texts of ancient India, has in it depths unfathomed by our present experience, and once discerning this, we can be liberated from the paltry existence that is now ours. All these sources give voice, I believe, to certain impulses present within a great many others of us as well.

Our thought about ourselves and the world in which we live is subject to division along several lines. This division, I believe, can be characterized as a single line that cuts, as it were, between worlds: Are persons bodies, or are they something more? Do value judgments refer merely to facts about this world, or do they extend in some way above it? Are seeming intimations of higher reality explainable in terms of natural events, or do they reveal something that lies beyond? In each case, we seem to be offered a choice between two basically different accounts of reality, one that leaves us within the material world, and one that takes us outside of it.

This division is often imagined to be one between philosophical camps and thus also between persons. It is indeed such a division, and yet, too, in many cases it is a division within individuals themselves. For it may well happen that a man may have within himself tendencies in each direction. Consider, for example, the intense concern that he may have for his outward appearance, and the effort he expends in order to maintain or increase his material standard of living and to secure his social status among competitors with the same aspirations. And yet consider again how the same man may, in a moment of solitude and desperation, turn himself from this world and throw himself to his knees to seek guidance. Think of how he may "visit" a departed loved one in a private moment and unburden himself, in full seriousness, of what is in his heart. The one whom he addresses is not physically present, yet somehow, he feels, this one is present in some other way, even if he cannot describe it. To this extent, it seems, such a man is not "deep down" a thoroughgoing materialist after all.

This nonmaterialistic tendency is reflected in many of the things that we say in ordinary conversation and in the course of daily life. We may, for example, hear a man criticized for being too "materialistic," as if to suggest that there is more to life, more to what is real, than the objects of his pursuit. We hear endlessly, from people who have achieved great material wealth, that despite their success there is "something" amiss that cannot be put right by further material acquisitions of any kind. A good many of us speak of values, on some occasions, as if they were somehow beyond the usual facts of human nature and society. We feel obliged to do things at certain times and feel as if this obligation transcends in its importance any fact about civil law or society's expectations. At times we entertain the prospect of a life after death, which suggests that we do not always take ourselves to be what the flesh would make of us.

What has philosophy in recent years had to say about this great divide? Its going trend, in some quarters, is materialism. That is to say, philosophy these days often explains, or hopes to explain, every aspect of human experience in terms of the world that is apprehended by the senses. It acknowledges, of course, the psychological tendency of people to speak and act in the ways described above and to entertain various notions of some reality outside the natural bounds. Yet philosophy aims to reduce the world to what can be seen and tested; in so doing, it aims to reduce all of human experience and all of reality to facts about the material world. This act of reduction subordinates any seeming "higher," or transcendent, reality to illusion, to a mere by-product of the forces that give rise to its appearance. The inquiry into things otherworldly, beyond the range of the senses, it deems false and undeserving of serious intellectual concern.

In the twentieth century, in fact, there has developed a tendency to regard such notions as being outright nonsense. The materialistic view, it is often supposed, is the stronger, the more responsible and realistic approach. In recent philosophy of mind, for example, there is little talk of souls. Moral philosophers seldom speak of values in any transworldly fashion. Religious and mystical experience is to many little more than a psychological curiosity. All reality, by this general line of reckoning, is to be found ultimately within the realm of nature. Any notion of a higher and "metaphysical" element in such inquiry is dismissed as being unrealistic and outmoded.

Granted, then, that each of these broad outlooks, the materialistic and the nonmaterialistic, exists as a psychological fact. The question arises whether either basic viewpoint has within itself any theoretical advantage over the other. What view of reality ought we to have? This book is concerned, in large part, with that alleged other reality—with that truth that is seemingly outside of the world investigated by the sciences, a truth that is immaterial, yet real and vital just the same. In this book I will argue that the materialistic conception of reality is unsatisfactory as a rational account of human experience. For I believe that reflection upon certain assumptions of ordinary life, such as rationality, freedom, and obligation, involves us implicitly in supernaturalism—in an outlook that goes, in its range, outside the bounds of the world of sight and sound that presently surrounds us. Certain assumptions of common sense, I believe, require us, if we wish to hold on to them, to suppose that there is more to us and to reality as a whole than materialism will admit. The conception of reality I thus propose is one that involves the immaterial; one that embraces truths and realities that transcend the material world and that cannot, in principle, be explained in terms of it. I believe that reflection upon a number of ordinary beliefs and attitudes—those shared by laborer, scholar, and theologian alike—sends us head over heels into metaphysics and into supernaturalism, whether we like it or not.

In this book I will not attempt anything so ambitious as a proof of the accuracy of the otherworldly view of life. A view of this kind, as I see it, is not so much the result of argument as the starting point from which an experience of the world begins. The basic differences of philosophers, it appears to me, owe to differences very deep within their personal makeup.[6] If they have different outlooks, perhaps that is because they begin their enterprise as fundamentally different kinds of persons. Philosophy, I believe, would do well to acknowledge this fact as a basic starting point of its own activity. The materialist and the nonmaterialist have existed side by side throughout the ages and probably will do so for as long as philosophy is practiced. The reason for this is that each begins his inquiry with his own vantage point and his own base-level notion of what is reasonable. Often the assumptions of each do not coincide. Every age has its believers and its skeptics, its otherworldly types and its types tied firmly to the earth. Their difference is not to be found, I think, in the basic aptitude of either or in the logical force with which each makes his case. Very likely, I suspect, it resides further down in the psychic forces shaping each personality.

My aim, accordingly, is not to prove the rightness of my own outlook, but to show that the basic tenets that compose it do not, of themselves, run afoul of rationality—that they do not violate established principles of logic or good sense or contradict the standing evidence of the material sciences. It may well be, I suspect, that there exists no such thing as a conclusive argument for such things as the freedom of the will or the immateriality of the human soul. And none, I suspect, to the contrary, either. Perhaps I cannot be sure on theoretical grounds and in my present condition that there exists another reality behind material appearances. But suppose that I am one of those persons who experience life with some sense of this greater reality. Do I commit some logical error, am I guilty of some excess of philosophical generosity, if I abide by a sense of this kind? I wish to argue, to the contrary, that this feeling can be trusted—that we may take it as a sign of the truth without any compromise of realism or rationality. I believe, in fact, that a number of our common-sense assumptions, if we take them seriously, involve us in a conception of reality that runs in this direction. This extended world picture, I contend, is also the one that best accords with our own deepest thoughts about who we are, how we ought to behave, and what ultimate purpose, if any, our lives may have in the greater scheme of things. I believe that certain assumptions about ourselves—that we are in some basic sense free, that we are rational, goal-directed, and morally conscious creatures—require from us, if we are to be consistent, a worldview that transcends this present realm. To this end, and following Kant's example,[7] I invoke in several places the notion of a postulate, that is, a claim that is not proved, but that ought nonetheless to be accepted if we are to make sense of our practical outlook upon the world.

There are basically three areas of inquiry addressed in this book—first, that of consciousness itself and the various accounts of its nature; second, moral truths and what they imply in the way of claims about reality; and third, religious experience and its interpretation. In the first chapter I run through several of the more prominent historical answers to the problem of consciousness, taking note of both materialistic and nonmaterialistic approaches. I argue in Chapter 2 that the nonmaterialistic view is not only the more intuitively satisfying but that it is also consistent with the data of material science. I argue further that this view, in some version, is actually presupposed by our assumption that we are rational beings in the first place.

In Chapters 3 and 4 I discuss a few historical efforts to deal with the problem of moral value. I contend that the efforts to explain values along materialistic lines—to reduce value judgments, that is, to judgments about events within nature—are unsatisfactory, and that value judgments, when taken in full seriousness, involve us once more in truths that transcend the natural world. I argue that in principle no amount of truth about this world can ever provide us with grounds for holding that one action or course of events is objectively better than another. I maintain also that our assumption that we are moral creatures requires us to suppose as well that we are capable of making choices that transcend the forces of material nature—that we are thus free, in some basic sense, to choose our actions in ways undetermined by the processes of the material world.

In Chapter 5, I discuss the problem of religion, taking some note of its historical relation to the scientific outlook and of attempts to explain religion as a by-product of the forces of nature. I then argue, in Chapter 6, against this reductionist view, that religious experience can in principle be understood, without any sacrifice of intellect or rationality, as genuine transworld revelation. I maintain that purported glimpses of a higher world are essentially trustworthy as an indication of both truth and personal destiny. In the seventh and final chapter, I return to a few of the preceding discussions and describe briefly the view of life that I believe is encouraged by them. The basic view of life that emerges from these conclusions is that of a spiritual enterprise extending beyond the confines of the life that we have at present. Herein I do not spend a great deal of time dealing explicitly with the particular conditions of a future life—something that will have to wait for another time. But I contend that the conclusions reached in this book, if accepted, do incline us toward belief in an existence hereafter.

I should add also that the work of philosophers in recent years has expanded the vocabulary of some of these issues, so that new terms have come into use and traditional ones are qualified by the use of special adjectives. Thus there is in some quarters a distinction between, for example, "hard" and "soft" materialism with respect to the nature of consciousness.[8] Some philosophers distinguish likewise between *constitutive* and *eliminative* versions of the theory,[9] the one holding that all reality is composed of whatever elements (such as atoms) are thought basic, and the other holding furthermore that all alleged realities except for these elements (such as common-sense physical objects) are but false appearances. Others forego the use of the term *materialism* and speak instead of *physicalism*,[10] which holds that all events can be described ideally in the language of the science of physics. I intend to avoid such jargon as much as possible and to deal with the issues in a much broader manner than does most of the literature in which such distinctions occur. A sufficient definition of 'materialism', for my purposes, is that offered by Robert Coburn,[11] which is that "everything that ever exists—or at least every concrete object—is composed solely of matter and every event or process that ever takes place consists solely of interactions among material things." As Coburn acknowledges, this definition remains unclear pending an account of just exactly what is involved in the notion of matter and material things.[12] But the definition seems to identify well enough the theory in question.

For my part, again, I will spend little time on distinctions of the kind just noted, for it seems to me that most of these variants come to the same thing in terms of their consequences for life and human destiny. If, for example, the events of consciousness are in any way dependent, at bottom, upon the events of the central nervous system, I doubt that it matters (except as an item of purely theoretical interest) which version of the theory is true. What I wish to encourage, by the same token, is a general account of reality that goes beyond this world as its principal focus of what is real. To this end I repudiate what some philosophers call "the primacy of the physical" as a basic point of view, however its details may be spelled out. I wish to propose instead a general outlook of mind and value that views the present world as no more than a stage, or level, of reality and the present life as but an inkling of something greater yet to come.

Chapter One

The Problem of Conscious Experience

Does my brain, which weighs only a few pounds and fits into a box about four by six inches, contain pictures or visual images as large as my perception of the Grand Canyon?
—Dale Jacquette, *Philosophy of Mind*

What sort of thing is a human being? Our situation in regard to this question is a bit odd, and more than one writer has noticed its irony. For, it seems, as our knowledge of the world around us continues endlessly to increase, we seem to remain as perplexed as ever about our own basic nature. What exactly are we? Our thought on this subject seems curiously divided.

We think of ourselves, at times, as being material creatures. Thus the mention of the word 'human' may call to mind a vague picture of a certain kind of physical object. I refer to a man by pointing out (what else?) his body. I say that the object in the mirror is myself, and I imagine that what happens to this object happens to me. We often describe one another by making reference to our physical attributes.

This is part of the story. But consider, again, the tendency, just as powerful, that we have in a quite different direction. Think of the resentment that a young woman feels when she is treated "merely as a body," for example, by a thoughtless suitor. Think also of the admiration that we have for "inner beauty" that somehow goes deeper than physical appearance. We speak often, and in a related vein, of the special *worth* of human beings. It is a worth that cannot be derived from, say, their mere usefulness to the rest of us or the sum total of the material components in their bodies. We find it hard, if not impossible, to capture this element of value in terms of any material facts or characteristics. At times we may entertain the notion of leaving the body at life's end.

This duality lies at the very core of our thought and speech. I refer, once again, to this collection of flesh and bone as being myself. But just as readily I refer to it as being my body,[1] suggesting (if one reflects for a moment on the nature of the locution) that the object is not exactly what I am, but is instead a thing that I some way control or possess. In speaking of the deceased, we say at times that such a person is dead and buried. In so doing we suggest that he is just that parcel of flesh, or what remains of it, that has been "laid to rest." Yet in other moments, we may fancy that he has in some way survived and perhaps is able somehow to observe the events in the world here "below." If we believe that such a thing happens, or even that it might happen, we apparently do not believe that a person is the same thing as that assemblage of flesh and bone that commonly identifies him.

Reflection upon human nature discloses one feature that is especially important and that lies at the heart of this general mystery. It is that of consciousness. In human beings the world contains a reality that is somehow aware of itself.

How the Problem Arises

As Keith Campbell observes, it is natural for human beings to feel that they are basically different from all else that exists in the material world. For men, he says, "can see and hear, ponder and resolve, suffer and enjoy"; they can "make plans, solve problems, and hunger and thirst after righteousness." They "can love, they can be amused, they can make music, they can worship. They can be heroic or cruel or ambitious." In all of this, says Campbell, they are utterly different from "the rocks and puddles, furniture and utensils, and even plants and animals" that make up our environment. So, he says, "has arisen the long Western tradition of contrasting man with the natural material realm. For Plato man comes into it as a prisoner, for Christians he journeys through it as a wayfarer, for contemporary Existentialists he finds himself thrown amid alien things."[2]

Consciousness, upon inward observation, does not *feel* like anything material. When we look inside, so to speak, and attend to the content of our experience, we seem to find a reality that is quite different from the world of rocks and trees and earth and puddles. This inner world, as it appears to us, is not a material world. It does not seem to be composed of objects or of such constituent elements as molecules or electrons. At least we would not describe it in terms of this kind. It is composed instead of such things as thoughts, feelings, sights, sounds, and choices. These events of consciousness, moreover, seem in some profound way to belong to someone, to that singular individual who is the subject of all these particular experiences that make up this conscious history.

Such events seem likewise to require in some cases a special mode of language if one is to do them justice. Consider, for one, the experience of being in love. How does one describe it? Artists of every sort have ventured to heights of eloquence in the effort. In so doing they give us expressions of word, shape, and melody that seem rather far removed from the world that we learn about through the physical sciences. Contrast, say, this expression of 'warmth', 'elation', 'magic', and 'rapture' with that of chemistry.

But experiences, it is commonly thought, however elevated we may think them, still owe in some way to the material events that give rise to them. The best candidate for explanation, it seems, is that collection of brain events, or some part of it, that occurs together with the experience. How might these events be described? Surely not in the terms just noted. (It is hard to imagine anyone, for example, describing a given brain event as being rapturous.) The nature of a brain event is physiological. It is described in terms of such things as neural cell structure and the electrochemical contact of one nerve appendage with another. Were one to attempt a description of each reality, the experience and the brain event, one would find that the two descriptions bear little resemblance to one another.

One the face of it, then, consciousness and particular conscious experiences are very different things from the material events with which they are associated. At the same time it must be said, even if consciousness does not seem like a collection of brain processes, it is nonetheless intimately associated with such events. What, then, is the likely relationship between the two realities? In the sections following I will provide a brief historical rundown of some of the more famous answers to this question. In Chapter 2, I will offer a defense of the view that consciousness is indeed something distinct from the material world and likewise from those material events (principally, the events of the brain) with which consciousness is associated.

Body and Soul in Ancient and Medieval Philosophy

The earliest Greek philosophy does not deal explicitly with the problem of consciousness. Instead it is devoted to cosmology, which is to say, it is a *logos,* or rational accounting, of the *cosmos,* or universe. Early philosophy is an attempt to make rational sense out of the world—to understand what reality is, behind its appearances, and what are its basic principles and components.[3]

What, for example, is the relationship between two fairly common-sense features of the world, namely, *change* and *permanence*? There seem, on the face of it, to be things in the world, such items as rocks, trees, and buildings, that last through time and retain their identity through all of their changes. What are these substances—these things, in other words, that stand under the flux of events that is forever shaping the world's appearance? Thales (fl. 585 B.C.) thinks that the best logical candidate is water. Anaximenes (fl. 545 B.C.) thinks it is air. Others think that perhaps there is really some primal set of elements, each of them distinct, yet endlessly divisible, and various combinations of these elements account for the plurality of things we find around us.

Some, like Heraclitus (fl. 500 B.C.), in a still more abstract vein, believe that change itself may be the only thing that is real. The metaphor of reality, thinks Heraclitus, is the river, which changes every moment and endures only in its outward pattern. Others think, on purely logical grounds, that permanence itself—unity, changelessness—might be the only real truth. Parmenides (515–445 B.C.), for one, believes that change implies that a thing becomes what it is not, which he alleges is a contradiction. The related common-sense notion of movement he rejects as well, for movement requires empty space. But what is empty space, except nothing at all? And of nothing at all, reasons Parmenides, one can say nothing.

Still others maintain that reality consists fundamentally of two things, namely, tiny enduring particles and the void in which such particles moved. Against Parmenides' earlier and somewhat restrictive logic, they hold that empty space is not utterly nothing, and that objects thus have a medium in which to travel, as common sense seems to report. The particles themselves, they hold, are indivisible and unchanging. These "a-toms," or "un-cuttables," are what gave the world its permanence.

The atomists make no exception for consciousness in their account. They believe that even mental activity is atomic in its structure, and that it faces the same prospect—that is, one of dissolution—as does everything else. They believe likewise that human beings are subject to the same forces as those that govern reality as a whole. Human beings, on the view of Democritus (460–371 B.C.), are a part of nature. They are composed of atoms, so abide by the same laws as those that govern atoms elsewhere. This claim raises issues in turn about such ordinary notions as good and evil, freedom, life purpose, and responsibility. A commentary on this view is offered by Terence Irwin:

> We sometimes suppose that we differ from rocks, trees, and dogs because we have free will; we choose freely and are morally responsible, open to praise or blame, for what we have freely chosen to do. We don't blame a rock for falling on us, or a bee for stinging us, because we agree they have no free choice. But if we agree with Democritus, we may easily conclude that we are no different from rocks and bees; they are just collections of atoms and so are we, since we are determined by the same laws.[4]

Irwin cites likewise the "naturalist determinism" of Leucippus, who holds that nothing happens "at random," but always for a reason and "by necessity." In later anecdotes, Irwin adds, Democritus is portrayed as the laughing philosopher, owing perhaps to the mockery that his view makes of human life. As Irwin observes, a view of this kind has an affinity with the view of the classical historian Thucydides, who maintains that social events (the Peloponnesian War being his chief case in point) are explicable, at bottom, in terms of the guiding forces of human nature.

For all of this, there is a strong element of the otherworldly in the popular beliefs of ancient Greece. From the time of Homer, and perhaps long before, it was commonly thought that the gods watched with interest over the affairs of men and even took part in them. Oracles were consulted, and their advice was heeded. The related notions of mediumship and possession were taken seriously, and the talents of song and poetry were thought to be the gifts of the Muses.[5] Although in Homer's epics there is not a clear sense of the difference between mind and body, some notion of an afterlife is expressed in both the *Iliad* and the *Odyssey*.[6]

The concept of a soul, as distinct from the body and wholly immaterial, is found in the thought of the philosopher-mathematician Pythagoras, who teaches both conscious survival of death and reincarnation. He believes likewise that the soul existed prior to its earthly career, a doctrine that is explicit in some of the dialogues of Plato.

It is in Plato that one finds what is very likely the most cultivated spiritual voice in all ancient literature. His is an otherworldly philosophy, and in this respect it is perhaps the very reversal of the attitude that prevails in the Western world some 2,400 years later. We today are in the habit of equating reality with tangibility—that is, what is real (or what is important, at any rate) is what can be picked up, examined, taken apart, and studied in its smallest components. It is no accident that the word 'immaterial' is presently a synonym for 'irrelevant' or 'worthless'.

Plato believes that what is real—what is good, enduring, and worth one's real concern—is not at all what is here in front of us and present to the senses. Rather, he thinks, the best and highest truth is the one that is apprehended by the soul, by the *intelligence*. It is not composed of matter, and indeed it is not even located within time and space.

Perhaps the best way to approach this conception of reality is through examples. One of the handiest of these (favored by Plato himself) is geometry. Consider our knowledge of such a thing as the *square*. We know that it has four sides, four angles, sides that are equal to one another and parallel to their opposites, and so on. How do we know these things? The answer of most people is that such a thing is common sense, that we learn them by seeing what is right in front of us, or perhaps by the formal study of geometry. But this answer, Plato thinks, is inadequate. For we know all of this, not about the square things that we have seen, but about squares in general. And of course those things that we have seen (blackboard diagrams, for example) are not themselves perfectly square. They are invariably flawed in some way. They come haphazardly into being; they alter and eventually perish. How, then, do we come by the idea of square-ness?

Plato's answer is that knowledge of this kind is really not knowledge of what we see in front of us but of another reality altogether. This knowledge is actually a kind of *recollection*. He believes that although we may see an object or a representation of an object with our eyes, we apprehend another, more enduring, reality with our intelligence. Our contact with material squares (which are imperfect and temporal things) occasions in us the awareness of another reality, namely, the square itself, an entity that is perfect and timeless and that we recognize from the existence that we had in that higher world before descending into this one.[7]

Plato summarizes his philosophy of the human condition in a famous story contained in Book 7 of his *Republic*. It is commonly known as the "Allegory of the Cave." In it he describes the condition of a man who has been kept all his life in an underground prison. During this time he has sat chained and facing a wall on which he sees shadows of events that (although he does not yet realize it) transpire behind him. With no point of comparison, he takes the shadow images to be reality.

Then one day he is set free. Unchained, he turns from this wall and sees for the first time what has cast the shadows. He then ventures upward to the outside, where he beholds still greater wonders in the full light of day. As his gaze lifts higher, he beholds eventually the moon, the stars, and at last the sun.

The story is a picture of our condition. The shadows on the wall—fleeting and insubstantial—represent the material world. The turning of the prisoner from the shadows to the objects is a turning, as it were, from the things of this world to the things of eternity. His ascent ("steep and rugged," as Plato would have it) is the journey of philosophy. It is the task of life to make this journey, and the soul, believes Plato, fares better or worse, both here and hereafter, depending upon its willingness to absorb these philosophical lessons.

The soul, Plato contends, does not belong to this world. It is distinct from the body, profoundly and essentially different from the world of composite things that come into being and pass out of being again. Its nature is to rule and to lead, hence it is like unto what is divine, to what is deathless and indissoluble. It is the very *Form* of life that "cannot admit its opposite" in annihilation.[8] By its nature, then, it belongs to the higher world, to which it has an affinity and in which it must one day reside. It is fated to reap the consequences of its choices in the life to come.

Complementing Plato, and representing, in effect, that other human impulse toward naturalism and against otherworldliness, is Aristotle (384–322), who tends to find the locus of truth to be this world and who rejects the notion of any realm of essences wholly removed from it. Form and matter, on

Aristotle's view, are inseparable aspects of a single reality, and there is no content in the notion of a form in the absence of any of its concrete instances.

To ask, says Aristotle, whether soul and body are one is like asking whether the *wax* and the *shape* are one; or again, whether the matter of a thing and the thing itself are one. One would not, he imagines, say that an object is the same thing as the sheer aggregate of its parts in any arrangement. (One would hardly think that a house, for example, is the same thing as the collection of smoke and ashes to which it has been reduced by a fire.) The collection of matter constituting the body, then, is not necessarily the same thing as the living and purposive organism.[9] In this way Aristotle suggests that a man is more than mere collections of atoms, but still that he is nothing apart from that sum total of matter that (in a given state of organization) makes up his body.

The Western world saw vast changes in the centuries following Plato and Aristotle, and these changes were reflected in the philosophies of the times. With the rise of Alexander and later of Rome, empires were created; these were societies on a cosmopolitan scale and thus quite different from the city-states of Athens and Sparta. In the centuries after the golden age of Greece, a number of philosophical schools arose. The most significant development for philosophy was the rise of Christianity, which began as a seemingly obscure movement within Judaism and grew into a major world religion.

In 313, Christian believers were granted freedom of worship by the emperor Constantine. Twelve years later, the Council of Nicaea produced an official doctrine concerning the differences of many ideas and philosophical strains of the young faith, thereby establishing the difference between orthodox religion and heresy. With the outlawing of paganism in 392 by Theodosius I, Christianity became the state religion. Philosophy in the Middle Ages, for this reason, is in large part Christian philosophy.

According to Augustine (354–430), the soul is an immaterial substance created by God. It has inherited sin from Adam and Eve and is predestined to spend eternity in heaven or hell.[10] Alexander of Hales (1170/80–1245), like Augustine strongly influenced by Plato, maintains that the soul stands in relation to the body much like a sailor to a ship. It is created by God out of nothing and has the capacity for making free choices. Bonaventure (1221–1274) holds a similar view and maintains that the soul exists principally to enjoy God.[11] Though distinct from the body, it will be reunited with the body in resurrection.

According to Thomas Aquinas (1225–1275), soul and body are distinguishable, yet they are not in the contrary relation that Plato and some Christian philosophers have held. Following Aristotle, Aquinas emphasizes the unity of man: The conscious activity of an individual, he reasons, is not only reasoning but also feeling and sensation. Yet the body is necessary for sensation, so it, too, is essential to an individual's identity.[12] There is thus nothing unusual, nothing punitive, in the union of soul and body, as others have maintained.[13] By the same token, the soul is not intrinsically dependent on the body and can function on its own when the two are separated at death and prior to resurrection.

The Modern Tradition

The modern philosophical tradition might be characterized in large part as a series of efforts made either for or against the key tenets of Christian faith, set amidst the developing worldview of modern science. At the outset of this tradition is René Descartes (1596–1650), who seeks to make room for religious belief while embracing the new conception of the world that has been opened by the progress of physical science and astronomy.

The best known expression of Descartes's philosophy is his *Meditations on First Philosophy,* in which he undertakes to set the whole edifice of human knowledge upon a logically certain foundation. As a means of beginning this project, he subjects his own beliefs to the test of logical doubt. He provisionally casts aside any given belief, or kind of belief, that is open in principle to the possibility of correction. Thus beliefs based upon sensation, for example, may be judged fallible on the grounds that the senses can (as in the case of mirages or optical illusions) deceive.

Are all sensory beliefs open to doubt? What of my belief that there is, say, a coffee cup on this table right before my eyes? Even this belief, thinks Descartes, is open to some doubt, if for no other reason than that my perception in this case may actually be part of a vivid dream. In this case, I am once again deceived. Descartes does not mean to encourage practical doubt about things of this kind. But he does believe that such considerations show that beliefs based upon sensation are less than perfectly reliable. Thus, he reasons, they cannot provide the foundation he is seeking.

But what of things seemingly still more certain, for example, that $2 + 2 = 4$ or that a triangle has three sides? Descartes maintains that even such things as these can be called into some rational question. For imagine, he says, that there exists an evil genius who (for whatever reason) wishes to plant such notions in my head when actually they are false. If the genius is sufficiently powerful, Descartes reasons, he may be able to create this experience contrary to fact and leave me none the wiser for it.

Then is nothing certain? Descartes believes that this experiment in doubt reveals to us the existence of at least one thing that can be known and that can serve as the starting point from which to build knowledge anew. For suppose (taking seriously, for a moment, his worst-case scenario) that the genius exists, and I am indeed the subject of one illusion after another. On this hypothesis, my own existence is implied, just as it would be in the other case, that is, where things are as I ordinarily take them to be. Whether my experience is hallucinatory or veridical, I must, qua experiencer, exist in any case. Thus my existence is established as a point of undeniable certainty.[14]

Descartes goes on to show that my own existence is not the only thing that can be established as certain. Reflection upon the concept of God, he believes, as a being containing, by definition, all perfections shows that God's existence is a logical certainty. And God's greatness, he argues, rules out the possibility of that basic deception entertained in connection with the evil genius. Thus, ordinary perception of the world, although imperfect, must be fundamentally reliable.

This exercise also provides Descartes with an argument for the immateriality of the soul. For my own existence as a conscious subject, reasons Descartes, is certain no matter what the status of the material world. Even if all the external world is an illusion, I am still as much "around," still as much a conscious experiencer as otherwise. Thus I myself, as a conscious subject, seem to have a property that is lacked by anything in that outer world, namely, the property of being directly evident to myself as an inquirer. Accordingly, Descartes reasons, I am not identical with anything (such as my own body) that is composed of matter.[15]

What Descartes believes he has discovered, by way of this introspection, is not merely a stream of experience but moreover, a conscious *substance*—an *I*, or *self*, that lies at the heart of this conscious flow; it is, he imagines, a thing possessed of various mental qualities, which persists through time amidst all of the varying conscious episodes (thinking, feeling, willing, and so on) that make up its experiential history. All created reality, Descartes maintains, is thus of two essentially different kinds. One he calls *res extensa*, or the reality that is fundamentally extended, in other words, material reality. The other is *res cogitans*, whose fundamental property is consciousness. The two kinds of reality, Descartes maintains, are in no way reducible to each other. They are nonetheless causally linked (the pineal gland of the brain being the locus of contact), whereby events in one realm can produce events in the other. Descartes is not sure how two such thoroughly different substances can influence each other, but he accepts their interaction as being a self-evident fact of experience.

Not all philosophers of his era share Descartes's spiritualistic outlook. Some indeed are thoroughgoing materialists. One such example is Thomas Hobbes (1588–1679). The universe, Hobbes maintains, is a plenum; there is no part of it that does not contain material of one kind or another. That portion of the universe occupied by human bodies (and on a larger scale, by the political state) is merely a part of the greater sum of machinery that operates according to specifiable laws of nature. The notion of immaterial substance Hobbes rejects as being a contradiction in terms. Life, on his view, thus consciousness as well, is merely the material life-process.

Materialism, according to Hobbes, is the natural consequence of rationality; it is scientific, and it paves the way for a rational investigation of the human being on both an individual and a political level. If human beings are material, then both they and their society are open to the possibility of analysis and quantification. Thus Hobbes's view accords well with the spirit of investigation that pervades the sixteenth and seventeenth centuries.[16]

The eighteenth century sees another and strangely different approach to the problem of consciousness taken by the Episcopalian bishop George Berkeley (1685–1753). Like Descartes before him, Berkeley is a religious philosopher who feels motivated to provide a defense of certain tenets of Christian faith. His solution to the problem of mind and matter is one of the most extraordinary ever attempted. Satisfied with neither the dualism of Descartes nor the materialism of Hobbes, Berkeley proposes that *all* of reality might actually be consciousness. To this end he attacked the common-sense notion of matter as a passive and lifeless entity lying somewhere outside of the consciousness that perceives it.

The emerging science of the day, of course, held that matter was just what Berkeley denied it to be. It held furthermore that the real, or "primary," properties of matter were the purely quantitative ones—such properties as those of mass, speed, shape—whereas its other alleged properties, such as color, sound, and temperature, were in fact "secondary" and had no objective existence apart from the mind that perceived them. Against this tendency Berkeley argues that one cannot in principle separate the secondary properties from the primary ones (how, after all, does one imagine an object without color?), and that the very notion of an object existing independent of consciousness is a contradiction in terms. To be real, on Berkeley's view, is to be perceived, which means that all of reality is consciousness. Thus a rock or a tree, for example, is not a collection of inert stuff out somewhere in space, waiting to be discovered by the senses; rather the truly real thing is just the *experience itself* that one has of such a thing.

Such an assertion does not mean, as some imagine, that Berkeley regards everything we perceive to be an illusion. What he claims is not that there is no reality, but that we must begin to conceive reality in a very different way if we are to understand it. The reality that he offers in place of the material universe of his contemporaries is one no less substantial than that of more conventional science and philosophy. It is a wondrous event of sound and color, the primary elements of which are the elements of experience itself. His most famous expression of this doctrine comes in a work called *Three Dialogues Between Hylas and Philonous,* in which his advocate Philonous argues for the immaterialist view of reality. Accused of denying reality by Hylas, Philonous replies that conventional thinkers seek the real world in the wrong place. They likewise underestimate the reality that lies within experience. Are not the fields, he asks:

covered with a delightful verdure? Is there not something in the woods and groves, in the rivers and clear springs, that soothes, that delights, that transports the soul? At the prospect of the wide and deep ocean, or some huge mountain whose top is lost in the clouds, or of an old gloomy forest, are not our minds filled with a pleasing horror? Even in rocks and deserts, is there not an agreeable witness? How sincere a pleasure it is to behold the natural beauties of the earth![17]

All of what we experience is real, as experience. There can, he thinks, be no reality besides experience. The error of conventional thought lies in making a passive and inanimate universe the theater of reality, when in fact experience itself abounds with the rich fabric of truth every moment. Reality is a spiritual event, and it is and can be nothing more.

Although Berkeley thus has no use for the popular notion of material substance, he agrees with Descartes that people themselves are substances of a certain kind. Later in the *Dialogues*, Philonous tells Hylas that although he does not, properly speaking, have a perception of himself as a soul,

I know what I mean by the terms *I* and *myself*; and I know this immediately, or intuitively, though I do not perceive it as I perceive a triangle, a color, or a sound. The mind, spirit, or soul, is that indivisible, unextended thing, which thinks, acts, and perceives. I say indivisible, because unextended; and unextended, because extended, figured, moveable things, are ideas; and that which perceives ideas, which thinks and wills, is plainly itself not an idea, nor like an idea. Ideas are things inactive, and perceived: and spirits a sort of beings altogether different from them.[18]

The concept of a soul or spiritual substance comes under attack in the work of David Hume (1711–1776), a truly radical inquirer who undertook to show that many of our common-sense assumptions do not stand up to the test of logical investigation. Hume denies, for example, that our observation of the world reveals to us the element of causal necessity, an idea that lay at the heart of the worldview that was developing out of the work of pioneer scientists like Galileo and Newton. For suppose, by way of illustration, that I let go of the ball that I hold in my hand. What happens? It drops to the floor. Why? Because, someone will say, its behavior is governed by some force or set of forces that somehow ensures that such a thing will happen. It is an instance, they will say, of the law of gravitation that is confirmed by experience practically every moment of our lives.

All we see, contends Hume, when we are reading off the content of our experience, is the succession of my letting go of the object and its subsequent fall. Wherein lies the element of necessity? Perhaps next time the ball will float off into the air, or vanish, or explode, or do some other thing quite different from what it has done until now. Granted, the ball has behaved in this way up to now. But how do we know that it will continue to behave in this manner? It will do no good to say that the hitherto constant succession of such events, of the letting go and the falling, is evidence to the contrary. Why, after all, do we think that the prior instances of this succession are any rational indication of what will happen the next time?[19]

Hume likewise challenges the idea that there persists a self, a "me," at the heart of experience, as philosophers like Descartes had imagined. Looking within ourselves, he maintained, we do observe *particular events,* such things as moods, pains, and volitions. But what else is left? In Hume's famous words, "When I enter most intimately into what I call *myself,* I always stumble on some particular perception or other, of heat or cold, light or shade, love or hatred, pain or pleasure. I never catch *myself* at any time without a perception, and never can observe anything but the perception."[20]

We are, he says, nothing except a "bundle," or collection, of different perceptions in constant flux. The mind is a theater in which these perceptions "pass, repass, glide away and mingle" in their endless variety. There is, he claims, no identity in its contents from one time to the next. Were the particular events of consciousness removed, as by deep sleep, there would remain no self of any kind whatsoever. Thus the notion of a soul, he maintains, is a confused or perhaps even an empty one.

Hume's skepticism raises troublesome questions, and his general approach to philosophy (as will be noted again later) has persisted in various ways into the twentieth century. Perhaps the greatest development in the history of modern philosophy is the synthesis of rationalism and empiricism that Immanuel Kant (1724–1804) effects in his reply to Hume's challenge. Kant agrees that the rationalists have overstepped themselves, but he thinks also that a pure empiricism is inadequate to deal with the central problems of philosophy. Ideas without sensory content, he maintains, are empty, whereas sensation without ideas is blind. Kant agrees with Hume that experience itself does not reveal the existence of an enduring soul. But he maintains that consciousness must involve more than successive episodes of sensation if it is to contain experience of the kind that we presently have. Were the mind a mere blank slate, as the empiricists tend to think, onto which the raw data of sensation is recorded, it could not independently of itself have the apprehension of a persisting world.

Hume, as noted earlier, argues that we never actually see *causality* (i.e., the force or principle whereby one kind of event has to be followed by some other), but instead only a (hitherto) regular succession of one event happening to follow another. It is for this reason that Hume believes that the future is open to some rational doubt. Kant follows a different tack. We know, he reasons, that causality is a permanent feature of our experience. We know (though we have not literally seen it and cannot deduce it as a fact of pure logic) that all events have causes. How so? Or again, we know that the shortest distance between any two points is a straight line, even though we can never test all such cases and (so Kant believes, at least) cannot know the fact merely by way of reason. We know, upon reflection, that any two points in time are successive. Things of this kind, Kant maintains, are knowable a priori, which is to say, they are known "prior," or without need of appeal, to any particular sense experience. And yet they are not analytic, that is, they are not things true merely by virtue of the definitions of the terms used to describe them. What must be the nature of consciousness if such is the case?

What Kant proposes, by way of solution, is a "Copernican Revolution" in the enterprise of philosophy. The data of the heavens, Copernicus (1473–1543) claims, were accounted for most reasonably by the hypothesis that the earth was not (as the earlier astronomy had claimed) a mere passive observation point around which the heavens turned. The movement of the heavens, relative to the observer, was more easily explained by supposing that the earth itself contributed something to the phenomenon by way of some action of its own, that is, by its orbit around the sun. Likewise, Kant maintains, the data of consciousness make more sense on the assumption that the mind actively contributes something to its experience. Against the absolutist view that space and time exist objectively on their own, he holds that each is instead merely a way in which consciousness organizes the reality with which it is in contact. Thus the form of our experience, the quality of distance, dimension, sequence, and the like—of things being to the left or right, above or beneath, each other, of one thing necessitating another—is supplied from within the mind itself. Reality on its own, as it exists independent of this experiential framework, he terms *noumena*—things-in-themselves, unfiltered, as it were, by the mind's activity. And reality as we know it is not a reading off, as one might say, of things objectively present in the world, but a product of activity from the side of the observer.

In a similar vein, Kant argues that there must be more to consciousness than a moment-by-moment succession of perceptions of the kind that Hume maintains. Were consciousness merely a succession of this kind, we would not have experience as we presently have it. A mere succession of mental states does not "add up," as it were, to conscious experience of an objective and enduring world order. Take, for example, my perception of the desk at which I now compose these words. What exactly is the raw data of this experience?

My perception of the desk, when looked at in its particulars, as Hume would have it, is a continuing sequence of individual perceptions, perhaps no two of them perfectly alike, and some of them (depending on such things as lighting, distance, and vantage point) very different from one another. I spend a good part of the day observing things other than the desk, during which time it is perceptually absent from my consciousness altogether. And yet I experience the desk, and other things around me, all of the time—as things "out there," so to speak, with a reality of their own quite apart from

whether or not I happen to catch sight of them. These individual perceptions, distinct and varying, are thus in some way successively united as the
experience of a single enduring object. I somehow know as well that the desk
did not come into being out of nothing and that it will not vanish without
reason into thin air. I experience the world, in short, as being a real, independent, and relatively stable thing that goes on, in its own right, regardless of
the manner in which I happen to perceive it and whether I perceive it at all.
How does one get this knowledge out of the mere facts of perception—the
varied and intermittent blotches, bumps, and noises that make up our frag-
mented contact with it? There must be more to consciousness, Kant concludes, than what Hume has made of it.[21]

Developments in the Twentieth Century

A wide variety of theories about consciousness appear in the twentieth century. Materialism, in one form or another, tends to dominate much of the
discussion. One of the more popular variations of materialism is logical be-
haviorism. The central thesis of the latter is that "mental" language—involving thought, knowledge, feeling, intention, and the like—is found to be upon
examination a reference to outward behavior and behavioral disposition.
The classic statement of this outlook is Gilbert Ryle's *The Concept of
Mind*.[22] Consider, says Ryle, the so-called mental characteristics that we
commonly attribute to individuals. Knowledge, for one: Would we say that
someone was *knowledgeable* in a given area if he did not provide us with the
appropriate behavioral criteria? What would it mean to know, say, a particular language, if one could not use it or could not give the appropriate answers
upon a test? To cite another example, what would it mean to have a sense of
humor unless one gave observable evidence of this trait? We ascribe these
qualities to people only in the event of some outward reason, and hence,
Ryle says, there is no need to suppose that such qualities involve any separate world (à la Descartes) of ghostly or spiritual events over and above the
world of nature.

By the same token, the obvious relationship between brain states and
events of consciousness has led some to think that conscious events, though
real, must be the very same things as the brain processes with which they are
associated. These people think that such things as thoughts, moods, sensations, and acts of will are identical with the neural events taking place simultaneously within the brain. This *identity thesis,* as it is called,[23] is one of the
current favorite materialist accounts of the nature of consciousness. Not
only does it seem to be supported empirically, but it also provides a rather
neat solution to the problem of the relationship between mind and matter.

This view has been criticized on a number of grounds. One popular com-
plaint raised against it is that an episode of consciousness, on reflection, just

seems so very different from the material processes of the nervous system. A pain, for example, seems to be more than merely an event of electrochemistry. It is, after all, disagreeable. And this peculiar feature seems very hard to capture in terms of any given material process.

It is for this reason that John Hick, in discussing the theory, maintains that it lacks face-value plausibility. Consider, writes Hick,[24] the conscious experience of seeing the night sky, "a visual field consisting of millions of points of light against a dark blue background." It does not seem in the least like the events that go on in the brain's gray matter. In fact, any theory identifying one kind of episode with the other is "paradoxical in the extreme." But again, as Hick acknowledges, identity theorists do not insist that conscious experience seems like electrochemistry to the individual that has it. Nor, in general, does it seem to be a logical requirement that a thing seem like whatever elements that actually compose it. Consider, for example, the fact that a cloud actually consists, in the main, of particles of water. Surely a cloud does not seem like this sort of thing when we view it from a distance. Small children do not think of clouds in such terms, and poets (fortunately) do not describe them in this manner. But it so happens that water particles make up a cloud just the same. A similar point can be made with respect to lightning and its constituent charges of electricity. Why not suppose then that consciousness may really be identical with brain processes?

Much recent work in the philosophy of mind has tended similarly in the direction of materialism. Dissatisfied with the traditional options—such things as dualism, idealism, and identity theory—philosophers have tried to find some new twist on the problem that will do justice to the features of conscious life without falling into anything so outmoded as the position of Descartes.

Why, asks John Searle, has this problem of consciousness persisted for practically the whole period of Western philosophy?[25] Why do we have a mind-brain problem in a way that we do not have, say, a digestion-stomach problem? The trouble with the going materialist conception of the mind, he believes, is that its proponents tend to deny that there is any such thing as a mind in the way that we ordinarily think of it.

There are four features of the mind, Searle maintains, that make the mind-body problem especially difficult. One is *consciousness*, "a central fact of specifically human existence," without which all the other specifically human aspects of our existence—love, language, humor, and the rest—would be impossible. Yet how, asks Searle, can "this grey and white gook inside my skull" be conscious? A second feature is *intentionality*, the quality by which our loves, beliefs, hopes, ambitions, and so on, are directed outward toward objects beyond themselves. How, again, he says, "can this stuff inside my head be about anything? How can it refer to anything? After all, this stuff in the skull consists of 'atoms in the void,' just as all of the rest of material reality consists of atoms in the void. Now how, to put it crudely, can atoms in the void represent anything?"[26]

A third key feature of the mind is *subjectivity*. Every sentient person can feel his own pains and not those of another; he can see the world from his own specific point of view and not from someone else's. Yet since the seventeenth century, writes Searle, we have come to think of reality as being something that is equally accessible to every observer. How, then, can subjectivity be objectively real?

Fourth, we feel that our own thoughts and feelings "make a real difference to the way we believe, that they actually have some causal *effect* on the physical world." (I decide to raise my arm, for example, and the arm somehow goes up.) But how do we account for this feature of the mind? It does not seem, once again, to be just the same thing as the matter within my skull. If it is indeed not this but something radically different, how can it bring about changes in the world of matter?

The answer Searle proposes is that mental phenomena—conscious or unconscious, visual or auditory, thought or sensation—are in fact caused in every case by processes going on in the brain. And all mental phenomena are themselves features of the brain as well. It is the failure, he believes, to see that both of these claims can be true simultaneously that has given rise to much of the trouble.

We are used to thinking that only one of these claims, at most, can be true. How can it be that brains cause minds while minds are themselves just features of brains? It is tempting, writes Searle, to think that whenever A causes B, there must be two discrete events, one being the cause and the other the effect—that all causation, in other words, is like one billiard ball striking another. Thus if mind and brain have a causal relationship to each other, we imagine, they must be two distinct things, existing perhaps in two entirely different realms.

But we are not, explains Searle, restricted to this model of causality in relationships found elsewhere in our investigation of reality. There is a common distinction in physics between the microproperties and the macroproperties of systems—between "small" and "large" scales. Consider, he then observes, the desk at which I sit or the glass of water in front of me. Each object is composed, beneath the level of ordinary perception, of particles. Such particles have certain features at the level of molecules and atoms, and again at the still deeper level of the subatomic. But each object also has, going back up, as it were, certain other, more obvious, properties, such as the solidity of the table, the liquidity of the water, or the transparency of the glass, which are "surface" or "global" features of these systems.

Many such surface features can be explained in terms of elements at the microlevel. The liquidity of the water is explained, for example, by the interactions of H_2O molecules. This, thinks Searle, provides a model for understanding the relationship of the mind and the brain. We have no trouble in thinking that surface features of the kind just mentioned are caused by the behavior of elements at the microlevel. The surface feature, in each case, is caused by this behavior and at the same time is realized in the system composed of events at that level. The surface features are simply "higher level" features of the system whose behavior at the microlevel gives rise to them. There is no division of realms involved in this situation—the same solidity that is "rigidity" and "resistance to touch" at one level is the lattice structure of molecules at another.

Applying this lesson to the study of the mind, says Searle, we can account reasonably well for the relationship between mind and brain. Just as liquidity, a "macro" feature, is caused by and realized in the system of its microelements, so the properties of consciousness are related to the microelements of neurology. The features that obtain at the higher level, in each case, do not obtain at the lower. One can say, for example, that a given system of particles is 10°C, or is solid, or is liquid, but one cannot say the same of the particles themselves. (Thus one cannot, says Searle, reach into a glass of water, pull out a molecule, and say that it is wet.) In the same way, one can say things of a system of neurons—that it is conscious, is experiencing thirst or pain, or whatever—but not that such things are true of the individual neurons themselves.

The foregoing does not mean that all accounts of consciousness in this century are materialistic. Contrary views are expressed by a number of philosophers, and not only by religious types. One finds a different and decidedly nondeterministic account in the writings of the atheist Jean-Paul Sartre, whose existentialist philosophy rejects the notion that human activity can be reduced to facts about the world of material fact.

Existence, Sartre insists, precedes *essence*: It is an error to think that human beings have any pre-given nature that decides their actions.[27] They make themselves and shape their own nature by the choices they freely make. It is likewise wrong, thinks Sartre, to suppose that my parents, or my culture, or my chemistry have made me the sort of person that I am. Rather my nature is just what I myself make it by my response to the conditions that I encounter. Thus if I am generous, it is because I have chosen to give of myself to another; my generosity owes to me and does not flow from some existing reservoir of generosity inherent in my nature. If I am a coward, it again is of my own choosing and not of anyone or anything else's. I may in fact inherit a weak constitution, but I cannot inherit a cowardly one. And no amount of past choice, for better or worse, can determine what my choice will be on the next occasion. It is thus an act of dishonesty to maintain that the material circumstances of the world have somehow necessitated my behavior.

Resistance to the notion that consciousness can be equated with any sort of material process is present as well in contemporary discussion. In an article called "The Ineffable Soul," Zeno Vendler criticizes the belief that materialism, in one form or another, can ever provide a satisfactory account of what is involved in conscious experience. The elements of human consciousness, writes Vendler, are in principle beyond what science can ever explain. And, curiously enough, he explains,

> my objections are not based upon the so-called "higher" mental abilities we possess, but on the "lower" ones. Not on the powers of understanding, reasoning, or choice, but on the modest functions of sensation, feeling, and emotion. To put it in a nutshell: the chess-playing computer Deep Thought, or an improved successor, may one day beat Kasparov, but it will not enjoy doing so.[28]

Although not willing to accept the classical dualism of Descartes, Vendler maintains that certain aspects of consciousness are outside any possible scientific domain. Consider, he says, the "utter impotence" of science to explain a thing like color. Physics tells us something, of course, about the material situation of color perception, with respect, for example, to various frequencies of electromagnetic radiation herein related. Neurology tells us about the activity of the retina and the optic mechanism of the brain. But where in this account, asks Vendler, is there anything about what a color looks like?

Such things as pains, colors, and images, thinks Vendler, are not a part of the world that science investigates. An alien might know all that one can know about these experiential episodes in terms of their effects on human behavior and never know what they are for the subject who experiences them. For such experiences are not, after all, things independent of experience that wait for us to come upon them. One example, I think, might be as follows: My awareness of a tree owes to the fact that the tree has first an existence on its own apart from my sensory experience of it. But what of this sensory experience itself? I do not have a sensation (say, the visual green image of its green leaves) because it is first there; rather it is the other way around—the sensation exists by virtue of the fact that I have it. The elements of conscious experience are irreducibly subjective and cannot be equated with any material fact that one may identify.

In a related vein, Richard Swinburne[29] rejects materialism in two different proposed forms as an answer to the mind-body problem. The first of these forms, "hard" materialism, holds that there exist only material substances, all of whose properties are physical. The second, a "soft" version of the doctrine, holds that there exist only material substances, but that some substances (such as human beings) have both mental and physical properties. Swinburne argues that neither version holds up to analysis.

It cannot be true, Swinburne reasons, that a person simply is a body or that a person's mind is the same thing as his brain. For my sensations—such things as the seeing of a red afterimage or the smelling of roast beef—are available to me (that is, I can know about them) in a way that they are not available to anyone else. Hence sensations cannot be the same things as brain events or any other events that are available to people other than myself.[30]

Nor, he argues, does the modified version of materialism suffice to cover all the relevant facts of the case. Soft materialism, according to Swinburne, "says that you have told the whole story of the world" when you have stated which material objects exist and which properties (of whatever kind) they have.[31] But this inventory of facts seems to leave something out of the picture, as witness the following scenario: Suppose that my brain, stem and all, is divided between its hemispheres and each half (together with whatever augmenting tissue is needed for its survival) is transplanted into a vacant skull. If this operation were done and we now had two living persons, both having conscious experiences, which one, asks Swinburne, would be me? Conceivably each would behave in a manner like myself and would have memories purporting to identify him with the person I am now. Yet surely they cannot both be me, for then they would be identical with each other. Perhaps, then, I am the left-brained one. Or perhaps the right. Or again, I may be neither. However much we know about the outward facts of the case, says Swinburne, we can never tell. Yet an answer must exist—it is "clearly a crucial factual matter" whether or not I have survived this strange operation. There must, then, he concludes, "be more to me than my brain, a further essential immaterial part whose continuing in existence makes the brain . . . to which it is linked my brain . . . , and to this something I give the traditional name of 'soul'."[32]

This contrast of materialistic and nonmaterialistic accounts of consciousness has been present from the early stages of Greek philosophy to the present day. It remains to be asked whether either basic type of account has any advantage over the other. In the coming chapter I will argue that one of the latter kind, although it may seem extraordinary, may well turn out to be the more rational.

Chapter Two

The Inadequacy of Materialistic Accounts

Strange dualism between the theory and practice of us moderns—electrons are the only real things, but yet by applied science the world of electrons has been reduced as never before to a means for the achievement of ideal ends!

—E. A. Burtt, *The Metaphysical Foundations of Modern Science*

Conscious Phenomena and Unconscious "Metaphysical Bias"

In the previous chapter I summarized some of the more noted historical accounts of the relationship between consciousness and the material world. Such accounts might be divided very broadly into two kinds—those that seek to reduce consciousness to events within the material world, and those that view consciousness as being something apart from that world. In this chapter I will explain why accounts of the former kind, those that seek to reduce consciousness to some event or aspect of the material world, are inherently unsatisfactory.

One problem with materialistic accounts of consciousness is that they never seem to capture, in any intuitively convincing manner, what is involved in the facts of conscious experience. To anyone who attends to these inward facts, the materialistic accounts—those, principally, that try to analyze consciousness in terms of physiology or outward public behavior—do not seem remotely accurate. This point is made succinctly by Curt Ducasse in his discussion of the problem. Let us consider, he writes,

> the assertion that 'thought' or 'consciousness' is but another name for subvocal speech, or for some other form of behavior, or for molecular processes in the tissues of the brain. As [various writers] have pointed out, no evidence ever is or can be offered to support that assertion, because it is in fact but a disguised pro-

posal to make the words 'thought', 'feeling', 'sensation', 'desire', and so on denote facts quite different from those which these words are commonly em-
ployed to denote. To say that these words are but other names for certain chemical or behavioral events is as grossly arbitrary as it would be to say that 'wood'
is but another name for glass or 'potato' but another name for cabbage.[1]

What these mental events are like, he continues, is observable by introspection. And what this look within reveals is that "they do not in the least
resemble muscular contraction, or glandular secretions, or any other known
bodily events."

No tampering with language can alter the observable fact that thinking is one
thing and muttering quite another; that the feeling called anger has no resemblance to the bodily behavior which usually goes with it; or that an act of will is
not in the least like anything we find when we open the skull and examine the
brain. Certain mental events are doubtless connected in some way with certain
bodily events, but they are not those bodily events themselves. The connection
is not identity.[2]

It is debatable just how much theoretical weight an objection of this kind
should carry. As noted in the previous chapter, identity theorists acknowledge that such things as thoughts, feelings, and moods may not seem like
events of neurochemistry. But they believe that these so-called mental
events could turn out to be events of this kind nonetheless. As identity theorists have pointed out, it is not a logical requirement that a thing seem, to
any given observer, to be identical with what happen to be its actual con-
stituents. One may thus agree with Searle, who argues that a system can
have features at a given level that it lacks in its individual constituent elements.

And yet there is something problematical, I think, in this kind of effort to
bridge the conceptual gap between consciousness and the neurological
events of which it is allegedly composed. For the features that Searle uses as
examples (tangible qualities like wetness and hardness) seem to be the very
ones that depend upon conscious perception for their existence. What, after
all, would these sensuous properties be, in and of themselves, in the absence
of some perceiving consciousness to experience them?[3] For this reason one
still wants to ask, I think, how it is that this other level of reality—that of
consciousness and of the various sensuous qualities that it makes possible—
comes into being.

Aside from this problem, there remains the question of whether we have
some positive reason not only to entertain the identification of consciousness with material processes but also to affirm it. There is a tendency in some
quarters to think that empirical science has in it (potentially, at least) the answer to every question in the universe, and thus to the problem of mind and
body. Consciousness, on this general view, although it may be elusive, is still

within the purview of scientific investigation, a part of the greater story that comprehends all of reality within one homogeneous picture. The notion of an immaterial entity, of something thus outside of this domain, of something not directly observable, is viewed as a kind of intellectual violation and as a holdover from a less sophisticated era of human understanding. The idea that consciousness should be an exception to the material nature of reality is thought by some to be philosophically out of the question. For example, J. J. C. Smart, an identity theorist, says, "that everything should be explicable in terms of physics . . . except the occurrence of sensations seems to me to be frankly unbelievable."[4] Although by Smart's own admission, this statement is "largely a confession of faith," its motivation, I think, is understandable.

From one point of view, consciousness as an exception to material reality seems indeed a bit fantastic. Let us try for a moment to picture the whole universe, lifeless in its entirety save for a few bits of organic material on this and perhaps a few other planets out somewhere in its dark reaches. Life, when seen in this way, may strike us as being a rather negligible part of reality. Life looks like very little in comparison with the world in which it is contained. Its chemistry, moreover, is reducible to that of the environment of which it is an integral part and from which it has evolved. Regarded in these terms, life represents an unimaginably small part of reality as a whole. The states of consciousness associated with it seem to be inconsequential as well. To suggest, then, that they may represent a break with the whole order of physical reality does seem perhaps a bit audacious.

But again, whether one is impressed with this line of approach depends, I think, on what basic interpretation of experience one has in the first place. Granted, the universe is a very big place and we who live in it are very small. In this context it may seem that our conscious experiences are likewise minuscule and hence unimportant. But perhaps we have the wrong perspective. For it is conceivable, I think, that the universe has a purpose in relation to us—perhaps it is the arena in which we are given the opportunity to develop in spiritual terms according to the lessons and challenges that it offers us. This, of course, is the view of most of the world's major religious traditions, the majority of which seem to have adjusted fairly well to the modern understanding of the universe in which we live. The merit of this broadly religious view is, of course, an issue unto itself. But belief in an ultimate purpose of the universe does not seem to me to be discouraged by what we may learn as to its physical nature, such as, for example, its immensity. (As for the reasonableness of this broadly religious interpretation of life, I will say more in Chapter 6.)

Why is it so often taken for granted that an immaterialistic account of consciousness must be somehow dubious or irrational? The reason for this tendency, Ducasse maintains, is that some people approach the subject with what he calls "an unconscious metaphysical bias."[5] They suppose from the beginning that a realistic view of the world contains nothing except what can be subjected to outward examination. They imagine, without considering the alternative, that reality is coextensive with what can be brought within the domain of scientific investigation. This attitude disposes such people to think that any theory that deals with immaterial entities is "unscientific" and thus irrational. Intangible entities, they imagine, are not worth taking seriously, the assumption being that to be *real* is to be *material*. And this assumption, he contends, is itself without rational warrant.

There is no reason in principle, thinks Ducasse, why material reality should be the only reality of any kind. Nor is there any reason to think that a putative reality outside the investigatory bounds of science is somehow less reasonable or legitimate than any other. It is true that an immaterial entity is in a sense "unscientific." But that does not mean that an immaterialistic account of consciousness should be thought any less reasonable than the alternative. For it is one thing to say that science deals only with verifiable realities and another to say that the only real things are those lying within the range of scientific verification. The assumption, writes Ducasse,

> that to be real is to be material is a useful and appropriate one for the purpose of investigating the material world and of operating upon it; and this purpose is a legitimate and frequent one. But [most of us] do not realize that the validity of that assumption is strictly relative to that specific purpose. Hence [we] continue making the assumption, and it continues to rule judgment, even when ... the purpose in view is a different one, for which the assumption is no longer useful or even congruous.[6]

Materialism, he concludes, is not attentive to the inner facts of experience. The insistence that consciousness is, or will likely turn out to be, material does not take stock of the most intimate data that can possibly be brought to bear on the question, namely, the content of introspection. What this inward look reveals (recalling the discussion in Chapter 1) is a world of events that resist description in terms of material reality of any kind whatsoever. The proposed reduction of consciousness to events within nature is prima facie implausible, and it is not warranted by any consideration of either science or philosophy.

A similar point is made by philosopher and psychotherapist Viktor Frankl, who speaks in a related vein about our "exaggerated respect for the so-called sciences." We accept without question, Frankl writes, the picture of the world that is presented to us by the science of physics—to cite an example, the eventual collapse of the universe from organization into disarray. But how real, he asks, is this cosmic doom that physics reports to us by virtue of the principle of entropy? If the universe is winding down into nothing, then all our moral effort seems to dwindle to naught. Do we really believe this?

Are we not rather taught by "inner experience," by ordinary living unbiased by theories, that our natural pleasure in a beautiful sunset is in a way "more real" than, say, astronomical calculations of the time when the earth will crash into the sun? Can anything be given to us more directly than our own personal experience, our own deep feeling of our human responsibility?[7]

The gist of these discussions just cited, I believe, is that real and honest objectivity means a willingness to read consciousness at its face value, free of the assumption that all reality must fall within the province of one or another category of our theoretical making. And what consciousness discloses to us, when we attend to its contents, is that reality is a far richer thing than materialism would care to admit. This disclosure does not mean, of course, that we should believe things that run contrary to the data of the sciences, but merely that science may reveal to us only one aspect of reality.

Our very trust in science, as Frankl suggests, is grounded in the data of conscious experience, which provides the justification for all that we believe about anything. Thus we believe on the basis of sensation that there is, for example, a material world, and we believe in general terms the story about this world that science tells us. But our experience informs us of other truths as well. We have reason, says Frankl, to accept the broad picture of the world that science gives us. But is that our only mode of apprehension? How much more certain, for example, is *conscience*, which is given to us directly and with greater vivacity than is any theory about the external world or any speculation to the effect that human emotion is merely "a strictly organized dance of molecules or atoms or electrons within the grey matter of the brain"?[8] The assumption that all reality is material is warranted by neither science itself nor rational principle of any other kind.

Consciousness and Mind-Brain Correlation

Nevertheless, many people are turned away from immaterialistic accounts of consciousness by the data of modern physiology. For, they suppose, even if the details of the materialistic account are as yet unclear, there is an obvious and intimate connection between brain activity and conscious experience. Certain parts of the brain, after all, correspond in identifiable ways to various sensory and cognitive functions. Loss of a given portion of the brain is apt to result in loss of that related conscious ability. Brain death, to all outward indications, means the death of consciousness altogether. And throughout all of nature there is an obvious relationship between the level of an organism's development and its level of sentience. Thus it is natural to think that consciousness is really in some way organic activity or that it is at least a closely related by-product.

Perhaps, then, whether or not identity theory is correct, the obvious correlation of mind and brain does at least show that mental events are causally dependent upon the brain mechanism. We all know, observes Bertrand Russell,[9] what brain injury can do to the memory; we see that a virtuous person likewise can be rendered vicious by encephalitis lethargica, that a clever child can be turned into an idiot by a lack of iodine. The connection between consciousness and brain condition is both certain and intimate, in which case, it seems, consciousness is at best a by-product of physiology and has no viability apart from it.

As William James summarizes:

> Every one knows that arrests of brain development occasion imbecility, that blows on the head abolish memory or consciousness, and that brain-stimulants and poisons change the quality of our ideas. The anatomists, physiologists and pathologists have only shown this generally admitted fact of a dependence to be detailed and minute. What the laboratories and hospitals have lately been teaching us is not only that thought in general is one of the brain's functions, but that the various special forms of thinking are functions of special portions of the brain. When we are thinking of things seen, it is our occipital convolutions that are active; when of things heard, it is a certain portion of our temporal lobes; when of things to be spoken, it is one of our frontal convolutions.[10]

This relationship, he says, is being established constantly and in ever greater detail, so that at this time practically no one "can be found holding back, and still talking as if mental phenomena might exist as independent variables in the world." Thus, says James, it seems right to set down, as a verdict of science, the claim that thought is a function of the brain.

But this fact, he continues, need not be viewed as ruling out the independence of consciousness nor, furthermore, its viability apart from the organ with which it is associated. For the notion of functional dependence is open to crucially different kinds of interpretation.

> When the physiologist who thinks that his science cuts off all hope of immortality pronounces the phrase, "Thought is a function of the brain," he thinks of the matter just as he thinks when he says "Steam is a function of the tea-kettle," "Light is a function of the electric circuit," "Power is a function of the moving waterfall." In these latter cases the several material objects have the function of inwardly creating or engendering their effects, and their function must be called *productive* function. Just so, he thinks, it must be with the brain.[11]

But there exist other kinds of function, that is, other kinds of dependent variation as well. One of these, says James, is *transmissive* function. Take, for example, a prism, or a colored glass. The energy of light, however it is produced, is "sifted" by the glass and is limited by its material characteristics. It is determined by the prism to a certain color, path, and shape. In this situation, the nature of the light cast varies together with the condition of the instrument through which it passes. But it is not produced by that instrument; rather, it is transmitted through it. Perhaps the functional dependence of consciousness upon brain states may be thought of similarly: "When we think of the law that thought is a function of the brain, we are not required to think of productive function only; we are entitled also to consider permissive or transmissive function. And this the ordinary psycho-physiologist leaves out of his account."[12]

Thus it may be, writes James, that the whole material universe is "a mere surface veil of phenomena, hiding and keeping back the world of genuine realities."[13] Our brains may be places in that veil where consciousness is filtered into its various qualities and quantities of expression. James quotes the affirmation of Shelley:

> Life, like a dome of many colored glass,
> stains the white radiance of eternity.[14]

So, says James, as the white radiance of consciousness "comes through the dome" (i.e., as it is modified by the properties of the brain), it may break through "in all sorts of restricted forms, and with all the imperfections and queernesses that characterize our finite individualities here below,"[15] In this way consciousness has a certain outward dependence on the structure of the organ with which it is associated, yet it is not identical with that structure, nor is it a mere passive by-product of that organ's activity. For this reason, the intimate relationship of consciousness and brain process is not per se an argument in favor of materialism. Mind and matter may well be an irreducible duality.

The Inherent Mystery of Causal Relationships

A dualistic account of consciousness, then, is consistent, I believe, with the data of the sciences and is even encouraged to some extent by our attention to the immediate facts of conscious experience. But such an account has its detractors, who continue to think that the reduction of consciousness to the material world is a sounder and perhaps philosophically neater alternative. Dualism does, of course, have its problems. The most troubling, by some estimates, is the question of how an immaterial agency can *interact* with the material world when the two things are so basically different from each other. A few words might be said at this point concerning the problem of causal interaction.

Dualism entails that mental and physical events are indeed quite dissimilar. For mental events, on this account, are altogether nonmaterial and thus lack the properties of extension and location in space. Physical events, in contrast, are fundamentally spatial. So the question arises, how can two such very unlike events have any sort of causal relationship? If mental events are not materially composed of anything, if they have no material substance, then how can they "get hold" of anything in that other realm? The relation is equally mysterious in the other direction—how can physical events bring about changes in the conscious world if, again, there is no common connecting ground?

But as C. D. Broad points out in his classic *The Mind and Its Place in Nature,* a basic dissimilarity of events is not of itself a conclusive objection to the possibility of their interaction. No one, says Broad, can deny that there exists a close relationship of some kind between bodily events and events in the mind. The two kinds of events vary together with obvious regularity. What, then, is the objection to the claim that there exists a transworld causal relationship between the two? The common argument, he explains, is that mind and body, when conceived dualistically, are so very unlike each other that their interaction seems impossible.[16]

The underlying assumption of such an argument, he observes, is that the co-variance of two given things, together with their high degree of likeness, is sufficient to demonstrate their causal interaction, whereas no amount of such variation between unlike entities can demonstrate the same thing. Causal interaction, Broad agrees, involves more than co-variation, but why is unlikeness such an obstacle? Surely there are examples of unlike things that seem to have this relationship. Take, for example, the case of drafts and head colds. No one, writes Broad,

> hesitates to hold that droughts and colds in the head are causally connected, although the two are extremely unlike each other. If the unlikeness of droughts and colds in the head does not prevent one from admitting a causal connexion between the two, why should the unlikeness of volitions and voluntary movements prevent one from holding that they are causally connected? . . . I am willing to admit that an adequate criterion of causal connexion needs some other relation between a pair of events beside concomitant variation; but I do not believe for a moment that this other relation is that of qualitative likeness.[17]

Thus, it appears, the interaction of mind and matter is not ruled out merely by the dissimilarity of the two entities. Of course, it might be added, the interaction of drafts and head colds is locatable within the world and so is not of the same order as that of the proposed interaction of mind and matter. The former interaction may be accounted for in terms of the body's material conditions and chemistry, whereas the latter involves a relationship that extends across whole dissimilar worlds. But Broad's point, I think, is still valid. Why should a basic likeness between two things be a necessary condition for their causal interaction? Hume, as Ducasse reminds us, shows us that "no kind of causal connection is intrinsically absurd. Anything might cause anything; and only observation can tell us what in fact can cause what."[18]

This observation has relevance to the problem of mind-body interaction. Hume, as noted in Chapter 1, is troubled by the notion of *necessity* as it is taken for granted by most philosophers. What, he asks, is really contained in our observation of this phenomenon? When, for example, one billiard ball strikes another, we see the proximity of the two objects and the sequential pattern of their motion. We do not see, over and above this pattern, the element of *necessity* that is supposed to figure in this event. How then do we know that the balls will do the same thing next time? Perhaps they will behave in a new way altogether. Hume maintains that nothing in our observation and nothing in the *concept* of the given object (round, white, wooden, and so on) provide us with any guarantee otherwise.

The skepticism engendered by this account was a scandal in its day, though no one at that moment seemed to have any notion of how to reply. For without this vital element of necessity, how could the sciences have any reliable foundation? No one, of course, entertains serious doubt that the world is in some sense regular and predictable in its behavior. Thus Hume's attack upon the presuppositions of science has little impact on anyone in terms of a practical outlook on the world. For this reason his skepticism, although it is conceptually interesting, has not really undermined the activity of the sciences. It may, however, have some other value. The import of Hume's own argument was skeptical, but it may serve to turn our thinking about causality in new directions and allow us to entertain notions of causality that reach beyond the usual bounds. There is, after all, nothing in the concept of a mental event that logically forbids the possibility of its influence upon matter. And nothing, either, in the concept of matter that rules out its reciprocal influence upon the world of consciousness. It will be said perhaps that such an interaction is "mysterious." But then again, as Hume observed, this mysteriousness seems to attach itself to instances of causality of any kind. And no form of causal relationship seems to be intrinsically absurd. Perhaps then the relationship between mind and matter is no more mysterious in principle than is any other. Only habit (i.e., habitual acquaintance) determines what we regard as natural or likely in this domain.

I suspect that those people who view material interaction as being the reasonable kind and who find the interaction of mind and matter anomalous have not reflected sufficiently upon the sheer mysteriousness of the causality that lies before them at every moment. It is, in fact, a bit remarkable that no one stops to consider just how mysterious is the interaction that they presently take for granted.

Gravitation, for one: It is the most common fact of experience that objects (under given conditions) fall to the ground when they are not otherwise supported. The fact is so much in evidence that it hardly occurs to anyone to wonder about it. Yet it is possible to view this fact in such a way that it seems not only odd but even wondrous. Why, after all, do objects fall *down* and not *up*? This question, as legend has it, occurred one day to Isaac Newton when an apple fell upon his head from the tree branch under which he was sitting. It dawned on him, at that moment, that there was no reason why the apple, or why objects in general, might not do all manner of other things instead of falling to the earth.

The story, of course, is a popular fancy and may have no connection with historical fact, but it illustrates a certain point about the world in which we live. There is nothing in the *idea* of an apple, or in the idea of a material object of any kind, that requires its downward behavior. One can, with perfect consistency, imagine a world in which apples (or objects, at any rate, that look and taste just like them) do not fall but instead remain suspended in midair when they are separated from the branches that hold them; or a world in which such objects at times explode, or fly off, in wild fashion, in ways that cannot be foreseen. A moment's reflection suffices to show us that in such a world the behavior of these objects would seem as natural as does the behavior of apples that we know at present. Observers in that world might devise their own formulas to describe that behavior, and the notion of *falling* apples would be as odd to them as that other behavior seems to us.

It might be said in objection that we know how apples must behave, since (owing in large part to Newton himself) we know of good and scientifically confirmable laws that govern the whole business of objects and their behavior. The "fall" of objects, for example, is quantifiable as the product of the masses of the two objects (in this case, earth and apple) and the inverse of the squares of the distance between them. And there is a tendency to think that this formulation (still quite good, within practical limits, even in an age of relativity and quantum mechanics) has demystified the world—has made sense of it so that we no longer need be puzzled by what we see around us. For what we now have at our disposal is an explanation of falling apples in terms of the law of gravity.

But then we must ask, what is the real content of this law? Is it not just the statement that objects do happen to behave in the manner as a matter of observed fact? If someone asked further *why* they behaved in this manner (why not the cube of the distance instead?), what possible reply would we have? What more could be said on the subject but that objects just behave this way in regular fashion for heaven knows what reason, if indeed there finally is any? It is hard to imagine what other, more basic, fact one might offer by way of explanation.

Or if, again, it is asked why one billiard ball moves another on impact, what final answer is forthcoming? One can imagine another world where the contact results in no movement at all or where the first ball passes through the other without collision. But instead it happens otherwise. One can only appeal once more to certain "laws," which translate in each case into facts about whatever facts we happen to find, and nothing more.

This explanatory stopping point is not, I think, a mere fact about the current (and presumably incomplete) state of science. It is not as if time and further research with the aid of more powerful investigative devices will provide the logical end point. For no empirical fact, in principle, can make logical sense of the phenomenon. Even as older ideas about matter (as conceived, for example, by the natural philosophers of the seventeenth century) give way to the myriad new conceptions of such things as space-time warps and wave-particle duality and to whatever new ideas may lie ahead, we will always be able to ask why it is this way and not some other. How can we ever find, say, a wave, a particle, a field, or any imaginable constituent thereof, that will be self-explaining? For this reason, I believe, the whole of science must at last acknowledge its ground in mystery. For this reason too, it seems, a similar admission must be made with respect to the phenomenon of causality. If the alleged interaction of mind and matter is mysterious, it is no more so than is the interaction that science describes.

Bodily Change and Personal Identity

Our ideas about personal identity over time furnish another example of the tension between reductionist philosophy and the convictions of common sense. Hume, as noted earlier, denies that there is any evidence of a lasting selfhood within the data of conscious experience. What introspection finds, says Hume, is not a substantial and persisting individual but only a rapid succession of discrete conscious episodes. Thus the concept of selfhood, on this view, is dissolved into the particular thoughts, feelings, actions, and sensations that constitute a given mental history.

Apart from the problem already noted (namely, how these varying episodes become united into a single coherent experience of anything), there is another difficulty with this account. For it is at odds with our own deepest instincts with regard to who we are and what is our relation to the world through which we seem, as persisting individuals, to be making our way. We commonly speak and behave, for example, as if we are single persons who are born, develop, age, and die in a single drama, whatever may become of our bodies over that duration. We know in fact that "the body" is not a single entity but instead a changing thing that undergoes a complete turnover not once but repeatedly over the course of an average lifetime. And yet we often imagine that we are "there" through all of it.

This notion, then, of a persisting selfhood at the core of passing experience is a part of our fundamental common-sense outlook. It also serves, on occasion, as a point of departure for those who seek to find a deeper insight into the nature of conscious reality. As Huston Smith observes, reflection upon the mystery of the self and its relation to the body is integral, in the Vedic Indian tradition, to the practice of *jnana,* or philosophically based yoga. A disciple, Smith explains,

> may be advised to examine our everyday language and ponder its implications. The word 'my' always implies a distinction between the possessor and what is possessed; when I speak of my book or my jacket, I do not suppose that I am those things. But I also speak of my body, my mind, or my personality, giving evidence that in some sense I consider myself as distinct from them as well. What is this "I" that possesses my body and mind, but is not their equivalent?[19]

Through endless change of body and mind, Smith observes, one remains in some way the same entity, "the same person who believed now this, now that; who once was young and is now old." What is this thing, he asks, more constant than body or mind, that has lasted through these changes? When meditated upon in full seriousness, he writes, this question "can disentangle one's Self from one's lesser identifications."[20] The essential tenet of orthodox Indian philosophy is that there is indeed a profound self-identity beneath the ongoing waves of ordinary conscious experience. It is alleged to be something more, something fathomlessly greater, than the selfhood that we ordinarily take for granted. And within this mode of life, it appears, there is firsthand experiential confirmation of the profound sense that we are the same persons across the whole span of a natural lifetime and perhaps beyond.

Apart from its conflict with intuition and with the esoteric tradition of the sages, there is another problem with this dissolutionist view. For it is also out of accord with our most basic attitudes about our relationship to other persons. Consider, for example, the way in which we view relationships involving vows, contracts, debts, and the like. If I promise to repay an amount of money to a friend over some period of time, I assume (as does he) that it is indeed he to whom the repayment must be made. If that is not the case, then the man who receives the repayment will not be the one to whom the promise was made. And the one who repays it will not be the one who made the promise. Thus it is hard to see what obligation could exist under such conditions.

It may be said that the future self causally connected with him will expect the payment, and that the world is a better place if our future selves, respectively, follow through with the arrangement that he and I have made with each other at the present time. But that is not the way in which such arrangements are presently understood, nor can it explain why anyone will be obliged to carry out the promise I have made to my contemporary acquaintance—a promise made, after all, to *him,* not to his causal descendent. Nor can it furnish any prudential reason for him in the meantime to maintain any interest in whether the outward conditions of the promise are fulfilled.

The Postulate of Rationality

In addition to what has been said to this point, there is another reason that materialism is unacceptable as a solution to the mind-body problem. In brief, materialism is self-defeating because it undercuts any claims we may have as to the purposefulness of our own actions and the rationality of our own beliefs and actions. This argument, or one version of it, was first stated, as far as I know, by Socrates, awaiting execution for having corrupted (so it was alleged) the youth of Athens. It was recorded by Plato in the *Phaedo*.

Philosophy, as noted in Chapter 1, had its beginnings in cultural Greece roughly a century before Socrates was born. It was, for the most part, cosmology, a speculative, protoscientific inquiry into the makeup and founding principles of the natural world. Late in the *Phaedo* Socrates mentions his early interest in those cosmological issues, which had been the fashion in his youth. The interest, he recalls, soon gave way to disillusionment, for this inquiry, he says, involved only physical explanations of the world, which he considered inadequate for the purpose of explaining human action. A physical explanation, he maintains, overlooks the most important and most obvious element of human behavior, namely, that of purpose.

He recalls Anaxagoras, who proposed (quite promisingly, it first seemed) that Mind was the ultimate cause of all that exists. But Anaxagoras, he says, quickly put aside this idea in favor of an explanation of the ordinary kind. That, says Socrates, was a disappointment. It was also irrational. For to say that Mind is a genuine cause of reality and then to posit instead explanations involving such things as "air and ether and water," he contends, is

> much like saying that Socrates' actions are all due to his mind, and then in trying to tell the causes of everything that I do, to say that the reason that I am sitting here is because my body consists of bones and sinews, because the bones are hard and separated by joints, that the sinews are such as to contract and relax, that they surround the bones along with flesh and skin which hold them together, then as the bones are hanging in their sockets, the relaxation and contraction of the sinews enable me to bend my limbs, and that is the true cause of my sitting here with my limbs bent.[21]

Similarly, he continues, a material account of his speech would enumerate "sounds and air and hearing, and a thousand other things," but

> would neglect to mention the true causes, after the Athenians decided it was better to condemn me . . . it seemed best to me to sit here and more right to remain and to endure whatever penalty they ordered. For . . . I think these bones and sinews could long ago have been in Megara or among the Boeotians, taken there by my belief as to the best course, if I had not thought it more right and honorable to endure whatever penalty the city ordered rather than escape and run away. To call those things causes is too absurd.[22]

Socrates' argument might be summarized by saying that a wholly material explanation of our behavior overlooks its *telos*—that is, it overlooks the purposive end to which that behavior is directed. If matter is the real explanation of all that happens, then the notion of such an end is superfluous in an account of human action. For what explanatory difference can it make, when in every case the real cause of such an action is the set of material events that *precedes* it? But this end, reasons Socrates, is logically indispensable. It has to figure into any plausible explanation of the choices that we actually make. Since the physical explanation neglects this element, it cannot be adequate.

It may be helpful to consider an example. Let us look at the choice of a freshman college student to persevere in a first philosophy course despite its difficulties. Suppose that he asks himself why he is seated at his desk one night doing his best to take in some author's discussion of Plato. The materialist explanation presumably is that his body is constituted in such a manner, and is subject to such antecedent and surrounding forces, as to land him at that desk, with his eyes trained upon that page, at the present moment. Given the makeup of the student's body and the forces acting upon it, nothing else is possible at this moment than that the body now seated here be arranged in this posture at this moment. But is this explanation adequate? Were one to ask the student why he is here at this time, would he (even if he had the relevant sophistication) consider offering such an account? Surely he would say instead that he is here, not merely from a cause, but for a reason— that he considers it better to be here than to be somewhere else.

Granted, his reasons might be several. They might also differ in certain ways from those of his classmates. Perhaps he wants the education. Perhaps he wants instead only to obtain the required distribution credits or to impress some acquaintance who, he has learned, has taken up a philosophy major. Or there might be other reasons besides. But his answer, in any case, would involve *purpose*—a goal or ideal toward which his actions are consciously aimed. And a solely material account does not provide a place for explanation of this kind. On a materialist account, the "real" explanation is mechanical, and the reasons he cites are incidental.

A comparable statement can be made about choice making of virtually any kind. Consider the example of a young woman who has found herself pregnant and weighed the options regarding her situation. She decides, say, to have the child despite the hardship it will involve on herself and those around her. How does one explain this series of events? On a materialist account, it is nothing more than the onward roll of matter in motion, one lump of matter (i.e., her body) spawning one other squalling little lump in accordance with the laws that govern events of this kind. Would such an account be the one given by the woman herself? Surely she would maintain otherwise. She would say that she has chosen this course of action because she thought it (for whatever her given reasons) to be in some way a wiser and better one than the alternative.

Or suppose, to cite another case, that a group of soldiers holed up in a fortress finds itself confronted by insurmountable odds and cannot hope to survive in its present situation. Let us imagine that it is faced with the choice of either capitulating to the enemy or fighting to the end in hopes of furthering the greater cause of which it is a part. Suppose it chooses the latter. How do we explain this choice? The materialist explanation of this phenomenon is that the material constituting the situation—the matter making up the soldiers' bodies, the forces acting upon them, and so on, yielded this result owing to the laws governing it. Any further commentary along the lines of ideals, heroism, weighing alternatives, surmounting fear, conforming to principle, and making, as far as possible, the higher and better choice, it will deem a mere accident. Such notions are beside the point of the real event, which is simply a result of the collisions of particles.

It should be said, before going further, that I do not mean to provide a theoretical disproof of materialism by an argument of this kind. It may be that the real story is the less appealing one and that our ideals do not enter into the actual story of the world in the way that we commonly imagine. It may be that the seeming role of the *telos* is an illusion. I do not know how such a claim can be disproved. I am only saying that if the worth of an end enters into this story, as common sense would have it, then we must suppose that more is involved in our behavior than the accident of matter in motion. We must think that the universe pulls, as it were, as well as pushes—that the noble end for which we may strive is not merely incidental to a given instance of human activity but a real and essential part of it.

In a similar vein, our assumption of being able to reason at all requires us, I believe, to think that something more is involved in our consciousness than material events. I maintain that materialism must be rejected on methodological grounds if we are to suppose ourselves to be capable of rational activity in the first place.

The gist of this argument is that materialism of any kind presupposes that our mental states are in every case a result of our brain activity. Such activity, according to the materialistic account, is determined by events in the world that have no bearing themselves upon the truth or falsity of beliefs of any kind. Thus our beliefs, if materialism is true, are determined, not by their rational merits, but by those external (and logically unrelated) physical events that determine the brain's development. But in that case, we can have no rational grounds for holding beliefs of any kind; nor, then, can we have such grounds for being materialists.

The argument is expressed in succinct form by J. B. S. Haldane when he says: "I am not a materialist . . . because if materialism is true, it seems to me that we cannot know that it is true. If my opinions are the result of the chemical processes going on in my brain, they are determined by the laws of chemistry, not those of logic."[23]

In other words, if materialism is true, then my beliefs about materialism itself are incidental to their rational worth. If, say, I hold that materialism is true, this event is itself only an accident of my physical circumstances (my brain composition, the events that trigger the synapses, and so on), not a result of the ideal merits of the position. Thus ex hypothesi, I can never have rational grounds for being a materialist. I cannot claim to know that materialism is true or even that it is probable. For any such claim depends for its support on my ability to function in some measure as a rational agent; it depends, therefore, on my ability to judge and select beliefs according to their rational worth. But if materialism is true, the rationality of a given view has no bearing at any time on whether I happen to accept it. My acceptance of that view, once again, is the result of my brain states, which are determined not by rational principles but by unrelated events in the material world. As A. C. Ewing observes:

> it is exceedingly difficult to see how we can be entitled to have faith in our intellectual processes at all if they originally spring from unconscious matter alone. The case seems clearest if we start by thinking of the epiphenomenalist. According to him the only cause of a mental event is a physical change in the brain. In that case we do not believe anything because we have good reasons for it, but only because something has changed in our brain. It would follow that all our beliefs were unjustified.[24]

Nor does it seem to matter just which version of materialism is under examination—whether it is, for example, identity theory, or Ryle's account, or any view that makes consciousness the mere by-product of brain activity. Some theorists, Ewing observes, may allow that mental processes are not a mere passive by-product of the brain and that they may have some capacity to effect changes of both a mental and physical kind. But again, says Ewing, "if they believe, that these, even ultimately, originate solely from an unconscious material source," itself incapable of purpose, then such theorists "are only putting the difficulty further back." For if matter, in the end, is responsible for thought, then thought is decided by events that have no allegiance to the canons of rationality.[25]

A reiteration of this argument is offered by John Hick in his extraordinary work *Death and Eternal Life.* He examines several of the ways in which philosophers in recent decades have dealt with the problem of consciousness. One proposed solution, Hick notes, is that of epiphenomenalism. On this view, as we have seen, consciousness is not itself identifiable with any material event but is dependent for its existence upon the brain's activity. Thus it has no autonomy or survival prospect apart from the events of matter.

The "Achilles heel" of this theory, as Hick sees it, is its entailment of determinism. For if the mind is in fact a material by-product, it is wholly determined by those events that are part of the material events of the world as a whole. If so, Hick reasons, then the ideas that arise in consciousness are determined by the causal system that governs the material world, and those ideas are without allegiance to truth or falsity. Thus in saying that consciousness is so governed, one is saying, in effect, that one's own thinking is materially governed as well. But in that case, Hick reasons, one's thinking is governed, not by rational principle, but by matter in motion. In this respect epiphenomenalism is self-defeating. If the mind, Hick writes, "has the intellectual freedom to come to rational conclusions, it cannot rationally conclude that it is not free rationally to conclude."[26]

It may be objected by some that a material process could, in fact, conform to rational principle. For certain kinds of machines, they will say, can be logical (i.e., can be designed to operate in accord with the dictates of logic) in their operation. Consider, for example, an arithmetic calculator or the chess program of a computer. The operation, in each case, is a material event. And it seems to be logically reliable; indeed, it may outstrip the best efforts of a human being to obtain the same result.

Hick does not dispute the claim that a material object (be it a machine or a collection of neurons) might in fact be structured to operate in a rational manner. It might, he says, be programmed or causally determined to print out or utter a series of propositions constituting an argument (or even a proof, if one ideally exists) for determinism. But a problem emerges when we try to universalize the picture in accordance with the deterministic thesis. Thus imagine, he says, a totally determined world with determined inhabitants who are in some way programmed to discuss the problem of free will. Half of them are determined to conclude that determinism is true and half that it is false. Let us imagine also a nondetermined observer who is able to look in upon this conversation from the outside, and who judges the argument for determinism to be sound and thus judges also that these inhabitants are themselves determined.

But we must, says Hick, suppose that *his* belief (that they are determined) is on a different order than *theirs*. For their belief arises, not from the merit of the argument, but from the material circumstance of their own programming. His own belief, in contrast, arises from his own rational appreciation of the argument itself. But if the determinist thesis is true, then in fact only the first kind of belief-state can ever occur. In such a case, the only kind of belief in determinism that can exist is a programmed belief that arises, not from reasoning, but "from physical causes which go back in an unbroken chain coterminous with the history of the physical universe."[27] Our concept of rational belief, Hick concludes, is inseparably linked with that of intellectual freedom. A world in which there is no such freedom would be a world in which there is no rational belief. Hence the belief that the world is totally determined cannot claim to be a rational belief.

I think that Hick's version of the argument, although essentially on the mark, is in need of slight rephrasing. The basic dependence of mind on matter, it seems to me, does not entail determinism. For a universe in which mind is dependent on matter could well have in it random events, that is, events free of events elsewhere, and so not necessitated by the nature of the world as a whole. The real problem with a view like epiphenomenalism, I believe, is that it entails the dependence of consciousness upon material events, whatever may be the situation with respect to determinism. And that, I think, does make the thesis of epiphenomenalism "logically suicidal" in the way that Hick claims.

The issue of rationality and material causation is discussed in a related vein by Paul Badham in his book *Christian Beliefs About Life After Death*. Concerning Haldane's argument, he writes:

> My first response to this argument was to think "Why not?" After all, the conclusions reached by my Volkswagen Service Station's Diagnostic Machine are "merely the effect of a causal chain of physical processes all blindly and mechanically determined," and the machine cannot help finding what it does; yet I take the greatest notice of what it finds.[28]

He cites likewise the report of Francis Crick that a machine programmed to prove various theorems of Euclid has come up with a new proof, in one case, more elegant than any previously devised. And no one, Badham observes, would seek to refute the validity of this proof on the grounds that its derivation was mechanical.

Thus again:

> As J. J. C. Smart points out, we decide whether or not an argument proves what it sets out to prove by considering its internal validity, not by finding out whether it was the product of a programmed machine or a free human agent. And it is on this consideration that Smart seeks to defend the Identity Theory against the charge that it is self-refuting.[29]

Yet as Badham points out, the case is different when we wish to examine our own rationality. We trust the processes of technology only because we ultimately trust our own; but "we can only check the validity of our own reasons if we are free agents." A computer, he explains, can make calculations, check figures, and prove theorems, but it cannot check the validity of its own programming. If we, too, are programmed by material elements, "we have no way of deciding between the merits of different theories of knowledge, for any conclusions we might come to would merely indicate the nature of our brain's programming and not whether its conclusions were true or false."[30]

As Badham explains, the basis of this objection is not that a physically determined system cannot work in accordance with the laws of logic. A calculating machine, as was noted, is thus determined and yet is logical in the structure of its operation. Rather, the point is that we cannot claim to have confidence in this operation except to the extent that we believe ourselves to be able to understand its mechanism. But that, again, requires us to assume that our beliefs are a product of rational activity, not of physical causation.

The upshot of this argument, to put it somewhat paradoxically, is that if we have rational grounds for accepting materialism, then we have no such grounds at all! As various writers have observed, that does not mean that materialism itself has to be false. It does mean, however, that we must always be mistaken in thinking that we have some reason to think that it is true. In this respect, materialism is self-defeating.

Once again, I do not claim that materialism implies determinism. Materialism allows that there may exist random events, such as those alleged by some to take place at the subatomic level. The problem with materialism is that it implies that our beliefs arise from causes (whether deterministic or not) that have nothing to do with their rational worth. Nor, incidentally, does it seem likely that indeterminism in nature would by itself add anything to the case for cognitive freedom, since a randomness of this kind need not proceed from any human agency.

It might be claimed by some that materialism is consistent with human freedom as well. For perhaps certain brain processes are themselves undetermined, in which case our beliefs may not be constrained by their materiality in the way that has been suggested. I grant that the concept of an undetermined brain process is logically consistent. But I am less sure of the grounds on which one might hold that such events take place. For the brain itself is a continuous part of the natural order. It is reducible in its composition to materials that are found elsewhere in the world and that appear to conform in specifiable ways to laws that govern nature on the whole. Although brain processes could represent an exception to this conformity, I see no reason to think that such is the case. For on what basis, it may be asked, is a given brain process exempt from this conformity while others are not? Thus I find it more plausible to think that any such exception of the brain to the causal order owes instead to the separate and immaterial agency of our own intelligence.

To summarize, if materialism is true, then our beliefs in every case are physically determined by the material nature of the world in which we live. But in that case, our beliefs are determined, not by rational insight, but by material accident, in which case we thereby sacrifice any logical right to claim that our beliefs are rationally sound. In short, we cannot have any rational grounds for maintaining beliefs of any kind. But if we have no such grounds, then our beliefs about the mind-body problem are groundless as well. In that case, materialism entails the groundlessness of our beliefs about the mind-body problem. But again, whenever we accept a given claim, we must also accept its consequences. Thus, if we accept materialism, then we must also accept that we have no justification for so doing.

If we are to think that we hold our beliefs on the basis of their rational worth, we must think that consciousness is something more than the material process with which it is associated. We must suppose that it is in some sense above these processes and, furthermore, that it is active—that it has an efficacy that it cannot have if it is a mere product of matter in motion. I conclude, then, that materialism is self-defeating and so is any view of the mind that denies it an active role in the formulation of its own beliefs. For this reason, epiphenomenalism—the view that mental events are mere by-products of brain activity—must be ruled out, along with more thoroughgoing materialistic accounts like that of identity theory. The freedom and the immateriality of the mind are warranted postulates of our own intellectual activity.

Chapter Three

Defining Moral Truth: A Variety of Accounts

If Quality exists in the object, then you must explain just why scientific instruments are unable to detect it. You must suggest instruments that will detect it, or live with the explanation that instruments don't detect it because your whole Quality concept, to put it politely, is a large pile of nonsense.

On the other hand, if Quality is subjective, existing only in the observer, then this Quality that you make so much of is just a fancy name for whatever you like.

—Robert Pirsig, *Zen and the Art of Motorcycle Maintenance*

The Nature of Value Judgments

A good part of our daily thought and speech concerns value. It thus concerns not merely what exists, or what has happened, or what is liable to happen at some time in the future, but also what we find to be good and bad about these events, what states of affairs we believe to be desirable in themselves, and therefore worth our efforts. We speak likewise, in this connection, of standards by which we can measure the worth of things.

Much of this discourse concerns the standards by which we may judge ourselves. Our thought and speech are laden with ideas of how we should behave, of what qualities of character constitute a good example of humanity, of what kind of society we should strive to promote, and so on. Our notions of such things as good, evil, praise, blame, obligation, resentment, and others related to them—which is to say, our *moral* notions—are among the most basic in our conceptual scheme. They influence our view of the world and how we behave toward it. Such thinking decides, in large part, our actions, our attitudes, our choices of companionship, our overall life plans and the various social causes that we may embrace therein.

What is the nature of good and evil? What distinguishes, for example, a right action from a wrong one? In this chapter, I provide a brief historical sketch of some of the major efforts that have been made to offer a basis for these distinctions and to define an ideal code of human behavior. In Chapter 4 I discuss what general theory of ethics best accords with certain popular convictions of moral common sense.

Ancient and Medieval Conceptions of Good and Evil

The inquiry into human conduct is very old and predates even the formal discipline of philosophy itself. Homer's *Iliad*, for example, sings the praises of battlefield courage. An exemplar of that is Achilles, a warrior without peer, and the story's central figure. Early on in this epic, he makes a fateful decision. A petty quarrel with the allied chief Agamemnon, in the middle of the siege of Troy, leads Achilles to abandon the cause in a rage of pride. Both he and his fellow Achaeans suffer losses as a result.

The *Iliad* is not commonly reckoned to be philosophy, for Homer, as W. T. Jones[1] observes, lacks the element of logical consistency that is essential to the enterprise of philosophy. Homer's patriarch god, Zeus, at times seems to be all-powerful; at other times it appears that the ultimate determining source is instead a "fate" that lies beyond even the will of the gods. Homer has no conception likewise of nature as a coherent and self-determining whole. He is a bard, a storyteller. His world may have in it some measure of regularity—day follows night, and the seasons observe their cycle, and so on. But that world has in it no explicit governing principle. It is open, for example, to divine interventions, owing to the occasional (and sometimes quite capricious) actions of the residents of Mount Olympus.

Homer offers no systematic treatment, either, of ethics. That is not to say that he has no sense of value. Men like Achilles and Odysseus, after all, are his heroes. There are many lessons in his stories on the subject of how human beings ought to conduct themselves. It is a good thing, for example, to give the gods their due in prayer and sacrifice and a bad thing to place one's mortal self on a par with them. But there is no distinction between good and evil in any systematic terms.

This changes in some measure with Hesiod, whose *Works and Days* voices a criticism of the greed and injustice of certain nobles who oppress the poor around them. Hesiod, writes Jones,

> deepened the conception of wrongdoing, he radically changed the way in which the sanctions against immoral conduct operated. For Homer these sanctions had operated, on the whole, capriciously: Zeus was virtually at the mercy of whichever relative happened to catch his ear. For Hesiod, on the contrary, Zeus had the moral integrity to choose, and the power to enforce, the rule of law.[2]

This law, Jones explains, whereby the good are sooner or later rewarded and the wicked are punished, operates with a certainty. Zeus is no longer a magnified version of a human ruler but a source of justice who sees even those things that are hidden and who metes out a consistent retribution.

Philosophy, as it is presently understood, has its roots in Greece. The nature of Greek thought and likewise of Greek ethics can be set in bolder outline by noting the contrast between two ancient and highly influential peoples, the Greeks and the Hebrews. These two peoples, writes William Barrett, are the two great roots of our civilization.³ The Greeks give us science and the ideal of rationality. The Hebrews give us the Law. Each of these contributes something to the worldview and moral consciousness of Western civilization.

Hebrew sensibility, explains Barrett, finds its core expression in the Book of Job, specifically in Job's confrontation with his maker. Job is not a philosopher in the usual sense of the word, but a man of flesh and blood who demands an accounting from God himself of his own difficulty. This encounter, writes Barrett, using Martin Buber's words, is the relationship of an *I* and a *Thou*. The resolution of Job's problem is not a theoretical solution of the problem of evil but "a conversion of the whole man."⁴ The ideal man of Hebraism is the man of faith. He is a man breathed out of the dust of the earth, a man who describes himself, as Barrett notes, "in starkly physical terms" and who must trust in his creator to raise him back up out of that dust if he is to live anew. His principal virtue is not insight but obedience.⁵

Socrates, by contrast, is "much at ease in Zion"; he is on easy conversational terms with eternity. Biblical man, on the one hand, is pervaded with the awful sense of his own sundering from his creator. The eternal, writes Barrett, "is a rather shadowy concept for the Hebrew except as it is embodied in the person of the unknowable and terrible God." Eternity, for the Greek, on the other hand, is something to which a man has access by clear intellectual vision. Beauty and goodness are for him virtually one and the same thing. Justice, says Socrates, is *kalon*—it is fine, fair, a beautiful thing to behold. It does not come thundering down from Mount Sinai, and it is not a cause for terror. It is instead a thing to be loved both for its own sake and for the benefit that comes from practicing it.

The tendency of the first Greek philosophy, as noted earlier, is a kind of protoscience, wherein certain individuals begin to develop a view of the cosmos and its origins. The emphasis of this inquiry, at first, is cosmology, and not human conduct. But all this begins to change in the fifth century when the old aristocracy begins to fall by the wayside and questions about life and values move into the forefront of Greek consciousness. A group of professional teachers called *sophists* ply their trade in the major urban centers and offer to their students, many of them from a newly wealthy and upwardly

striving industrial class, the arts of speech and persuasion. The sophists, on
the whole, are worldly and world-wise types, well traveled and having little
use of the older provincial ideas; their principal stock in trade is a practical
training geared toward material success and participation in the affairs of the
state. They tend to be skeptical about the reality of good and evil or even, in
some cases, of truth itself[6] of any kind that transcends the social structures of
the day. The laws of the land, maintain the sophists, are not *physis*, which is
to say, not an objective part of reality, but instead only *nomos*, or a product
of human manufacture. It was a view shared by many by that time, for no
educated man, as Jones explains:

> believed any longer in the gods as a possible source of law's reality. Every "en-
> lightened" man knew that laws were, as a matter of fact, the product of the ac-
> tivities of men—either individuals like Lycurgus or groups of men in assem-
> blies. Hence, how was it possible to maintain that law is anything more than
> "mere" convention? And why, if it is merely convention, should it have any
> claim on us? Why obey it if it is not to our advantage to do so?[7]

Much of Plato's writing involves public confrontations between these men
and Socrates, who objected to their generally skeptical and relativistic approach to the topics at hand.

And yet Socrates himself was dissatisfied with traditional assumptions
about the nature of good and evil. He is depicted, in Plato's *Euthyphro,*[8] as
challenging one of his friends to tell him what it means to say that an action
was "pious" or "holy." His question may be rephrased today to ask what it
means to call an action "righteous." Euthyphro's answer—that to call an action pious means to say that it is approved by the gods—does not fare well
under scrutiny. What if, for example, the gods are divided in their preferences? And this is not the only problem. For if righteousness *means* divine
approval, there is no reason, in principle, why the gods may not change in
their preferences and approve something quite different tomorrow. Today,
for example, they may approve of kindness, say, and disapprove of cruelty.
But what if tomorrow they feel otherwise? Will kindness then be a vice, and
cruelty a virtue? One cannot object that the gods will never do such a thing
on the grounds that they will not approve what is immoral, since what they
will is by definition righteous. Nor can one rule out that the gods will
change in their preferences, since there in no basis, on this theory, for saying
that change itself is in any way inconsistent with integrity.

Moral philosophy in ancient times receives perhaps its most elevated development in the writing of Plato, who believes, once again, that the source
of truth is not this world but another. Moral truths, thinks Plato, are timeless
and beyond the happenstance of human opinion or social structure. They are

likewise objectively real and like other such truths, such as those of mathematics, are discoverable by the intelligence.

Plato shares Socrates' conviction that moral truth cannot be defined in terms of the divine will. Goodness, on his view, has an existence of its own. It is uncreated, and as such resides above even the gods themselves. Plato, as we have seen, believes that things in this world are but pale reflections of those perfect and timeless things that they represent. The square things of this world, for example, reflect the eternal square—the square-ness, which exists above the happenstance of time and space. He believes that something analogous is true of moral knowledge. Take, for one, our knowledge of *courage*. It is occasioned by our encounter with a certain kind of behavior— say, an act of daring on the battlefield. What exactly do we see when this happens? We see outwardly, perhaps, a man facing attack and carrying his comrade to safety amidst the fire of the enemy. The content of this sensory experience is a variety of sights and sounds and various other sensations. But what we apprehend, thinks Plato, is a good deal more than this: What these sights reveal to us, in addition to the particular and material facts of the case, is a certain moral quality of which the present action is but an instance.

Plato's expression of this claim reaches its culmination in his "Allegory" (see Chapter 1), in which the escaped prisoner leaves the cave and beholds the wonders of the outside world. These new sights—the plants, animals, moon, and stars that greet his eyes, more real and more wondrous than anything he has yet seen—are an illustration of the greater truths that lie outside the darkness of worldly preoccupation.

Last of all, thinks Plato, he sees the sun, a thing too great, too brilliant, to be seen until his eyes are ready. Likewise in philosophy: In the realm of things knowable, he contends,

> the last thing to be seen, and that with considerable effort, is the *idea* of the good; but once seen, it must be concluded that this is the cause of all that is right and fair in everything—in the visible it gave birth to light and its sovereign; in the intelligible, itself sovereign, it provided truth and intelligence—and that the man who is going to act prudently in private or in public must see it.[9]

Herein is expressed, on Plato's view, the apprehension of ultimate reality. It is the Good that stands above all of reality and by virtue of which there is such a thing as truth and goodness at all. This *idea*, as Plato calls it, is not a mere psychological event within the consciousness of human beings. It is not a god, nor is it the creation or commandment of a god. It is perhaps not even a fact, in the usual sense of the word, but the very origin of truth and intelligence that transcends the usual categories of thought altogether.

This Good does not vary with time, or with place, or with custom. Plato will have none of that relativism espoused by his contemporaries, the

sophists. He would be no friendlier toward modern theorists who seek to reduce talk of good and evil to mere incidental facts about the shifting conven-
tions of different societies. A man, thinks Plato, can be enlightened about the
Good or he can be ignorant of it. The same is true of a whole society. Moral
truths are real, and they endure regardless of what human beings may think
about them.

Knowledge of the Good is not merely theoretical. It is essential to the or-
dering of a good life. To understand justice is to see that one's own good is
inseparable from it. The real task of life, on Plato's view, is not material success but knowledge. Without knowledge, man is rather like a sailor cast
adrift with no sense of the right direction of his vessel. He may have license
to steer the ship as he wishes or may have the ability to persuade others to do
it. But what can this license be worth as long as he is without knowledge of
how the ship ought to be steered? The end of this power is shipwreck. In
knowledge is salvation.

This equation of wisdom and virtue has an interesting consequence. Injustice, on Plato's view, is simply ignorance. For no one, he believes, will harm
himself voluntarily. Yet injustice is just that—the doing of profound injury
to oneself.[10] The psyche, like the state, thinks Plato, is composed of integral
parts of reason, spirit, and appetite. Its corresponding virtues are wisdom,
courage, and temperance. The man (like the state) who is well ordered is the
one who is governed by reason. Injustice, in contrast, is a strife, an upheaval
of the psyche, wherein the lesser elements of spirit and appetite rise up over
the proper rule of reason. The result is injustice—cowardice, ignorance, and
intemperance. Justice and injustice, believes Plato, are to the soul what
health and disease, respectively, are to the body. In the same way that this
unlawful rebellion against reason will ravage a state, so on an individual scale
will it ravage a soul. Injustice is harmful to oneself, and the offender who
goes undetected and unpunished is worst off of all. Persistence in injustice is
the soul's ruination.

The subject of moral philosophy is given a somewhat different treatment
by Aristotle, who differs from his teacher both in his basic temperament and
in his approach to philosophy. Whereas Plato imagines that form precedes
matter, Aristotle thinks of form and matter as inseparable and thus dependent upon each other. Form, on Aristotle's view, is not something remote
from the instances that remind us of it. Matter and form are instead a unity,
and one cannot exist without the other.[11]

Hence there is, to cite an example of Aristotle's, no triangle apart from triangularity and no triangularity without the triangle. Similarly, there is no
good apart from particular good things, and no ideal man or society prior to
any instances in the natural world. Whereas Plato is a mystic, Aristotle is a
scientist. This fact is reflected in Aristotle's approach to political theory,
which, as W. T. Jones[12] observes, is an empirical study of the actual societies

available to him. It is not an effort to construct, as if from some higher blue-print, an ideal that may hold independently of the world around us.

Aristotle's view is a middle ground of sorts between the relativism of the sophists and the absolutism of Plato. There is no perfection off on its own, beyond the world in which we live. The ideal structure of society, likewise, is a function of the conditions in which human beings operate. At the same time, Aristotle believes that there exists such a thing as excellence, and that there exists an ideal of conduct relative to the circumstances. Despite his basic difference with his teacher, Aristotle believes, as did Plato, that there exist identifiable virtues—qualities of character that distinguish higher and lower types of humanity. The Greek *arete*, translated roughly as 'virtue' in English, is a word that applies to human beings and inanimate objects alike. It refers to the functional excellence of a thing—as, for example, the *arete* of a knife, which is its shape, balance, cutting edge, and so on.

Aristotle shares also Plato's celebration of the intellect as the highest ele-ment of human nature and activity. The distinguishing feature of a human being, he thinks, is rationality. Thus the highest development of human char-acter is the exercise of the intellect.[13] It is an ability, thinks Aristotle, that human beings have in varying degrees. Although virtually everyone, he be-lieves, is capable of some excellence, only a minority are up to the task of contemplation.

All activity, maintains Aristotle, aims at some good.[14] Yet goods form a hi-erarchy—some goods are means to other goods. Bridle making, for instance, is good only insofar as it promotes the activity of riding, which is in turn subordinated at times to military activity. The good that is final and best for any human being, says Aristotle, is happiness. This happiness is called in the Greek *eudaemonia*, a personal and active flourishing in accord with one's potential. It is, in Aristotle's formulation, an activity of the soul in accor-dance with virtue.

Classical Greek ethics (the moral thought of the fifth and fourth centuries) is today called *virtue ethics*[15] by moral theorists. It focuses, not (as have most modern views) upon what duties one ought to perform, but upon what qual-ities of character make up an admirable human specimen. It is also thought by some to be, in the end, an ethic of self-interest. After all, there is no being to whom one gives obedience, no rule that may override one's own well-being. Instead, the cultivation of excellence is thought to constitute the high-est good for oneself—it is the life that one is advised to live, if one wants the best life possible.

A simpler and more frankly egoistic philosophy of conduct is advocated by Epicurus[16] (341–270 B.C.), who revives the earlier cosmology of the atomists. The soul, on this view, is itself atomic. It disperses at death, and with this dispersal comes the end of consciousness. The real end of life, thus the real business of philosophy, reasons Epicurus, is the avoidance of pain.

The cardinal virtue is prudence—the capacity to make discerning choices for oneself with respect to this end. Life's goal is *ataraxia*, a negative term indicating freedom from disturbance.

Chief among the pains, he observes, is anxiety. Two of the principal sources of this feeling are, first, our idle notions about the wrath of the gods, and second, our fear of death. Philosophy has therapeutic value, since it enables us to be rid of these fears by the method of rational examination.

Fear of the gods, Epicurus reasons, presupposes that the gods have an interest in human affairs. But if the gods, as tradition has it, are blessed and eternal and hence above mortal concerns, they cannot possibly be interested in the affairs of human beings. Should we have any doubt, observation suffices to show it. For if the gods really expect something from us—a code of social conduct, a ritual sacrifice in their honor, or whatever—we would find that those people who act accordingly have blessed lives, whereas those who act otherwise have wretched ones. But clearly that is not the case.[17] Actions, of course, have consequences, and some kinds of actions are apt to cause great harm to those who commit them. But this harm (the retaliation, for example, of a party whom one has injured) is a part of the natural order; it can be accounted for perfectly well within the bounds of nature. Fear of the gods is thus irrational.

Fear of death, reasons Epicurus, is just as absurd. For all evil—that is, all bad fortune—consists in sensation. And with death comes the end of sensation, in which case, no harm can come to the deceased. Those who have died exist no longer, hence they cannot suffer. Their pain is impossible, as much now as before they existed. If there is nothing unfortunate about their condition (or lack of one) prior to life, there is nothing unfortunate about their condition afterward either.

The earliest major philosopher of the Christian tradition is Augustine, who criticizes traditional approaches to moral philosophy discipline in light of revelation. The various Greek virtues, he argues, have no real value unless they are of service to the true faith. How, reasons Augustine, can one be prudent if one is ignorant of the real nature of good and evil? Where there is no true religion, he argues, there can be no true virtue: "For though the soul may seem to rule the body admirably, and the reason the vices, if the soul and reason do not themselves obey God, as God has commanded them to serve Him, they have no proper authority over the body and the vices."[18]

Thus, in the subsequent centuries, mainstream philosophers no longer look to the Greeks or to any pagan philosophy for their first authority. Yet the recovery of many of the works of Aristotle provide them nonetheless with an impressive source of information with respect to the world in which they live. For Thomas Aquinas, ethics is primarily an inquiry into what is the ultimate good and what must be done to attain it. Aquinas, like Aristotle, believes that there is an ultimate good, for the sake of which other goods are the means. But Aristotle, reasons Aquinas, is a pagan, and thus cut off from the Christian experience and from the knowledge of man's ultimate good and destination.

The supreme good of man, Aquinas believes, is his own perfection, which means the perfection of an intellectual substance. Such perfection involves, not merely the exercise of reason, but the apprehension of God. All creatures are directed to God as their last end. Each individual reaches perfection by attaining to some likeness of God as far as it lies within his nature. "To know God by an act of intelligence," he concludes, is the last end of a human being. But this knowledge, given human limitation, is not (unless it is granted by mystical insight) fully attained in the present life.[19]

Does that mean that Aquinas simply defines God as the good? It is sometimes thought that Christian belief equates the moral good with God's command, thus reviving the old issue of the *Euthyphro*. But as James Rachels[20] explains, Aquinas's view, and consequently the dominant view of ethics within Christian tradition, is not divine command theory, but the theory of natural law. On such a theory, says Rachels, the world is not merely a collection of valueless facts but constitutes a rational order invested with value and purpose. So-called laws of nature, on this view, describe not merely how things are but how they ought to be as well. Things are as they ought to be when they are serving their natural purpose. The distinction between morally good and morally evil actions is thus the distinction between natural and unnatural actions. We ought to be beneficent toward a neighbor, on this view, because such behavior is natural for us, given the kind of creatures that we are.

In this way, God's goodness means more than simply his own command. To call God good, says Alisdair MacIntyre,[21] in reflecting upon this tradition, "is to name him as the goal of desire." The natural man, unacquainted with revelation, can know the meaning of the good in his present condition, even if he does not yet realize what the ultimate good may be. Hence, says MacIntyre, the statement "God is good" is synthetic (i.e., it is not merely true by definition), and to cite God's goodness is to give a reason for obeying his commandments.

A different outlook, as MacIntyre notes, predominates in the later Middle Ages, with an increased emphasis within philosophy upon immediate divine revelation. In this period, says MacIntyre, there is a greater sense of the distance between God and man, and a corresponding diminution of the confidence in human reason to understand the ultimate questions of life. Man in his fallen condition can have no understanding of God but what God provides by grace, and man has no means by which he can judge what God says. Hence "God is good," says MacIntyre, becomes a truism and divine command theory prevails.

Ethics in the Modern Tradition

The dominant moral views of the modern era, reflecting the scientific spirit of the times, attempt to define good in a rational manner and (even if their advocates are themselves religious) in ways that make no explicit reference to the divine will. Perhaps the most famous example is Kant, who holds that an action is morally acceptable if it is consistent with what he called the *categorical imperative*.[22] This imperative, or command, says in effect that one should act only in such a way that one can consistently will that the maxim of one's act (in other words, the general rule that this act expresses) should become a general law of human nature. Or equivalently, Kant maintained, one should act so as to treat every human being (oneself included) as an end in himself and never solely as a means.

This requirement of willing one's own maxim is ingenious. Kant illustrates it with a number of examples. Suppose, to cite one case, that you desire a sum of money. Suppose, too, that your acquaintance will not lend it to you unless he is persuaded that you will repay the sum within a given period of time. You have no means or intention of making the repayment but decide to make a false promise in order to receive the money. You must then ask yourself, says Kant, what the world would be like if everyone in such a situation were to behave in the same manner. Would you choose to live in such a world? In that world, of course, there would be no point in trying to deceive others in this way, for everyone would take the words 'I promise' to meant simply 'I want'. Thus lying would have no advantage. A world where *everyone* lies is a world, in effect, where *no one* does—for were everyone in the habit of making false promises, such promises would have no effect. A would-be liar, then, cannot will that his maxim be a universal law of human nature. There could not be a world in which everyone persuades by deceit. There is, for this reason, something inconsistent (thus, Kant thinks, something wrong) with the act of lying.

Suppose again, says Kant, that you discover within yourself a talent of some kind. It is a talent that, with some cultivation, will provide the world with some benefit that it might otherwise not enjoy. But suppose that you decide, just the same, to neglect this talent, reasoning that a life of minimal subsistence is less trouble than one of sustained effort. Can you will that this maxim (roughly, that you demand of yourself no more than minimal effort when conditions of life are generous enough to allow it) become a general law of human nature? Surely you cannot. For what man would choose to live in a world where (owing to this shared lack of ambition) he himself would be deprived of the richness of experience that he enjoys through the painstaking cultivation of talent that now exists in this one? In this case, Kant reasons, the habitual neglect of one's own talents is wrong.

There seem to be two tests, in effect, posed by Kant's requirement. The first is universalization. There can be no lying in a world where everyone does it. Others must tell the truth, if my own lie is to have plausibility. Such an action, then, is self-canceling as a universal law of human behavior. (And similarly with other forms of deceit, such as bribery, tax evasion, counterfeiting.) Moral parasitism, as a universal law, destroys itself. Someone must give, so to speak, before another can take. But not all immoral actions are self-canceling in this way. For in some cases, thinks Kant, an action can be universalized (consistently imagined to be a general law of human behavior) and still fail the test. Consider, once again, the refusal to develop one's own talents. A society could function in this way, he observes, though it would be a society very different (and presumably less interesting) than our own. But one can hardly want to live in such a world. Another example is that of indifference to the welfare of other people. There could, says Kant, be a society in which people refuse to come to the aid of one another. Such a world, he thinks, might even be better in certain respects than a world in which people make a false show of sympathy for the sake of appearance. But again, a person cannot will to live in such a place, for who knows when he might find himself in need of the very compassion that his choice would have thus eliminated.

Perhaps the most striking aspect of Kant's philosophy is his profound respect for the moral law. His description of this law takes on supernatural proportions in some of his writing. There is, for one, an extraordinary passage near the end of the *Critique of Practical Reason,* in which he discusses the nature of the moral law and its place in human experience. "Two things," he writes, in all of our awareness, "fill the mind with ever new and increasing awe and wonder." These are "the starry heavens above" and "the moral law within."[23] Within us, Kant maintains, is the apprehension of something awesome, of a thing beyond nature that both demands and merits our obedience. In our more serious moments, thinks Kant, we cannot deny it, even if certain theorists may claim otherwise. It is a source of truth that speaks to us with grave authority.

Innate in Kant's sensibility is a powerful sense of justice, and so also of the value of retribution. Those who transgress this law, Kant believes, commit a profound offense, and society has both the right and the obligation to punish them in turn. The real basis of punishment, he insists, is not the rehabilitation of the offender; it is, in fact, a violation of human dignity to try to mold him to our own ideals. Rather it is just and deserved retribution. Our instincts, Kant observes, are satisfied by seeing pain inflicted upon a wrongdoer, for herein is the serving of justice.

Although Kant has had great impact on the moral thought of the past two centuries, the rigidity of his theory (its absolute prohibition upon lying, for example, under any imaginable circumstances) has struck some people as being somehow too severe in its formulation. Speaking to this sentiment is a theory that gives priority instead to the well-being of the human race and to the alleviation of its misery. It is called *utilitarianism*. Advocates of this view—among them Jeremy Bentham and John Stuart Mill—maintain that the real worth of an act lies, not in its agreement with any abstract law, but in its consequences for those who are affected by it. Mill's formulation of this ethic—the so-called greatest happiness principle[24]—states that an act is good to the extent that it causes happiness, and bad to the extent that it causes unhappiness. The moral worth of an act is thus determined, as a kind of net balance, by the amount and richness of happiness it causes.

By 'happiness' Mill means pleasure and by 'unhappiness', pain. What is good, he believes, is the promotion of a society in which human beings enjoy a wealth and richness of pleasant experiences and a minimum of unpleasant ones. Such things, then, as loss, pain, or sacrifice have in themselves no positive worth (for example, the ennobling effect of pain on human character or the good intention of a sacrifice). They are desirable only to the extent that they bring about some greater advantage (which is to say, some pleasure, or avoidance of pain) for someone in the long run. The notion that pain ought to be inflicted upon an individual for any other reason (say, for the sake of payback) is dismissed by the utilitarians as sheer barbarism.

This standard, thinks Mill, is the whole criterion of the moral worth of an action or a social policy. He has no use for such notions as those of *freedom* or *sacrifice* as goods in themselves. He does not appeal to the concept of *rights*, which figures so prominently in both British and American philosophy of the past several centuries. It is instead the principle of utility that provides us with the entitlement to speak, write, and convene as we may wish. Liberty is good only because it means greater happiness in the long run for the society that allows it. A citizen ought to be allowed freedom of expression for the simple reason that such a policy brings about a keener appreciation of truth and a resultant improvement in the condition of society over time.

In his classic essay on utilitarianism, Mill discusses various objections to the claim that pleasure and pain provide the criteria of a moral standard. One objection is that it is somehow degenerate to suppose that human beings have no greater end than pleasure. A pig, after all, is capable of that much. Surely human beings are meant for something more important than sensory enjoyment. Utilitarianism is thus labeled a doctrine of swine. Furthermore, it was said, man is not the standard of right and wrong; rather God is. We are given the truth about such things in the scriptures, and so it is to them that we must look for an answer.

In response to the first of these claims, Mill states that it is really the objectors who degrade the human race. For they suggest, by implication, that a human being is capable of no more elevated pleasures than is a pig. But surely a human being has faculties far higher and more complex, and is capable of enjoyments of which an animal has no conception. Human beings, too, can grovel, and some indeed are capable of little else. But anyone, insists Mill, who has experienced the pleasures of great music, or great literature, or the satisfaction of resolving a problem of mathematics knows firsthand that such enjoyments as these exceed, in their intrinsic value, those enjoyments of the baser kind. The greatest happiness principle, accordingly, aims to promote, not merely a maximum of pleasure and avoidance of pain, but an existence of varied enjoyments "both in point of quantity and quality."

As to the religious objection, Mill contends that Christian ethics and utilitarianism do not really conflict with each other. The utilitarian principle requires of us a strict impartiality between our own good and that of our neighbor. Does this impartiality not seem to be the requirement of the Sermon on the Mount as well? To do as one would be done by, to love one's neighbor as oneself—what is this but the utilitarian message? In the golden rule of Jesus, says Mill, "we read the complete spirit of the ethics of utilitarianism."

There is another reason, as Mill observes shortly afterward, that utilitarianism need not be subordinated to an ethic of religion. For if religious types believe, as they claim, in the *goodness* of God, they can hardly suppose that he disapproves of an ethic that promotes human happiness. It is thus irrational to cite scripture of any kind as evidence against the truth of utilitarianism. Or if we think that God does approve some contrary ethic, we must suppose that he is something other than benevolent.

Moral Subjectivism

Although philosophers like Kant and Mill have their differences, they at least have something in common: the belief that value judgments have some objective status. They believe, in other words, that statements like 'Murder is wrong' or 'Compassion is a good quality' are statements that aim at describing some feature of reality, thus are true or false according to their correspondence to the fact. The two men are clearly different in their approach and temperament, Mill's orientation being toward society and Kant's toward metaphysics. But a value judgment, each imagines, is something true or false, depending upon its relationship to the moral truth itself.

In the twentieth century, some philosophers adopt another and very different way of thinking about moral language and its function. These philosophers hold that the discipline of philosophy itself has suffered from a kind of delusion as to its proper task and limits and that much of its historical activity has really amounted to empty talk. So-called value judgments, they maintain, are not *judgments*, as traditionally supposed. Instead they are merely expressions that serve to vent the feelings of those who make them.[25]

This way of thinking about ethics has its roots in the moral philosophy of Hume. Whereas traditional philosophers had more or less taken for granted that value judgments were real and objective, Hume confessed that most of the literature of ethics was perplexing to him. Typically, he said, moral philosophers begin with observations about what *is* the case and then, by some odd transition, shift their discussion to claims about what *ought* to be. Where, asked Hume, is the logical warrant for such an inference?

Hume doubts, in fact, that one could find objective grounds for value judgments at all:

> Take any action allowed to be vicious: Willful murder, for instance. Examine it in all lights, and see if you can find that matter of fact, or real existence, which you call vice. In whichever way you take it, you find only certain passions, motives, volitions and thoughts. There is no other matter of faon into your own breast, and find a sentiment of disapprobation, which arises in you, towards this acct in the case. You can never find it, till you turn your reflexition. Here is a matter of fact; but 'tis the object of feeling, not of reason. It lies in yourself, not in the object. So that when you pronounce any action or character to be vicious, you mean nothing, but that from the constitution of your nature you have a feeling or sentiment of blame from the contemplation of it.[26]

The claim is revolutionary. For the great majority of philosophers, whatever their differences, have always believed at least that value judgments concern the real value of human conduct. They have thought that in calling an action wrong, for example, we are saying something (whether true or false) about the action. On Hume's view we are actually saying something about ourselves. Where, then, does this leave the whole enterprise of ethics?

In order to see this more clearly, we might pause to consider for a moment what really is contained in the outward and sensory characteristics of the act in question. What, for example, might a forensic investigator turn up in his investigation of a murder? Depending on the evidence available, he might learn such things as the nature of the weapon that was used, the blood type of both victim and assailant, the assailant's height, weight, and shoe size, the approximate time that the act was committed. With sufficient research he might determine with reasonable certainty the identity of the murderer and be able to reconstruct the act to the satisfaction of others involved in the case. But where, in this investigation of tangible fact, does the *wrongness* of the murder appear? It does not seem to be yet another outward and witnessable fact among the others. One could, in principle, reconstruct a complete description of the act without making a single reference to its value. (Such an investigator, in his role as scientist, would not report that the murder was *foul* any more than he would note that the murder scene was "yucky.")

In the act of murder itself, reasons Hume, we find no value present to the senses, nor does value seem to be evident in any fact of sheer logic. For this reason, he infers, we must turn our gaze back into the observer if we are to understand what moral language is actually about. It is here, he contends, that one finds the fact. It is a fact, not of value, but of feeling. Thus any talk about the value of murder, for example, of its evil and negativity, although it may seem to characterize the act itself, is really a statement, as it turns out, about the attitude of the observer. It describes, not the act, but instead the psychological reaction of the individual who makes it. Moral qualities, then, "may be compared to sounds, colors, heat and cold, which according to modern philosophy, are not qualities in objects, but perceptions in the mind."

Hume's account seems plausible to many who read it these days who vaguely imagine that judgments about the goodness or badness of things are merely "personal" and that one such judgment is as true as any another. Such judgments, it is often imagined, are grounded in the individual feelings of the observer and have nothing to do with independent fact. Therefore, it seems, moral differences have no objective resolution. They might be likened to other differences that can be analyzed in this way. Suppose, for example, that two persons have different reactions to a given event, say, a baseball game. One cheers on the home team and the other roots for the visitors. Which reaction is "right"? Or if one likes spinach and the other asparagus, which of the two is the better viewpoint? Surely, one must think, there is no such thing as better or worse in this case. If Hume is correct, moral issues are rather like this. There exists no objective value in actions themselves. Take, once again, his example of murder. It is not, objectively speaking, a good thing or a bad thing. If two persons, for example, witness a murder and have different moral reactions, there is no truth or falsity in either reaction. If one viewer approves of the action and the other disapproves, there is no sense in asking which attitude is the better or more elevated one.

Of course, it may be that the viewers have similar reactions. Hume, in fact, believed that human beings were enough alike in their constitution that they would have similar feelings about a given event if they had similar perceptions of it. But the psychological similarity of human beings does not provide value judgments with any foundation in objectivity. For they still amount to statements about the feelings of those who observe them. Or again, for the sake of illustration, let us imagine a race of beings—extraterrestrials, if one likes—who have emotional reactions radically different from our own. Suppose that they are basically unlike ourselves in their constitution and that they find the pain of others, say, not to be tragic or lamentable, but merely humorous. If Hume is right, we cannot say that we who are sympathetic with such pain are somehow more perceptive or more enlightened than these creatures, but only that we are different.

One can, as I suggested a moment ago, feel reverberations of Hume's philosophy in the thinking of certain philosophers in the twentieth century. His direct descendants are the logical positivists, a broad alliance of scientists and philosophers who believe that a good deal of traditional philosophy is misguided in its enterprise. The main tenet of this school is that a sentence has content (in other words, that it makes an assertion) only if it is analytic or is in some measure empirically verifiable. It has content, in other words, just in case it is either true by the definitions of its terms ("All bachelors are unmarried") or is capable of verification by some possible set of sensory experiences ("Water freezes at 32°F").

The logical positivists claim that meaningful language must stay within the bounds of the empirical world—the world that is apprehended by the senses. In going outside these bounds—venturing, as it were, into that alleged territory of metaphysics—we cease to say anything that makes literal sense. That is not to say that language has no function other than the making of assertions—there are, after all, such things as commands, exhortations, and poetry. But none of these things belongs properly to philosophy, whose real task, they imagine, is not any such higher inquiry but instead the somewhat more mundane task of the analysis of language—the clarifying, essentially, of the terms and concepts of human activity, especially of the sciences. Attention to the definitions of terms, they believe, is the key to solving (or perhaps one should say dis-solving) its traditional philosophical problems.

This principle has application to ethics. The classic discussion is that contained in A. J. Ayer's *Language, Truth and Logic,* which had its first printing in 1936 and has influenced a great deal of philosophy in the decades since. Ayer's contention is that traditional moral philosophy is really a fabric of several different kinds of language, and that much of it, on examination, is really not philosophy at all. The description of moral experience, for example, as appears in the research of psychologists and cultural anthropologists, is properly the work of the social scientist. The exhortation to moral virtue (i.e., the attempt of a speaker to move and motivate his audience in some direction) does not involve an assertion of any kind at all. Thus it is not philosophy either. And value judgments—seemingly the heart of moral philosophy as traditionally understood—can be dismissed on the grounds that they are unverifiable. The scope of ethics, and of philosophy in general, is hereby reduced to looking carefully at the words human beings use in various contexts and determining in each case their practical meaning.

Ayer criticizes traditional accounts of ethics as failing to pay attention to the nature of language.[27] He agrees with Hume that moral utterances (like "Murder is wrong") do not describe any objective feature of the events that they are commonly thought to describe. But he does not agree that such an utterance cannot mean simply that one has a negative feeling about it. For if that were the case, an expression like "I have no particular bad feeling about this action, but it may still be wrong" would be false by definition—it would, in other words, deny the very same thing that it asserts. But it seems that this utterance (whatever else it may be) is not a self-contradiction. For there is no explicit contradiction in saying that a given course of action is (or might be) wrong even though one does not have a negative feeling about it. Against the utilitarians, he offered a similar argument. If calling an action good simply means that it causes pleasure, an expression like "This action will cause pleasure, but it may be wrong" would contradict itself. But again, an expression of this kind does not seem to be a contradiction. Therefore, it seems, the utilitarian account is false.

Ayer also criticizes the notion that value judgments involve intuition of some intangible property that is somehow present in the situation and yet unavailable to the senses. For one thing, he explains, intuitions vary, and it would be hard to know which intuition is correct. And whether intuitions vary or not, their verdict cannot be empirically tested, in which case, the putative claims arising from them are really not genuine statements.

This line of thought, as we have seen, has appealed to a number of philosophers in the twentieth century. Thus Russell,[28] for example, says that the "chief ground" of moral subjectivism is "the complete impossibility of finding any arguments to prove that this or that has intrinsic value." We are, he thinks, prone to misunderstandings of our own language where claims about the good are concerned. When a man says "this is good," he seems to be providing us with an objective description of the thing in question. But what he really is saying can be better construed as something like, "I wish that everyone desired such thing," or "would that everyone desired it." Herein he does not say anything about the item in question but only expresses a wish concerning it; beyond that he says nothing at all.

Ethics, insofar as it renders judgments about what is good and bad, says Russell, "contains no statements, whether true or false, but consists of desires of a certain general kind." Nor, he thinks, does it matter if there exist other beings beyond the sphere of what is human, for the same analysis applies. Value judgments are concerned, not with facts, but with desires—those of human beings, and "of gods, angels, and devils, if they exist." The notion of just retribution, whether in this world or another, is thus irrational, since sin is logically in the eye of the beholder—what is a vice to one may be a virtue to another.

Ethics and Human Science

Positivism, then, aims at a rejection of traditional thinking about good and evil as an objective part of reality. There is a related tendency in the past century to reduce value judgments to the status of judgments about one's society or to see such judgments as expressions of sentiments instilled in a subject by the surrounding influences of his own culture. Alexander Sutherland, in his two-volume work *The Origin and Growth of the Moral Instinct* says that he finds it strange that so many philosophers should speak of what Kant calls the "inscrutable Origin" of the sense of duty. He wonders likewise how anyone could maintain that this sense of duty or conscience is a thing each of us has within him from birth. Asks Sutherland, "How can this be so? Do we not see its growth in the child? What sense of duty do we expect of a babe six months old? Do we not look for more of it when the child is a year, and still more when he is five years old?"[29] Do we not see, moreover, "that notions of duty vary from man to man and from nation to nation; while the strength of the general sense of duty is even more constant?"

"These transcendental views of duty," he concludes, "have no grounds to stand upon, and are possible only to those who have been too busy with theories ever to take an occasional look at facts." He provides instances of how public pressure has effectively shaped human behavior into its many different forms, and how it has at times created moral notions that no one in current society would consider even thinkable. Likewise, he ventures, "Much that we feel assured to be true morality today may seem as radically false 100 years hence." Reflecting on this seeming plasticity of the conscience, he contends,

> So far from the notion of duty having that permanence, that uniformity which, on Kant's supposition, would mark its transcendental origin, it has all the rugged look of a growth, here distorted and there knotted. There is absolutely not one of the moral virtues which the sense of duty has not at some time or other been defied. Is it the prohibition of murder? Then what of all the tribes whose most sacred duty is to gather human heads; what of the Australian who, if a relative has died, finds himself bound by the great duty of killing some one in expiation; what of that serious circle of respectable philosophers ... who ... but a century ago decided after long discussion, that a man was bound to fight a duel if his honour were impugned?[30]

Such considerations lead Sutherland to think that the locus of moral knowledge is this world, not some other. Although he grants that some moral codes may be more humane than others, he believes that moral awareness is inextricably bound up with our awareness of the world around us, and is not the mystical thing that Kant, for example, imagines in his *Critique of Practical Reason*. Moral knowledge, he reasons, is acquired naturalistically, not by means of some alleged higher faculty. I will say more about Sutherland's outlook in the next chapter.

A good deal of popular skepticism, as may be indicated by Sutherland's discussion, has been engendered by the phenomenon of moral diversity. An absolute moral law—one, say, of the kind that Kant has in mind—is supposed to have an existence that transcends the empirical world and so to apply to all individuals, independently of time and cultural accident. Yet if such a law exists, how is it that the moral consciousness of human beings varies as it does? Conscience, as Russell[31] observes, seems to tell different people very different things, depending upon their culture, temperament, and historical circumstances. Presumably not all of these different views can be right. One may think, perhaps, that one's own culture is the enlightened one. But when one looks at the matter objectively—viewing one's own culture from the outside and as one possibility among many—this choice seems strangely arbitrary. The question then arises as to whether we may continue to think that our own conscience informs us of any truth at all.

What fact is alleged to follow from this diversity? Reflecting upon the great variation of moral rules and attitudes across cultures, Ruth Benedict[32] concludes that morality is not "absolute," but that it is merely a product in each case of cultural expectation. Citing examples of behavior deemed wrong or pathological in our society, yet honored in others, she concludes that any notion of *normalcy* is defined, without exception, by the culture in which it has developed. Thus what is paranoia to us, or obsession, or blind vengeance, may be a sign of healthy adjustment elsewhere. Kindliness, likewise, may indicate high character in one place and silliness or befuddlement in another. We may be horrified by infanticide or by abandonment of the elderly. People in other cultures may have different views altogether.

In summary, she remarks that the selection of given traits of temperament and behavior are at bottom "subconscious and nonrational." Much like the articulations of speech, they are "historically conditioned by innumerable accidents of isolation or of contact of people." Thus developments of personality that seem to us to be altogether unacceptable may well make up the very foundations of social life elsewhere. Therefore, reasons Benedict, morality is but a culture-relative and ultimately subjective phenomenon with no reality apart from the variable human ideas, instincts, and attitudes from which it develops.

The past century has also seen various attempts to reduce human action itself and alleged freedom of choice to the laws of the sciences. This analysis generally advocates *determinism*, the belief that all events in the world are but the inevitable result of events that have preceded them. Human action, on this view, is but one such kind of event and thus is no exception to the wider causal scheme within which it transpires. Human action is necessitated, in every case, by the antecedent factors that bring it about. Opinion varies as to what bearing this thesis may have upon the common-sense notions of freedom and moral responsibility. On some readings, determinism rules out any meaningful conception of freedom whatsoever. For human beings, it is herein argued, are not the genuine authors of their actions, and so cannot be held to account for them. This effort has a number of variations, and in closing this chapter I will note a couple of the more prominent lines of such argument.

A classic formulation of the so-called hard deterministic argument is that made late in the nineteenth century by Paul Ree. To say that the human will is unfree, explains Ree,[33] is simply to say that it is bound by the law of causality. To say that it is free is to say that it is not bound by causality. But it is evident, he believes, that the will is indeed subject to the same causal laws that govern all other events and that freedom thus is an illusion.

Every instance of change, insists Ree, be it animate or inanimate, requires some prior "sufficient cause" if it is to come about. Consider, he says, for illustration, the case of a donkey that stands motionless at a given moment between two bundles of hay. Suppose that the donkey then turns to the bundle on the right. How may we account for this fact? The turning of the head, Ree explains, requires the contraction of certain muscles. This in turn presupposes the excitation of certain relevant nerves and the brain state giving rise to it. How does the brain come to be in this state? The answer is found in some set of conditions in the environment and in the organism itself that provide the stimulus. As a result of this whole sequence, the donkey now "wants," as we say, to turn to the right. Given this set of conditions, no other result is possible. Change these conditions, perhaps even slightly (the scent of one of the bundles, the position of the donkey, or whatever), and another result may obtain. But to think that the donkey could have willed on its own, independently of those conditions, a different result is contrary, insists Ree, to "the universal validity of the law of causality."

Everything, holds Ree, is essentially the same with respect to human beings. Although the causal factors may be more complex for humans, we can have no doubt that change requires cause. Every intention and, "indeed, every thought that passes through the brain, the silliest as well as the most brilliant, the true as well as the false, exists of necessity." So-called moral behavior is no exception: The capacity for pity or for taking pleasure in another's pain, the capacity for courage or for cowardice, or any change in such a capacity over time is born in every case of necessity.

The science of depth psychology provides another version of the deterministic theory. In the mind, writes Charles Brenner in his *Elementary Textbook of Psychoanalysis:*

> nothing happens by chance, or in a random way. Each psychic event is determined by the ones which preceded it. Events in our mental lives that may seem to be random and unrelated to what went on before are only apparently so. In fact, mental phenomena are no more capable of such a lack of causal connection with what preceded them than are physical ones. Discontinuity in this sense does not exist in mental life.[34]

This principle, says Brenner, is essential to the understanding of human behavior in both its normal and its pathological aspects. Of every phenomenon in the study, we must ask what caused it, and we may be sure, he maintains, that an answer exists even if it is not always easy to discover.

The application of psychoanalysis to the issue of free will is discussed at length in a seminal essay, "What Means This Freedom?" by John Hospers.[35] The concept of *unconscious motivation,* says Hospers, is of tremendous importance in understanding human behavior. It also bears strongly upon the issue of freedom and responsibility.

When are we rationally justified in holding an individual responsible for his actions? As Hospers observes, there are a number of popular criteria. Among them are (1) the presence or absence of premeditation; (2) the ability or lack of ability of that individual to defend his actions with reasons; (3) the presence or absence of unconscious forces of which the individual himself is ignorant; (4) the presence or absence of compulsion, in some form or other; and (5) the extent to which the actions can be changed by the use of reason. All these criteria, singly and severally, have been used by people in the field of psychiatry at one time or another. But even after one has made these distinctions, Hospers explains, there remains a serious question whether we are ever responsible for any of our actions. The issue, he writes, may be put this way: "How can anyone be responsible for his actions, since they grow out of his character, which is shaped and molded and made what it is by influences—some hereditary, but most of them stemming from early parental environment—that were not of his own making or choosing?"[36]

Consider, then, for illustration, a criminal who has strangled several people and stands condemned to die in the electric chair. Jury and public alike hold him responsible, for he planned the murders down to the least detail. So far, from this vantage point, the criminal seems to be an absolute villain. But suppose now that we learn more about the events in his life that have led up to the murders—the parents, says Hospers, who rejected him from babyhood; the childhood spent in one unloving foster home after another; the constantly frustrated early desire for affection; the hard shell he assumes to compensate for this pain and humiliation; and, finally, the attempts to heal his wounds to his shattered ego through "defensive aggression."

It all takes on a different look, Hospers claims, as we gain this new and more informed perspective. We may still institutionalize the man for the good of society, but no longer will we flatter ourselves by holding him responsible for his actions. Sometimes the key facts available to us may involve environment, as in the case of childhood trauma. In others, they may involve biology, as, for example, when an abnormal development of the skull precludes the normal development of the brain. But the implications are the same. "Let us note," Hospers writes, "that the more thoroughly and in detail we know the causal factors leading a person to behave as he does, the more we tend to exempt him from responsibility."[37] The more we learn about the criminal, it seems, the less we tend to think of him as being morally bad and the more we tend to see him instead as a victim. What is more natural, then, than to think that if we were fully enlightened as to that man's behavior, we would cease to think of him as being bad in any degree at all.

There are, as Hospers acknowledges, familiar objections to this general account of human behavior. It is immoral, say some, to exonerate people in this way: "I might think it fit to excuse somebody because he was born on the other side of the tracks," goes one line of response, "if I didn't know so many bank presidents who were also born on the other side of the tracks."[38]

What is most immoral in this situation, Hospers replies, is the caricature of the conditions related to the excuse. One is not excused simply for being born on the wrong side of the tracks, but for a whole set of conditions that are (according to the theory, at least) inevitably linked with the behavior in question. Suppose, says Hospers, it was learned that a man commits murder only if at some time in the previous week he has eaten, say, tuna fish salad along with peas, mushroom soup, and blueberry pie. Suppose that research into murder cases of the past twenty years turned up the fact that these factors were present in every murder case. Would not such a finding give us pause? The example, to be sure, is empirically absurd, but might there not be, Hospers asks, some combination of factors (no doubt more complex) regularly associated with such behavior? And when we discover this connection, will it not seem "foolish and pointless, as well as immoral," to hold people responsible for their crimes?

This theory does not deny that people may willfully *resist* the influences of a negative environment. Such people have in them, as a part of their psychic legacy, the energy that can be mobilized to this end. Others lack it. But in either case, the origins of the condition—the presence or absence of the capacity to react against outward circumstance—will be outside the doing of the agent. Whether one is the kind of person who can make the relevant effort is itself a matter of circumstance.

For this reason, there is something self-righteous, Hospers concludes, in our pronouncement that a condemned criminal deserves his punishment—"as if," Hospers says, "we were moral and he immoral," when in fact we are lucky and he is unlucky—forgetting that "there, but for the grace of God and a fortunate early environment, go we." He cites with approval the statement of Clarence Darrow, made in connection with Darrow's celebrated Leopold-Loeb defense, that a man is not to blame when "his machine" is imperfect. "I have never in my life," states Darrow, "been interested so much in fixing blame as I have in relieving people from blame. I am not wise enough to fix it."

The upshot of this line of argument is that human behavior involves no exception to the general and unexceptionable laws that govern the universe as a whole. The alleged autonomy of human beings, the seeming spontaneity of their actions, is an illusion. Freedom and the attendant notion of moral responsibility are but the remnant of our intellectual innocence.

It remains to be asked whether this general view of things is one that we should accept. I have already discussed the proposed reduction of our thought processes to events in the natural world. Any such theory, I have maintained, is plagued by the fact that the theory itself is presumably but one more of the conscious events that are determined, at some level, by those same material forces. A number of questions, however, remain with respect to the issues noted in this chapter. In Chapter 4 I will discuss several of these issues, such as the alleged scientific analysis of human behavior and the ultimate status of value judgments. I will argue that science, on the whole, does not incline us toward a deterministic account of human action, and that our common-sense ideas about good and evil require us, if we are consistent, to accept a theory of values and of human nature that transcends the scope of the empirical sciences.

Chapter Four

The Inadequacy of Naturalism

When a Roman father told his son that it was a sweet and seemly thing to die for his country, he believed what he said. He was communicating to the son an emotion which he himself shared and which he believed to be in accord with the value which his judgment discerned in noble death. He was giving the boy the best he had, giving of his spirit to humanize him as he had given of his body to beget him.

—C. S. Lewis, *The Abolition of Man*

Reductionist Theory and the Elements of Moral Common Sense

In the preceding chapter I gave a brief account of some of the major historical efforts to define value judgments. Such efforts divide themselves, I believe, into views of two kinds.

One kind seeks to reduce such judgments, in one way or another, to statements about the natural world. It finds expression, for example, in the outlook of the early atomists, who believe that all of reality is composed of tiny bits of matter in their various configurations in the void. The view finds expression likewise in the words of the skeptic Thrasymachus, who claims that so-called justice is merely the self-interested dictate of those who have power, and in the doctrine likewise of modern day relativists, who say that good and evil refer merely to the ways and traditions incidental to a given culture. It is voiced as well by the logical positivists, who seek to reduce judgments of value to expressions, in each case, of the emotional states of those who make them.

Alongside this basic view is another, quite different, outlook, which finds one expression in Plato and another in Kant. On this view, value judgments reach beyond mere facts about human feeling or culture, and indeed beyond the natural world altogether. Value judgments cannot be reduced to statements about matter, or society, or human preference, or custom. They are instead metaphysical.

Has either view any rational advantage over the other? In this chapter I will argue that our ordinary convictions about morality (that some actions are good and some evil, that we are under an obligation, at times, to do certain things, and so on) are better served by a view of the latter kind. I will maintain that such a view, however mysterious it may seem, and however out-of-fashion in its otherworldly character, is the one that best accords with our common-sense views about morality.

Few people these days, it seems, have use for a moral theory of this kind. Many are swept along on popular currents of thought that see value judgments as being in some way a matter of social circumstance—that they vary somehow with the changing attitudes of given cultures and have no reality of their own.

The grounds for this kind of thinking are several. Some people say that there can be no real truth in ethics on the grounds that general moral rules are so hard to formulate. Take, for example, the claim that one ought not to lie. It may serve well enough in most cases, but nonetheless, they observe, it seems to have exceptions—to cite one example, an act of subterfuge in time of war, when deception, it seems, may serve a legitimate purpose. In this case, the prohibition against lying is imperfect. And if such a rule has exceptions, it is supposed, it cannot be "absolute" and cannot apply to all people at all times.

It is true, I think, that moral rules tend to have exceptions, and that dependable guidelines of conduct are hard to formulate. But it is an error, I believe, to suppose that because a rule has exceptions, it has no real application. Indeed the same man who judges that lying is sometimes right and sometimes wrong does not thereby abandon the idea of an objective moral truth. He does, in fact, affirm it. For if, as he claims, lying is a good thing in one situation and a bad thing in another, then presumably there is some basis for this distinction—some rule or principle according to which each act of lying derives its respective value. The claim that lying is right in some cases and wrong in others implies that each given instance of lying has genuine value. The fact that lying has no constant status does not mean that value itself is not objectively real. If one cannot offhand find a rule for all occasions, it may only mean that the word "lie" ranges over too wide a variety of actions to allow for generalization.

Some people are troubled by moral differences between cultures. This phenomenon, cited by Benedict and others, has been adduced many times in favor of a moral skepticism of one kind or another. And there do exist, it seems, moral differences between various societies across time and place. What does one make of this fact?

It is actually a bit odd, I think, that so much emphasis has been placed upon moral differences between cultures, and that so little attention has been given to moral similarities. It is true that such differences exist, but just as impressive, one must think, is the tremendous amount of agreement of moral attitudes across the span of history and culture. Take, for example, physical courage. Who has not admired it? The prowess of Achilles and his faithfulness, at last, to his task[1] have been admired, as far as I am aware, by every audience that has encountered them. (Likewise, I think, has his excess of pride been discerned as a moral defect.) What culture has not admired physical courage, be it the culture of an Achaean, a samurai, a Cheyenne dog soldier, or an urban gang member on the streets of today's inner city?

Perhaps it will be said that it is only natural for such a quality to be admired, since a personal quality of this kind tends to serve the side that has it. But that, I think, is inadequate as an explanation. For what does it mean to say that a given quality, such as fighting spirit, is *admired*? It does not, I think, mean only that persons find it enjoyable to look upon or that they welcome heroes on their own side when they can have them. Everyone, of course, would want a warrior beside him in time of trouble, if one were available. But the attitude of admiration goes beyond this. To admire the hero is not merely to want him, but to want to be like him, which is a crucially different matter. To esteem a man is (to use a cognate verb) to estimate that he is of high worth—that is, to say not merely that he is handy to one's own cause, but that he is valuable, that he merits respect independently of one's own position with regard to the contest. It is possible, likewise, to admire an enemy or to admire, at least, some facet of his character, even in the midst of mortal combat. (We count it as a virtue, in fact, when an individual can rise above his immediate vantage point to see his adversary in this light.)

Granted, it may be said, there exist certain moral elements that are constant, or nearly so, across different cultures. What does one make of the remaining differences? Although such differences may exist, I believe that a word of caution is in order before going further. For some thought needs to be given to just what it is that constitutes a moral *difference*. In some cases it appears that outward cross-cultural differences, when examined in detail, may actually express a deeper sameness of basic principle. As Solomon Asch[2] observes, given cultural practices must be assessed within the context of the circumstances and the belief systems within which they appear. It may happen, for example, that one society condones the abandonment of one of its elderly members, whereas another will regard this policy as being unthinkable. Does this difference mean that the two societies have "different values"? We must be wary, writes Asch, of the assumption that in such a case "the same action which is tolerated under one set of conditions is outlawed under other conditions."

As he explains:

> The same issue arises in connection with the killing of parents. In the society that follows this practice there prevails the belief that people continue to lead in the next world the same existence as in the present and that they maintain forever the condition of health and vigor that they had at the time of death. It is therefore a filial duty of the son to dispatch his parents, an act that has the full endorsement of the parent and of the community.[3]

Thus what seems to be a moral difference at one level of assessment may turn out to involve moral agreement at another. It is true that a certain kind of action—say, the killing of a reasonably healthy parent—is outlawed in one society and is permitted (or even required) in another. But given the context of the action, there may exist a deeper agreement between the parricidal culture and the other—namely, a principle of concern for the ultimate welfare of one's parents, and a wish, likewise, to maximize their happiness. Given the presupposition, noted by Asch, of a next life and its continuation as described, the act of parricide may be authorized in one societal context by the same principle that forbids the act in another. Thus what is shown by this societal difference is not that the selfsame act of killing of one's parents is (or is deemed to be) right in one place and wrong in another, but that surface descriptions—those making use, without qualification, of terms like 'killing' and 'parricide'—are insufficient to tell us what are the real values of a given society.

Granted, between cultures there may be some moral differences that cannot be handled as neatly as this. Some differences may be more basic—as with the difference, perhaps, between a pacifist ethic and a nonpacifist one. And in fact we may not have to go outside of a whole culture to find them. Such instances of moral difference seem to exist, after all, in the moral attitude of a single culture over a period of time. They may exist likewise between two individuals within a culture at a given time or even, for that matter, within an individual at different stages of his own moral development. What might this tell us about the status of moral truths themselves? Does it tell us, as some might claim, that they have no objective reality?

There is something a bit curious, when one thinks about it, in an argument from the diversity of *belief*, of any given kind, to the denial of an objective truth at issue. One finds disagreement, after all, in a great many areas, among them the areas of history and mathematics. In no cases there do we suppose that the existence of diverse beliefs about the thing in question implies the absence of truth in the subject matter. Indeed the very fact of disagreement itself seems to involve an assumption shared by each side that some truth of the matter exists independent of those who argue over it. Thus moral disagreement, where it may exist, does not by itself seem to be a reason to deny the existence of moral reality.

Another curious feature of the moral diversity argument is the seeming gap between its premise and its conclusion. The argument purports to show that since there exist different moral beliefs across different cultures (or, again, across different periods of a single culture, or between different individuals, etc.), there can exist no truth independent of the differences themselves. But how exactly is such an argument supposed to work? This difference, after all, is an empirical fact about people and how they historically happen to think, or feel, or behave, and how their society is structured with respect to certain practices. The issue of a higher moral law, in contrast, is metaphysical and transcends, on the face of it, the data of the empirical sciences altogether. How can the premise, then, provide grounds for the conclusion?

But the real difficulty, it is sometimes said, is not mere difference. It is rather that moral differences cannot be settled in the way that others can. For in the case of history or mathematics, there are agreed-upon ways (in principle, at least) in which an answer can be reached. Or if not—say, in the case of certain problems of mathematics[4]—we think that this owes to a limitation upon currently existing methods of the science or upon the human understanding itself. We do not suppose that no ideal answer exists.

What, then, of moral differences? Can they be resolved? I think that Ayer, Russell, and others are right in saying that there exists no such thing as a scientific demonstration of moral truth. I do not think it follows that there can exist no such truth, or that values must therefore be reducible to facts about human psychology. Not, at any rate, unless we assume that all truths must lie within the scope of scientific investigation.

But that does not seem to be the case. Few persons, I think, would insist that mystical experience is a subjective phenomenon just because its insights cannot be outwardly measured. Of course, it may be said by some that mysticism, too, is really but another phenomenon of psychology—that it is something unusual, to be sure, but nothing more than an aberration of the mental state, and thus provides no real insight beyond itself into reality. Those who reject supernatural interpretations of ethics tend, in general, to be skeptical about mystical experience as well. But such aberration, I think, is not what most of us make of such experience. The more common feeling is that the mystic's experience differs from ours, not merely in its form, but in its range and in its level—in the extent to which it serves to apprehend the truth. The content of this experience may not be communicable to us in rational terms, but that does not mean that the experience reveals no truth. Rather its truth may simply not be available to our own limited range of apprehension.

But what, again, of the verification principle? Does it not render metaphysical claims of any kind meaningless? I contend that it does not. The meaningfulness of a given piece of language is not undermined, I think, merely by the fact that it transcends the facts of outward investigation. Granted, there are some types of minds that will reject metaphysical claims as being unreal or even meaningless. But to say that such claims are empty simply because they are not outwardly observable is to beg the question, I think, in favor of the position of materialism, and to give the verification principle a wiser reign than logic requires. Must all propositions be either analytic or verifiable? Judged by its own standards, the principle itself may be suspect, since it appears to be neither of these things.

I think it is important to see the difference in this principle as applied, say, to the following "rabbit" case and to certain others. If a rabbit is defined in the first place as a material entity with certain observable characteristics, then one cannot speak sensibly of a rabbit with those same characteristics removed. A rabbit minus its rabbit characteristics is no rabbit at all, in which case the claim that such an animal does (or might) exist is an empty claim. It is just this element of internal contradiction, I believe, that accounts for the absurdity of the example. In the case of certain other alleged realities, however, the same objection may not hold. Not all elements of human experience are defined in ways that involve the presence or absence of any given material fact.

Consider, again, Kant's encounter with the moral law. The object of this experience is not defined as something that has material characteristics—such things, say, as being brown, or furry, or long-eared. Therefore, the element of self-contradiction present in the rabbit case is not present in this one. It is for this reason, I think, that metaphysics in this latter context is not undermined by the fact that its pronouncements lie beyond the range of sensation. Granted, this moral law, as Kant describes it, does not have sensory qualities. But this lack does not make it empty. For it is the source of those judgments that have to do with such things as the real and objective difference between good and evil and the demand that this difference makes upon us. The actual nature of Kant's moral law may well transcend the categories of the empirical world altogether, but this law is, at the same time, the thing that enables me to ask certain questions that would be impossible to ask meaningfully were it not to exist. How far have I come in terms of moral wisdom? Have I grown beyond the person I was a year ago? Because I recognize this source of truth, I can speak of my development as being not merely change but progress. The outward, empirical changes in my behavior (that I am now, say, more honest or more compassionate) signify not merely change but *evolution*—a positive development with respect to what the moral law demands of me.

What is the difference between having this apprehension and lacking it altogether? Consider, for the sake of illustration, the difference between an individual of acute moral consciousness and one who is amoral. Is the difference between these two persons simply *emotional*? Perhaps the real difference lies in the fact that the amoral individual lacks the apparatus to understand values of the relevant kind. What his amorality may indicate is not that moral values themselves are illusory, but only that they require of us a certain faculty that may be present in some individuals and lacking in others.

There is a similar situation, perhaps, with respect to particular differences between morally conscious individuals. For if there does exist a truth in morality, it may be that we come to understand it only gradually, as our individual maturation process allows. Presumably not all people are at the same stage in this process, so it is reasonable to think that they may not apprehend moral truth to the same extent. Likewise, a given individual may understand some aspect of this truth while failing to understand another. And similarly, perhaps, with a whole culture: It may favor a certain aspect of moral development while at the same time it gives little attention to some other. Thus one society may prize in its members a keen sense of honor, whereas another may instill first and foremost a sense of compassion. Still another may honor above all things the worth of physical courage, and so on. Perhaps no single culture has a full apprehension of what is ultimately involved in moral excellence. But each may understand some aspect of it. It is for this reason that one culture may learn something from the ethic of another. But the fact that such differences exist, again, is not grounds for a denial of moral truth. Nor, I think, do cultural differences imply that moral truths are merely truths about the structure of society.

Perhaps an insight into the nature of moral truth can be found in the moral differences that develop within ourselves over a period of time. How do we come to be the moral persons that we are at present? If we reflect upon our own case, we will find, I think, that certain very important (and presumably ongoing) changes have occurred within ourselves over the course of our lives. We do not suppose that these changes are neutral in value. We say instead that they involve growth, which is to say, positive changes in the level of our character from one time to the next; changes for better or worse, not differences on the same plane. Change indeed is essential, we commonly imagine, to our own moral development.

Of course, our basis for saying that is intuitive. Furthermore, it is not always obvious when we have become truly enlightened upon a given moral issue or have acquired virtue with respect to some aspect of our behavior. Moral problems involve many gray areas and often they admit of no clear solution. (To cite one example, one may take the current controversy surrounding abortion.) But that, I believe, does not mean that there is no truth at stake. For perhaps the gray areas and the uncertainty that attends them may be part of the moral struggle itself. A respect for moral truth implies a willingness to seek it out insofar as our faculties will honestly enable us, in responsible fashion and without falling back upon skepticism or false authority in the process.

The doctrine of moral relativism is plagued further, I think, by the fact that it runs afoul of common-sense notions of *societal* progress. We commonly suppose that it is possible for a society to become better or worse in given respects over a period of time. We often imagine that it is our responsibility to do what we can to bring about, say, a wider range of freedoms and opportunities for those who live in our own society, and perhaps also a more equitable distribution of wealth. Such things, we imagine, constitute positive change—progress toward an ideal against which the society is measured. Yet what can progress mean if right and wrong are defined simply in terms of what is accepted by the society at a given time? In order for a society to better itself morally, there must be some ideal against which that society can judge itself in the process. A society, for example, in which slavery is practiced can presumably become a better society if it abolishes the practice. Yet if *right* only means what is accepted, a slave-holding society must, by definition, be right in its practice.[5]

Likewise with other cases—those, say, of child castration or of cruel and unusual criminal punishment. Most of us wish to say, against any relativistic claim to the contrary, that a society that lacks these is (all things being equal) a better society than one that has them. And we imagine that a society that moves to abolish such practices is improving—that is to say, not merely changing, but changing for the better. Yet if relativism is true, we cannot make moral judgments across societies, since there is no transsocietal basis on which to make them. But if we cannot compare two societies at a given time, neither, it seems, can we compare one society with itself over a given time period. And if the latter is the case, we cannot have any basis on which to propose moral changes (i.e., for the better) within our own. But surely that is contrary both to belief and to conscience. If we wish, then, to retain our belief that a society can change for better or worse, and that we ourselves are responsible in some measure for which course it may take, we must suppose also that some standard of value exists independent of which moral beliefs our society may embrace at any given time.

Ethics and the Limits of Social Science

Some people imagine that any notion of an objective moral truth is refuted in some way by the data of the sciences. In recent decades social scientists have made efforts to comprehend the human being as an object within the realm of nature, and to see him likewise as something that can be understood in purely clinical terms. Accordingly, there has been an attempt in this century to replace the language of ethics with that of a supposedly more objective analysis of human behavior. Thus old-scheme words like 'good' and 'evil', 'righteous' and 'unrighteous', have been replaced, in the name of sophistication, by those denoting such events as 'confusion', 'neurosis', and 'maladjustment' and their resolution. The more enlightened view of the human condition, it is claimed, takes us in the direction of moral neutrality.

Value judgments are thus discounted or are understood to be in some way relative in their basis. The real business of understanding and modifying human behavior is supposed to work instead in terms of such things as socialization, personality dynamics, and quantifiable stimulus and response. Misbehavior, it is said, is not a subject for blame or for sermons but for investigation by trained social clinicians. The substance of this analysis is causal, not evaluative. Value words, it is thought, add nothing to the fact; they have no active part in a science of human behavior. What should be said about this tendency from the standpoint of moral philosophy?

I think, first, that the notion itself of a thoroughgoing science of human behavior may rest upon a misconception. For a science of this kind presumably seeks to establish certain causal regularities that will allow for the prediction and control of the events within its domain. But that, in turn, presupposes that human behavior itself (involving such things as human will, thought, motivation) is determined in some way—presumably, at bottom, by material events—in ways that make this prediction possible. For reasons given in Chapter 2, I think that we must be wary of any such presupposition. Later in this chapter I will say more about the notion of determinism and its relationship to our supposed freedom of action.

But aside from such theoretical issues as these, it might be asked if the method of the social sciences can offer us a personally satisfying account of the facts of experience. Can it, for example, explain convincingly what is involved in so-called antisocial (e.g., dishonest or unduly aggressive) behavior?

The discussion by William Barrett in his classic *Irrational Man* is instructive. Barrett criticizes the recent tendency, in some quarters, to suppose that the study of human behavior is in fact a purely scientific undertaking. In the process he criticizes the related tendency toward moral neutrality. Reflecting upon the rather prescient insights of the nineteenth-century Danish philosopher Soren Kierkegaard, he says:

> We are in the habit nowadays of labeling morally deficient people as sick, mentally sick or neurotic. This is true if we look at the neurotic from outside: his neurosis is indeed a sickness, for it prevents him from functioning as he should, either totally or in some particular area of life. But the closer we get to any neurotic the more we are assailed by the sheer human perverseness, the skillfulness, of his attitude. If he is a friend, we can up to a point deal with him as an *object* who does not function well, but only up to a point; beyond that if a personal relation exists between us we have to deal with him as a *subject*, and as such we must find him morally perverse or willfully disagreeable; and we have to make these moral judgments to his face if the friendship is to retain its human content, and not disappear into a purely clinical relation.[6]

Kierkegaard, says Barrett, understands that what we today call sickness is really a kind of sinfulness. Thus our supposed "distance" from the neurotic in the interest of objectivity is not really in the service of the truth. Our wholehearted involvement in this situation requires a value judgment from us if it is to remain honest. In dealing with such misconduct, we reach a point where moral neutrality becomes a lie. The so-called neurotic must not merely be analyzed but *confronted*, if the relationship is to remain authentic, and if he is finally to be understood either by himself or by others.

A central area of concern for moral theorists is the means by which moral truth is learned. Those who reject the otherworldly conception of ethics sometimes do so on the grounds that we learn moral rules from our social environment. Moral knowledge, they say, is thus empirical; it cannot be knowledge of any remote or supernatural kind. We must therefore look, they reason, to nature, not to some higher realm, for the substance of ethics.

Is the foregoing a sound line of argument? There is a serious question, I believe, about whether we can really be said to learn ethics from our environment. Consider again Sutherland's discussion. He is correct in saying that moral beliefs are not found consciously within us, in any developed form, from our earliest years. One does acquire moral ideas by social contact, and indeed it is hard to imagine what moral experience would be possible for an individual in a world that did not contain other people. But it does not follow, I think, from the fact that moral knowledge is occasioned by contact with the world that it is knowledge *of* the world. It does not follow, either, that moral knowledge can be understood in terms of the natural process of an individual's social contacts.

In order to see this better, it may be worth a moment to reflect upon what sort of thing we actually acquire in gaining moral knowledge. What, after all, do we mean when we say that one course of action is morally better than another, or that an individual ought to do something? And if indeed some actions are better than others, how do we come to know that?

Sutherland thinks that moral knowledge is empirical. But empirical knowledge is knowledge of what is materially present in the world around us. Can any such information be said to constitute a knowledge of values? Consider the case of a small child (a moral kindergartner, as it were) who carelessly runs over a playmate with his tricycle and is taken to task for his behavior. What is the empirical content of his experience in this situation? An inventory of the relevant sensations presumably would include such things as the impact of the collision, the mother's stern look and disapproving tone, and the added swat that she may deliver to the back of his pants for emphasis. All of this the child absorbs by way of his senses. But wherein lies the moral lesson? A child may learn from his sensations that reckless behavior is dangerous, that it precipitates all sorts of experiences that he would rather not have. But how can he learn, from these sensations, that such behavior *is wrong in principle*?

Perhaps it will be said that moral knowledge is not gained at this stage of a child's development, but that it comes only through time and with greater sophistication of language and reasoning. A child, it may be claimed, will not yet acquire moral insight from such an episode, or not on the first occasion at least. Perhaps moral understanding comes only with his further social and cognitive development in the coming years.

But it does no good, I think, to say that such understanding comes gradually in the manner just described. For this further contact with playmates, peers, neighbors, educators, and associates—in short, with society in general—is essentially just more contact of the same kind. Suppose that the reckless tricyclist just observed takes to driving his car, a few years down the line, in residential areas at speeds far exceeding the legal limit. A judge may admonish him in the courtroom, swat him, as it were, with a hefty fine, and tell him that he ought to be more mindful of the safety of those around him. Where, again, are the makings of a moral lesson? This person learns, by way of his eyes and ears, that reckless driving is something of which the judge, and the legal system as a whole, disapproves. He can learn that such behavior has painful consequences—in the event, at least, that he is apprehended. But how can any amount of such contact teach him anything about what he ought to do? Moral knowledge is presumably not simply knowledge of cause and effect, or of what society happens to want from its citizens, or of what noises it may happen to make at some given time as to how its citizens ought to behave. Rather it is knowledge of what one ought to do for its own sake, independently of the price that one stands to pay when one acts otherwise. Hence it is hard to see how any such knowledge can be gained by way of sensation. It is for this reason that some philosophers have insisted that the knowledge of ethics lies beyond our knowledge of the empirical world.

It is sometimes thought that the science of ethics can be grounded neither in empirical fact nor in supernaturalism, but in the sheer fact of reason itself. It is claimed by some that Kant's ethics is an example of this. His categorical imperative, it is said, is actually a test of an agent's rational consistency: The man who lies, for example, counts upon the general honesty of his fellows in order to press his strategy; he wants likewise to live in a world where people tend to develop their talents even if he finds it too much trouble to develop his own. Thus when he lies, or falls into habits of sloth or dissipation, he wills, as Kant himself puts it, one thing for himself and another for his fellows. And that, it is thought, is irrational. Kant, it is thus said, equates the rules of conduct with the rules of thought; he bases his ethics upon rules of logic.

There is indeed a sense in which Kant's principle involves consistency. For a liar does make an exception of himself to the same rules (that of honesty, for example) that he hopes will be observed by others. But it is not clear from this, I think, that lying is *irrational* in the same way as is, for example, 2 + 2 = 5. After all, the liar does not wish, say, to be both honest and dishonest. And he does not expect the world, with no reason whatsoever, to weigh his own interests more heavily than the interests of others. His behavior involves an inconsistency in one sense; objectively speaking, there is no reason why one member of the human race should enjoy some advantage over all others. But this does not imply, so far as I can tell, that it is contrary to reason for one such member to prefer an advantage for himself. This imagined outside point of view (the view, it is sometimes said, of an "ideal observer") is in a sense objective in that it is not limited, as is the point of view of a particular individual. But this fact need not, on any logical grounds, determine the point of view of such an individual. From an outside point of view, the double standard may be arbitrary, but it does not follow that from this outside point of view, an individual *within* the world, with a specific (i.e., self-interested) point of view, should have the same detached outlook.

The Impossibility of Grounding
Judgments of Value in the Natural World

A bit more might be said here about the common-sense notion of moral obligation and its relationship to the problem of ethics. The discussion offered by Hastings Rashdall[7] in his two-volume work *The Theory of Good and Evil* is very much to the point.

Morality, says Rashdall, is at first glance neutral with regard to certain higher issues of philosophy. People of all different persuasions, after all, whether materialists or nonmaterialists, worldly or otherworldly in their basic outlook, are able to recognize moral values and to incorporate moral reasoning with full seriousness into their daily lives. Often they see no logical connection between this part of their lives and their views (if any) regarding the problems of religion and metaphysics. There is no contradiction, on the face of it, between a respect for conscience and undecidedness with regard to problems concerning the nature of such things, say, as freedom of the will or the possibility of a future life.

Says Rashdall:

> It is no doubt true that the Agnostic . . . cannot be convicted of any positive inconsistency, if he simply accepts the dictates of his moral consciousness as final, and says: "I know nothing as to the ultimate source of these moral ideas, except that they come to me in the same way as the rest of my knowledge, or anything as to the ultimate outcome of this moral life which I feel to be incumbent upon me. I simply know the meaning of the good, and that it is right for me to aim at it, and that I can, to some extent, bring it into existence by my voluntary action."[8]

Thus morality has at least a psychological independence from certain claims of metaphysics. An individual can recognize moral values and can live a good and decent life without ever taking up any higher questions about the nature of the universe. But, thinks Rashdall, certain common-sense views about our moral situation may turn out to have some very serious philosophical implications.

Granted, he says, that the agnostic attitude is psychologically possible. "It remains a further question whether the true meaning of Morality is capable of being made explicit, and of being reconciled or harmonized with other facts of our knowledge or experience without necessitating the adoption of certain views concerning the ultimate nature of things and the rejection of certain other views."[9]

It is possible to combine strong moral convictions in practice with agnosticism in regard to metaphysics. But it remains to be asked whether this combination is a reasonable one. We may avoid the issue by "shutting our eyes to a position of the facts," or by refusing to address the issue beyond a certain point. But a question about reasonableness requires that we look at all the available facts of the case. Indecision or avoidance of the issue is not reasonable when we may have the answer. So the question arises if we may have to choose ultimately between our "practical recognition of moral obligation," on the one hand, and "certain views of the Universe which reflection has shown to be inconsistent with that creed," on the other.

Let us imagine, then, that an individual has adopted a materialistic view of the world wherein the human mind has somehow emerged as an accident. How, asks Rashdall, would such a view affect his attitude toward morality? To the man who regards all spiritual life as being an accident—as "a mere inexplicable incident" in the career of a world that is essentially material and purposeless:

> There is no conclusive reason why all moral ideas—the very conception of "value," the very notion that one thing is intrinsically better than another, the very conviction that there is something which a man ought to do—may not be merely some strange illusion due to the unaccountable freaks of a mindless process or to the exigencies of natural selection.[10]

Yet we say, again, "that the Moral Law has a real existence, that there is such a thing as an absolute Morality, that there is something absolutely true or false in ethical judgments, whether we or any number of human beings at any given time actually think so or not. Such a belief is distinctly implied in what we mean by Morality."[11]

The idea of this objective law, Rashdall says, exists at least as "a psychological fact." A question remains as to its theoretical content. Where might such a law exist, and what manner or existence can be attributed to it?

Certainly this law is found wholly and completely in no human consciousness. Can it then somehow exist in the natural world order itself? On materialistic assumptions, Rashdall continues, the moral law cannot be regarded as being a real thing or as a property of a real thing. It is instead a product of the imagination that cannot itself "compel respect when we feel no desire to act in accord with it." An absolute moral law, he says, cannot exist *in* material things.

Where, then, does it exist? Rashdall believes that the moral law can exist only in a divine mind, and that is the source of all that is true in our own judgments of what is right and wrong. Thus the belief in God, he concludes, is a postulate of an objective or absolute morality.

I am not sure that the existence of God is the solution of the problem, since morality, if it is objectively real, seems to require an existence that is independent of divine will. To say that the moral law exists in a divine mind can mean either that the divine will is itself the law or that the law is comprehended by that mind. If it is the former, then the old problem arises as to what divine goodness can mean other than divine command. If the latter (if, in other words, the law has an objective reality that is not contained in, but only comprehended by, the divine wisdom) then an account of moral law is still wanting.

Can we make any sort of inference regarding the higher order of things from the presumed fact of moral obligation? I believe that we can, though I think that such an inference ought not to proceed from any "noumenal" assumption about the nature of morality in itself. Rather, it ought to proceed from our intuitive recognition that we ourselves are morally obligated at times to behave in certain prescribed ways. We may ask further what sorts of things must be true of a universe in which that is the case. In so doing we can obtain, not theoretical certainty about such further things, but a view instead that allows us logical consistency with our ordinary moral beliefs.

On such a view, the moral law is practically knowable insofar as we may know our duty, at times at least, in a given situation. Our inferences from this point should be taken, I think, not from speculation about the moral law as a thing in itself, but from its practical relationship to ourselves as presumed moral agents. And again, if this law is worthy of our efforts, it must be something more than simply a part of the natural world. This fact and its further implications are treated by John Hick in his discussion of the so-called moral argument for God's existence.

If, says Hick, morality were

> a human creation, consisting in the adoption by a group of people of rules of behavior designed to safeguard their common existence, it would not presuppose any ground beyond man himself considered as an intelligent and gregarious animal. But if we are sometimes aware of moral claims upon us that are absolute in the sense that no counter-considerations of personal self-interest can lift them from our consciences, then something more than man the gregarious animal must be involved. In acknowledging such claims upon our lives we are recognizing a source of moral obligation that is higher than ourselves in the scale of values and that rightfully summons us to faithful obedience. It is characteristic of the moral prophet that he is vividly conscious of an obligation that is

unconditional and that cannot rightfully be set in the balance with any other interest whatsoever, not even life itself. If there are such moral absolutes—and
Rashdall believed that most of us in our heart of hearts acknowledge that there
are—one cannot consistently accord to them the allegiance they demand and at
the same time be satisfied with naturalistic analysis of our obedience.[12]

Let us consider, for a moment, the general content of moral experience—
such things as pangs of remorse, pride in one's own integrity, and a desire for
social justice. The bare fact of this experience, as Hick recognizes, is open to
more than one theoretical interpretation. We may view it as being the product, once again, of natural forces that have shaped our social and psychological constitution. Moral conscience, so conceived, reveals to us nothing outside of ourselves. It may be understood solely in terms of its natural
mechanics, without reference to any higher realm of values therein revealed.
It can, however, be viewed as being a revelation of some higher truth that has
a reality of its own. In that case, morality is something different, something
indeed to be reckoned with, as a reality that makes a genuine demand upon
those of us who are conscious of it.

It is important to understand that no fact of moral experience itself can resolve this issue. For whatever such fact that we may consider will be consistent with either kind of interpretation. Thus we cannot use it to decide the
case theoretically in either direction. We can never find grounds to support
either view, since we can never get outside ourselves, so to speak, and assess
this epistemological situation in its entirety. We cannot somehow stand
above ourselves and see, as if from overhead, what our own deepest instincts
about value really mean, for these convictions lie at the very heart of our apprehension of reality and our place in it. They accompany whatever investigations we may make of the world and of ourselves. That is not to say that
we must remain undecided in our daily lives as to which interpretation is the
better and more natural for ourselves as a course of action. Indeed we cannot, for situations must be acted upon in one way or another, whatever we
may think. But the theoretical question, I think, lies outside of any solution.

Are there rational grounds, then, for accepting the higher interpretation?
Hick continues:

In trying to evaluate this position, much would seem to depend upon the credi-
bility of a naturalistic theory of ethics from the standpoint of the person who is
engaged in any exceptional and critically demanding response to the claims of
duty. There is no doubt that a variety of naturalistic ethical theories are possible.
But could a person rationally risk his life, as, let us say, a French underground
fighter in World War II, or embark on a career of poverty and hardship in the
struggle to win social justice for others, or sacrifice himself to save another, if he
believed that there is ultimately nothing more to human morality than group
compulsions which are basically akin to those of an ant-hill? It may be said that

self-sacrificial action is not usually based upon rational calculation at all, but expresses some altruistic impulse of our nature. But why, from a naturalistic point of view, should we not try to suppress such an impulse? Why should we respect it? The answer of the moral consciousness itself seems to be that in the call of some special and costing moral duty we are aware of a valid claim upon our lives, a transcendent demand that is authoritative and absolute. And it may be considered less than rational to acknowledge such an absolute claim in practice while denying it in theory.[13]

Perhaps the key phrase in Hick's commentary is "rightfully summons us to faithful obedience." The law, as we apprehend it, is not merely objective, but it is also worthy of our obedience. Its appearance in our consciousness does not merely inform, but it tells us, in effect, to do something. And this message is deserving of our respect, we feel, even when our own well-being hangs in the balance. What must we then suppose to be the case with respect to this law if we grant, at this practical level, that it has a claim upon us?

I have already said that morality cannot be satisfactorily explained simply as the divine will made evident to human beings. For once again, we must ask by virtue of what the divine will commands *this* thing and not some other. Yet it also seems that morality of common sense, once cashed out, requires the postulate of a reality that is beyond the material world. One is reminded, in this vein, of Lao Tzu's pronouncement[14] that "the Tao that can be expressed in words is not the eternal Tao." The Way, or Truth, that eludes the mind and senses is a mystery, and yet it is still the thing of primal importance. If we wish to say that there exists such a thing as real value, such a thing as genuine obligation, we must postulate that there exists likewise a source of moral truth that transcends the material world.

Moral Knowledge as Transcendental

I have suggested that certain reductionist views of ethics—those, in other words, that try to explain moral experience in terms of events in the natural world—are unsatisfactory. They fail, I maintain, to provide an account that we can square with our own deepest convictions of what it means to say, for example, that a given course of action is right, or that it is wrong, or that we are in some way obligated to behave in a certain manner. One may wonder, at this point, what I wish to propose as an alternative. In the following pages I will discuss another view of ethics, one that admittedly contains within it elements of mystery and elusiveness, but one that speaks more effectively, I believe, to certain issues raised in this chapter.

If moral judgments are in fact merely statements about one's own constitution or expressions of it, or if they are statements about the society within which one lives, then they cannot have the prescriptive force that we ordinarily suppose them to have. Suppose, for example, that Hume is right, and that my statement that *X is wrong* is nothing more than an autobiographical report of how I happen to feel about action X. Suppose that I am then confronted with a situation wherein action X (some given instance, let us say, of murder) seems to be both possible and to my advantage and that I may do X or not as I choose. On what basis might I make the choice?

It is commonly taken for granted that I should not do X if it is wrong but should choose some contrary action instead. Yet here a problem arises. For if *X is wrong* means only that I have a negative feeling about the action, what will it mean to say that I have done wrong in choosing X? It will mean, apparently, only that I have behaved in a way that runs contrary to my own feelings. Yet if the choice is profitable, what does it matter? Have I done anything truly objectionable? If the choice is to my advantage, then have I not made a wise choice in reacting against my own emotional biases (ungrounded as they are in any truth or principle beyond themselves) and going in the other direction?

Or again, suppose (following the positivists) that *X is wrong* is not really a statement about anything but is merely a venting of my (or someone's) feelings? Suppose again that act X is to my advantage. In having done X, what have I then done? I have acted, once more, in a way that runs counter to my feelings. But what is the problem with this, if I have benefited from the action? Perhaps it will be said by someone that it is wrong to act in this self-contrary manner. But of course, if the emotivist account is correct, the message will only mean that the one who proclaims it has contrary feelings about such behavior. And what concern is that of mine?

On the whole, I think, it is hard to square the naturalistic accounts of ethics with the attitudes that we actually have in daily life toward moral-choice making. If moral judgments are mere expressions of feeling, then there is nothing in principle to forbid us from doing what is deemed "wrong." Or if they are (recalling the moral relativists) mere reports of what "society" expects of us, what difference does it make whether we abide by them or not? Why should the general preferences of a person's society (whatever exactly this means—the general run of those in his neighborhood, in North America, in the English-speaking world, or whatever) be a cause for his own concern?

Perhaps the best and most telling criticism of the naturalistic view is that by C. S. Lewis in his short classic *The Abolition of Man*. In this book Lewis describes the tendency in modern education to discount the element of value in the curriculum. He begins with an anecdote, recalling the courtesy copy of an English text that was sent to him by two fellow educators, which purports to serve as a manual of composition for young readers. Early on, relates Lewis, the pupil who reads this text is introduced to the example of two persons who stand beside a waterfall. One of them reacts to the sight by calling it sublime and the other by calling it pretty. The authors of this text then declare that when we bestow predicates of value on various objects we seem to be "saying something very important about something," when in fact "we are only saying something about our own feelings." As Lewis observes, the young reader who absorbs this message will believe two things: first, that all statements making a value judgment are statements about the emotional state of the speaker, and second, that such statements are unimportant. In conveying this message, says Lewis, these self-professing educators are cutting off their readers from a vital source of truth. They are indeed cutting out a portion of their readers' souls. (This first chapter is thus entitled "Men Without Chests.")

What should children be taught about values? Across time and culture, Lewis observes, there has arisen in one form or another a certain doctrine regarding the nature of value. One finds this doctrine in classic Chinese and Indian cultures, likewise, in Greek philosophy, in Hebraism, and in Christianity.

> In early Hinduism that conduct in men which can be called good consists in conformity to, or almost participation in, the *Rta*—that great ritual or pattern of nature and supernature which is revealed alike in the cosmic order, the moral virtues, and the ceremonial of the temple. Righteousness, correctness, order, the *Rta*, is constantly identified with *satya* or truth, correspondence to reality. As Plato said that the Good was "beyond existence" and Wordsworth that through virtue the stars were strong, so the Indian masters say that the gods themselves are born of the *Rta* and obey it.[15]

The Chinese, he continues, speak similarly of the thing—the greatest thing—called the Tao. It is "the reality beyond all predicates, the abyss that was before the Creator Himself. It is Nature, it is the way, the Road. It is the Way in which the universe goes on, the Way in which things everlastingly emerge, stilly and tranquilly, into space and time."[16]

Just as important, he explains, it is "the Way which every man should tread in imitation of that cosmic and supercosmic progression, conforming all activities to that great exemplar."[17] It is, then, the objective source of all that is true in the moral consciousness of human beings.

A fair number of readers will be put off by the elusiveness of such a description. For what is a thing beyond all predicates, and how does something emerge ("stilly and tranquilly," yet) into space and time? And what can precede the "Creator Himself"? There is a reason, I believe, why Lewis chooses such language to describe the thing that he is after. And a reason, too, for his choice of such words as 'supernature' and 'supercosmic' in the bargain.

What Lewis sees, I think, is that any theory that locates the truth of value within the sphere of nature is bound to be inadequate as an account of what our own deepest apprehension of what value means. For if moral judgments are in fact merely expressions of a going social ethic, what prescriptive force can they have? If *X is wrong* means simply that X goes contrary to what is popular or to what is the current civil law, then it is an open question, I think, as to whether anyone ought not to do X.

There is a tendency, Lewis observes, for moral theorists in the present age to seek to ground judgments of value not in supposed higher sources, but in some empirical fact about human nature or human society. In so doing, such theorists imagine that they have taken a step toward the intellectual understanding of what is involved in moral experience. For such an account, as Lewis explains, seems "scientific" in contrast to the older and more mysterious way of thinking about the subject.

To this end it is adduced, for example, that human beings have some impulse or instinct to come to the aid of their fellows, or to do what will help "society," or to further the existence of the species. So-called moral behavior, then, is whatever expresses this instinct and brings about whatever state of affairs that such an instinct will encourage. The enlightened approach to ethics, it is thought, will be the one that is grounded in this tangible fact about the human organism, not in remote, unverifiable claims about what lies off instead in some more ethereal region. Ethics, on such a view, is properly a branch of psychology.

But the problem with such an account, Lewis explains, is that no fact of nature can ever provide us with a principle on which to act in relation to itself. Suppose it is true, for example, that I have an instinct to help others or to do some thing that will contribute to the welfare of the race. How ought I to stand in relation to this fact? What do I *do* with it? The instinct itself cannot tell me. It can only appear within my field of consciousness and leave me to decide.

Perhaps it will be said that the instinct is a "higher" impulse, that the man who abides by it is a better and more advanced specimen of humanity than the one who lacks this mental component or who acts contrary to it. But how does one decide, scientifically and on the basis of observed fact, which impulse is higher?

The problem with any naturalistic reduction of value is that it always leaves open the question of what relationship we should adopt toward those facts of nature to which values are being reduced. The fact (if it is granted) that I have some impulse to help others does not tell me whether I should abide by it. The fact that I may feel some pang of remorse over having failed to help another tells me nothing as to what I ought to have done. It is only when I transcend these facts of nature and appeal to some principle concerning them—that one ought, for example, to respect such feelings—that I have grounds for making a judgment of value. It is for this reason that Rudolph Otto, in his religious classic *The Idea of the Holy* writes that certain elements of human awareness cannot, in principle, be found within the natural world. Like the element of holiness, Otto explains, which lies at the heart of all developed religion, the notion of the good "as an objective value, objectively binding and valid," is a priori, that is, it cannot be acquired by any empirical means.[18] Knowledge of objective value requires a faculty that transcends the natural world. No amount of sensory experience—of facts about science, or history, or clinical psychology can provide us with it. Our senses can tell us what is in the world and how the world happens to behave, but they cannot tell us what we should do with respect to what we find.

The Postulate of Moral Freedom

What more is involved in this conception of morality? I have said that it involves, for one thing, the assumption that some states of affairs are better than others: Justice will be served, I imagine, if I award the promotion to that individual who has earned it independently of my own personal affections in the matter. A system in which citizens have a right of free speech is more enlightened and so is morally preferable (all things being equal) to one that does not. But with beliefs of this kind comes the further conviction that it is somehow incumbent on us to bring about this state of affairs insofar as it lies within our powers. And this requirement, in turn, implies that you and I are in some measure free to shape the world according to our ideals—that we are not, as hard determinists would have it, helpless recipients of our fate.

The message of the hard determinists, once again, is that there exists no such freedom. In support of this position, they appeal in some broad way to science, which shows us, they claim, that human behavior conforms to all the same laws that govern the world as a whole. A few things should be said with regard to this general line of thought.

The message of hard determinists is sometimes presented in a way that is inconsistent with the thesis itself. We are told, recalling Hospers, that it is immoral, in light of the evidence, to hold a man responsible for what he has done. This line of reasoning is supposed to extend not only to criminals but also to the rest of us, since each of us, in the end, is the product of his own psychic circumstances. But if that is so, then how can *anything* be immoral? Suppose that I am, say, a juror faced with the task of deciding the fate of an accused person. I normally suppose that I am under an obligation to review the evidence of the case in a responsible manner and render a decision that is in line with the facts. Hospers himself seems to encourage such a belief. But how, if he is correct in his general thesis, can I be under any such obligation? For if he is right, then my own behavior is subject to all the same psychoanalytical principles that govern, in perfect detail, the behavior of the defendant. Will not the same forces that landed the defendant in his current situation land me in whatever situation will be mine? If Hospers is correct, any decision I reach about the defendant, it seems, will be only one more outcome of this same deterministic mesh of psyche and surroundings. How, then, can I think that any such decision will be genuinely mine or that I can ever be responsible for it?

Perhaps it will be said, in reply, that the use of the word 'immoral' in this context means only 'irrational'—that it implies, not that anyone is truly responsible for his actions, but only that our traditional notions of good and evil are not supported by the facts. That may be so, although I suspect, for what it is worth, that men like Hospers and Darrow have not really given up the ideas of good and evil. In reading their words I get the feeling that they still believe, at some level, that some things are truly good and some evil, and that they themselves are responsible for the task of enlightening others about the errors (as surely they exist) to which the judicial system has historically been prone. But the question remains as to whether the hard determinist position is warranted by the facts. What more may be said in this regard?

Whatever else we may think, there is one curious feature of this position that is worth noting, namely, that it does not seem to be tenable when we try to apply it to ourselves. The deterministic argument holds, in one form or another, that the circumstances of a man's life determine what kind of man he shall be. He is not responsible, on this line of reasoning, since the things he will believe, his affections, his general level of ambition, the choices he makes in any given situation—all of these things—are supposed to be the product of his overall social and genetic inheritance.

But how does this proposition fare when we examine it in relation to ourselves? Take, for example, the case that is made for it on the basis of psychiatry. The clinician, if he agrees with Hospers, will say that the life experiences of a criminal (beginning, roughly, at birth) have effectively made him the kind of man that he is. The clinician may point to such details in the man's life story as the absence of a nuclear family, the constant and unfed hunger for emotional support, and his failed relationships in the educational system and the workplace. Such factors as these, it will be said, make it unreasonable for us to hold this man responsible for his actions. For they are—recalling Hospers's own choice of words—the factors leading him to behave as he does.

How does this argument work with respect to myself? Suppose that I examine the history of my own life and find that it matches, outwardly at least, the life of that criminal in all of the cited details. What inference may I draw from this fact? Ought I to conclude that I am no longer responsible for my actions? Should I suppose that I am causally fated to do the very same things that he has done? Of course, I cannot infer from the limited facts available that my life is just like his own. It may be that there exist significant differences between him and me, even if they are not conspicuous ones. Perhaps his life has been more difficult than mine, after all. But again, how do I know, without begging the question, that my own life has not actually been the more difficult? How do I know that my own life circumstances have been any less challenging, or my psychic constitution any more durable, than his? It may be said that the mere fact that he is the criminal, not I, proves the case. But that assumes the very thing at issue, namely, that the circumstances necessitate the outcome.

It is true, I must think, that my own life in fact has not been so unfortunate or so traumatic as it might have been. But what added pain, what multiplied set of troubles, would allow me, in principle, to say that I am no longer responsible for my actions? At what point, in my own life, or in my philosophical mind's eye, can I honestly say that I am now incapable of genuine moral-choice making? Offhand, it does not seem that any one added difficulty would give me this logical license. Nor any other one added on top of that.

Suppose that I assess the facts as best I can and decide that my life has been in certain respects more difficult than the average. Have I thereby (assuming my estimate, for argument's sake, to be realistic) grounds for saying that my moral responsibility has been diminished? It seems, on reflection, that any amount of excuse in this direction I might offer to myself, be it great or be it modest, is begging the question. Suppose that I add up my life troubles—bouts of childhood allergy, run-ins with a neighborhood bully, a failed teenage romance, the loss in later years of an adored and adoring parent—and say that I am thereby, in this given specified degree, exonerated from blame for my actions. What is this but to say that I now *choose* to count these losses in such a manner? And the question then arises, how am I justified in this choice?

The problem with this method of exoneration, it seems to me, is not that a person is apt to be too lenient in assessing his own case. Rather, I think, the problem is logically inherent in the situation: At what point, in the adding process, am I rationally justified in saying that *circumstances* have rendered me incapable of the right behavior? In truth, I would not be willing to grant myself any moral leeway of this kind. For it seems to me that any set of conditions, however much or little demanding, leaves open to me the choice of my response. But if I cannot, in good faith, allow some given set of conditions to cancel my responsibility for reacting in a responsible manner, how can I allow such conditions, in theory, to cancel the responsibility of another person?

That is not to say that extenuating circumstances do not exist, in given cases, either for myself or for others. It is only to say that conditions of a given kind cannot, as a point of logic, provide me with conclusive reason to insist that I lack moral freedom. Nor have I shown, by my example, that determinism is false. It may well be, in the end, that all our choices are determined in roughly the way that Hospers thinks they are. Perhaps my stubborn resistance to the thesis of determinism is itself one of the things that has been necessitated by the forces that have (so it is said) shaped my character.

But can determinism be incorporated into an honest philosophy of life? It does not appear to me that it can. In the remaining part of this chapter I will briefly address two related issues in connection with determinism: first, the question whether the theory is somehow supported by empirical fact, and second, where the thesis stands with respect to our ordinary assumptions about our own conduct and our obligations to other people.

Is determinism warranted, as a theory, by what we see when we look at the world? In his essay "The Dilemma of Determinism," William James makes an ingenious observation that merits acknowledgment, I believe, in any discussion of the free will problem. James cites the example of a rather ordinary choice, namely, his decision to walk home from the lecture hall by one of two imagined routes, via either Divinity Avenue or Oxford Street.

If the choice is real, he explains, either eventuality is consistent with what is the case at the present moment. Thus either may yet come to pass, may yet form the continuation of the world history that has preceded it. Imagine that he walks home via Divinity Avenue. And then imagine, he says, that "the powers governing the universe annihilate ten minutes of time with all that it contained" so as to set him now back at the door of the hall and once again about to make the choice. If we as spectators are determinists, then we must believe that one of the two universes has been from all of time necessary and the other impossible. For only one can be consistent with the stream of events causally preceding it.

But looking outwardly at the two universes, he asks:

Can you say which is the impossible and accidental one, and which the rational and necessary one? I doubt if the most iron-clad determinist among you could have the slightest glimmer of light on this point. In other words, either universe after the fact and once there would, to our means of observation and understanding, appear just as rational as the other. There would be absolutely no criterion by which we might judge one necessary and the other a matter of chance.[19]

If that is the case, he wonders, what warrant have we for interpreting either choice, when it is actually made, as being inevitable? James's example can be generalized to apply to the world as a whole. Virtually any choice can be put to the same logical test with the same result.

It may be said, to the contrary, that we as readers cannot be sure which choice would be the real one, but that closer observation of James himself, in the real world, would provide the answer. He might, after all, be in the habit of choosing one course over the other because it is shorter or because it has more pleasant scenery. Suppose, then, that on a given occasion he chooses the usual route. Has he done that of necessity? Let us rewind the event in our imagination and roll it out so that he chooses the other way. Might that have happened instead? The real world, after all, contains exceptions to the rule. People sometimes do things contrary to habit and even out of character.

Suppose that next time he does in fact choose contrary to habit. Will we insist once that nothing else could have happened? Suppose again that we are shown two choices, without being told which is the actual one. Which of these events is the one necessary? We would be hard-pressed, I believe, to defend our answer.

Consider also moral choices. Suppose that some individual has been confronted with a situation requiring (as it seems to us) a choice between good and evil. Do we interpret his choice as having been causally necessitated? There is no reason, I think, to assume that, based upon the outward facts of the case. It makes little difference either, I think, what may have been his past habits in similar situations. Suppose that a man with a history of antisocial behavior commits a violent crime. Can we be sure (rewinding, as it were, and now rolling out the episode differently) that a contrary choice was impossible? Or if such a man rises up out of this moral slough and chooses nobly his next time out, must we think that the universe contained no other possibility than that?

If we cannot say, in principle, which sequence of events is the necessary one, then we have no warrant for supposing, in the actual world, that either sequence is necessitated by the events that have preceded it. Thus determinism has no obvious advantage over the chance hypothesis with respect to what we observe. Either hypothesis seems to be consistent with the facts. If so, it does not appear that determinism has any particular advantage in terms of science or sophistication.

Can anything then be said in a positive vein on behalf of the chance hypothesis? I believe that one thing further can be said in its favor, namely, that it is warranted as a postulate of what we commonly refer to as moral obligation. An obligation is a demand. It entails choice. When confronted with a situation involving an obligation, we commonly imagine that the world stands open with regard to which of these eventualities may yet come to pass. If we think ourselves obligated in a given situation, we must also, if we are consistent, think that there exist at least two possibilities with respect to it.[20] At least two things may happen, given what is now the case. Suppose, for example, that I feel myself obligated to pay back a debt to a friend who has lent me money. If I say that I ought to repay the money, I must suppose that two different outcomes are contained potentially within this situation—one wherein I repay it and another in which I refuse.

There may, of course, be yet other states of affairs that can, as yet, emerge—perhaps the situation will change in some relevant way (the friend may decide that the debt can be canceled by some consideration on my part or, perhaps, the whole world will end in nuclear holocaust). But obligation, in any case, entails multiple possibilities regarding the future. It entails likewise that what may yet happen depends in some degree upon my own act of will. The question then arises as to what must be the relationship between this will and the material forces that shape the world in which it operates.

If determinism is true, then there exists only one possible state of affairs with respect to any given time in the future. There likewise exists only one state of affairs with respect to my repayment (or not) of the debt as just mentioned. But the notion that I *ought* to repay the money implies, I think, that my paying it or not is still an open question, that it is not somehow already in the cards, so to speak, which of the two envisioned outcomes may yet come to pass. Saying that I ought to repay it implies that there is something that should happen and something that should not. The world, it is thought, will be (in this respect, at least) a better place in the former case than in the latter, and either eventuality is still potentially a reality. Justice may yet be done. Or it may not.

But if determinism is true, only one of these imagined outcomes is causally possible, and the actual cause of this outcome lies, not in me, but in the mechanics of the world as they have existed throughout all of time. I can "choose," as it seems to me, a given course of action but can add nothing to that material flow of events that has been in motion from all of time, a flow that decides my frame of mind and putative choice making at every moment. But if that is the case, then the obligation, as the common-sense morality would have it, is illusory. Thus I am forced to choose philosophically between hypotheses. If I believe that the future is in some degree in my hands, and that it contains multiple possibilities, I must reject as a working hypothesis the view that all events are determined. Determinism may well be true, but I cannot accept it if I am to take seriously the idea that I am subject to the demand of the moral law. I must suppose that my will is in some measure undetermined by the material system with which it is associated.

It is sometimes held that determinism and freedom are compatible. For, it is thought, the so-called laws of the universe are merely descriptions of how things happen. To say that my action is determined by these laws is not to say that I am constrained in some way—that these laws somehow force me to do things that I would not do otherwise. It is only to describe how in fact I do behave. True, my nature was given to me by these laws, and I was not able to choose what sort of creature I would be. But I must have some nature, or I could not have wants of any kind. And provided, then, that I am free to realize my wants, to achieve my goals, I am free in the only sense that can matter.

It is correct, I think, to say that determinism is consistent with freedom in this respect. As long as my choices are self-interested ones, I am indeed free whenever I am able to act in accord with my desires. Indeed I cannot imagine any other kind of freedom apart from that. But it is different, I believe, where moral choices are concerned. A world in which I must not choose evil is a world in which either eventuality may yet come to pass, and in which I am the sovereign force responsible for which of those it will be.

I conclude, then, that our ordinary convictions about ethics—that some actions and some types of character are better than others, that we ought to choose some actions over others, that we are responsible, in some degree, for what may come to pass—require of us some conception of moral truth and of human agency that goes beyond any analysis in terms of the natural world. Although naturalistic accounts of ethics, I have argued, may be theoretically possible, they do not allow us to retain our ordinary ways of thinking about morality and human action. If we wish to continue in our beliefs about good and evil and about free choice making, then we must embrace a theory of reality that extends beyond the world of nature.

In this chapter and the preceding one I have looked at moral experience and its interpretation. In Chapter 5 I will direct my attention to the phenomenon of religious experience and its historical relationship to the enterprise of rational inquiry. In Chapter 6 I will address once again the question of interpretation and will argue once more that we have reason to accept the view that reality is not confined to the material world.

Chapter Five

Religion and Rational Inquiry

The Ethiopians make their gods black and snub-nosed; the Thracians say theirs have blue eyes and red hair.

—Xenophanes (fragment)

A major part of philosophy concerns the nature of religion. What is religion, and what essentially does it purport to tell us about reality? In this chapter I will examine, in broad fashion, the nature of religious experience, and how this aspect of human experience is related historically to the enterprises of philosophy and the sciences.

The General Nature of Religion

First, what is religion? One way to understand the word is to consider its etymology. The word 'religion' comes from *'religio'*, a word that the ancient Romans used to refer to their relationship to the gods. *'Religio'*, in turn, is related to *'ligare'*, a verb that means "to bind together." This root may suggest that religion serves to bind together persons in worship or, perhaps, to bind together human beings and whatever powers, beings, or forces that ultimately rule the universe.

The general nature of religion, and the further issue of its interpretation, are discussed at length by William James in his classic *The Varieties of Religious Experience*. It is not easy, as James says, to come by any single characterization of the subject. Many gods, after all, have flourished in religious history, and their nature has varied. As a general description, James states,[1] we may say that gods are conceived to be "first things" in the way of being and power. Religion, likewise, is man's "final reaction upon life," which is to say, not a casual attitude, but a final and serious one.

To get at the nature of this attitude, James continues, one must "go behind the foreground of existence" and "reach down to that curious sense of the whole residual cosmos as an everlasting presence, intimate or alien, terrible or amusing, lovable or odious, which in some degree everyone possesses." The religious life, put in general terms, "consists of the belief that there is an unseen order, and that our supreme good lies in harmoniously adjusting ourselves thereto." This belief and this adjustment, he writes, are "the religious attitude of the soul."[2]

What does that mean to us? Science, writes James[3] in a famous essay, "says things are; morality says some things are better than other things; and religion says essentially two things." First, "she says that the best things are the more eternal things, the overlapping things, the things in the universe that throw the last stone, so to speak, and say the final word." Her second affirmation is that we are better off ("even now") if we believe the first affirmation to be true. The basic idea of this *religious hypothesis* is that reality is a far greater thing than we imagine and, accordingly, that there is more to ourselves as well than is evident in the general run of our day-to-day conscious experience. The present world, seen in religious terms, is but a brief stage through which we pass and beyond which our destiny extends. The right perspective on life is the one that is focused on that greater reality. It is the unseen order that is truly real and that deserves our allegiance.

On what basis does anyone suppose that there exists such an order? The history of philosophy is replete with alleged proofs of such things as God's existence and the immortality of the soul. Although those arguments are interesting, they do not appear to have produced a great deal in the way of either scholarly consensus or personal conviction. It seems instead as if religious belief grows out of a deeper wellspring than that of the intellect. The real basis of religious belief, it seems, is religious experience.

This experience can take many forms. In some cases, it may consist simply in the vague sense that there exists some greater reality of which the present world is but a part. This sense, at times, can be extraordinarily powerful, even if it does not have specifiable content. In such cases it is, writes James, "as if a bar of iron, without touch or sight, with no representative faculty whatever, might never the less be strongly endowed with an inner capacity for magnetic feeling; and as if, through the various arousals of its magnetism by magnets coming and going in its neighborhood, it might be consciously determined to different attitudes and tendencies."[4] Such a bar of iron, although it could not provide an outward description of the realities by which it was affected, would be aware of their presence and of their significance, and its understanding of reality would be deeply altered as a result.

In other cases this experience may have more definite content. It may involve, for example, the putative encounter with a person of some kind or other. God, claims Julian of Norwich, is our father and so, in truth, is he our mother. He is "nearer to us than our own soul," the source of our love and strength, and his truth is that *"all shall be well, and all shall be well, and all manner of thing shall be well."*[5]

Religion, on the face of it, is revelation. It is a portal, of sorts, through which we find another and greater reality and an insight into the significance of the world that we currently occupy. Some people, of course, fail to see anything compelling about testimony of the kind just noted. Such experiences, they may say, are psychologically interesting, but they do not provide us with any sort of real knowledge. For, they imagine, these experiences can be explained quite well in terms of events within the world itself. In the following sections I will look at the religious element of human experience in relation to the development of critical inquiry and the sciences. I will give particular attention to several efforts in the past two centuries to account for religious belief in terms of events in the natural world. In Chapter 6 I will explore the question whether we are rationally justified in taking religious experience to be a genuine indication of reality.

The Development of Science and Its Impact on Religion

The relationship between science and religion is a long and somewhat uneasy one. This tension owes, it seems, to the basically unlike nature of the two activities. Science, of course, is confined to the natural world; its method is empirical. As such it has no use for alleged supernatural elements in its investigation. To no surprise, its verdicts have run afoul at times of certain religious doctrines.

As B. R. Tilghman[6] observes, the earliest Greek philosophy may well have begun as a result of dissatisfaction with more traditional explanations of the world such as that found in Hesiod's account of the origin of the gods. This philosophy was a kind of protoscience; it aimed at a rational explanation of the world—its origin, composition, and first principles of movement. As such, it rested its case upon observation and argument. Traditional Greek religion, by contrast, had been storytelling; it was *mythos*, legend, stirring and dramatic, appealing, perhaps, to some element deep within the psyche of those who listened to it, but having no theoretical force. For this reason conflict was inevitable. Anaxagoras, for one, was tried on charges of impiety for alleging that the moon and stars were not gods but were instead natural bodies composed of materials like those found in the world below. The ancient physician Hippocrates, reacting with disdain against the belief in chance and in divine intervention in earthly affairs, says of disease that each "has its own nature, and none comes about independently of nature. . . . For when chance is examined it turns out to be nothing; for everything that comes to be is

found to come to be for some cause." Xenophanes (570–475 B.C.), in a related spirit, ridicules the gods of his day, saying that "if oxen and horses or
lions had hands, and could paint with their hands, and produce works of art
as men do, horses would paint the forms of the gods like horses, and oxen
like oxen, and make them in the image of their several kinds."[7]

The Greek theory of atomism purports to offer an account of reality that
is self-sufficient and independent of any supernatural reality. Epicurus, once
again, maintains that common attitudes toward the gods are without foundation. The Roman atomist Lucretius has no need of gods as a principle of explanation. He maintains, in a distinctly rational tone, that no thing comes
randomly into being out of nothing. For if it did, there would be no limit on
physical possibility, "every kind might be born from all things," and the
world would cease to have its present regularity. By the same token, nothing
is ever destroyed, for in that case there would come a time, over the aeons,
when all things would eventually have disappeared. Lucretius also argues
that there must exist an empty space wherein the atoms can move, and that
space is infinite, since the notion of limit is itself a spatial concept implying
both an "inside" and an "outside" in relation to itself. It follows that the
number of atoms is likewise infinite, since over time a finite number of
atoms would become so much dispersed in the universe that the interaction
of one atom with another would become impossible.[8]

By no means have science and religion always been at odds with each
other. As Tilghman observes, the major conflicts of the early Christian
church had more to do with moral and cultural issues than with science. In
the last centuries of the Roman Empire and the subsequent Dark Ages, there
was little intellectual life of any kind, let alone any development of science.
Even so, the church was antagonistic to all philosophy that ran contrary to
its own message. In A.D. 529 the emperor Justinian, who ruled over the east-
ern half of the Roman Empire, closed the classical schools of philosophy in
Athens. Many of the best scholars found sanctuary in Syria, where they
reestablished the teaching of the old school of philosophy.

Arab expansion in the seventh and early eighth centuries brought Arabs
into contact with Greek thought, which stimulated advances in science, med-
icine, and mathematics. A good deal of effort was also devoted to establishing intellectual support for Islamic religious belief. Eventually, however, the
tension inherent in the relationship between Islam and philosophy became
outright conflict and, by the end of the twelfth century, gave rise to reaction
against philosophy. In the meantime, Europe was beginning to recover from
its long period of economic and intellectual stagnation. Increasing contact of
the Christian West with Islamic Spain resulted in a rediscovery of Aristotle.
This vast corpus upon many areas of science and philosophy soon became a
source of authority on the created world.

Aristotle's picture of the world lends itself very well to the view of the church. For the earth, on his view, is at the center of the universe. This notion agrees nicely with a religious outlook that sees the earth as being not only a physical center but a spiritual one as well. The earth, in religious terms, is God's special creation and a stage on which the drama of man's salvation is being carried out.

The world that took shape in the work of men like Copernicus, Kepler, and Galileo was one markedly different from that of the Middle Ages. The scientific picture of that earlier day was chiefly the one of Aristotle, who described the world in terms of its perceptual qualities and its alleged purpose, or "final" cause. The enterprise of the sixteenth and seventeenth centuries had a new conceptual scheme. In place of such things as qualities and purposes were *quantity, measurement,* and *description.*

In this new approach, observation took precedence over pure reason. It had been traditionally thought, for example, that the planets made their revolutions in perfect circles, since a pattern of this kind seemed like an appropriate expression of the higher order of things. The astronomer Johannes Kepler maintained instead, on the basis of his observations, that the planets traveled in ellipses. He found also that (using the sun as a focal point) a planet "sweeps out" equal areas in equal times during its revolution, and that the ratio of the squares of any two planets' revolutions is equal to that of the cubes of their mean distances from the sun.

This new world owed to the work of a great number of investigators, perhaps none so much as Galileo Galilei, who reacted at an early age against the worldview that prevailed at the time. Aristotle had said, for example, that the speed of a falling object was the product of two things—the weight of the object and the nature of the medium (air, water, or whatever) through which it fell. Thus, given the same medium, a heavier object would fall faster than a lighter one.

Aristotle's views carried great authority among the philosophers of the age, who thought that they represented the final word in regard to truths about the natural world. Some of his claims—such as that there existed an essential difference between the earthly and heavenly spheres, found great favor with the church, which, on scriptural grounds, held a similar view. But were Aristotle's views correct? It seemed to some that they were out of accord with the testimony of the senses, which tell us that no such relationship exists between the weight of an object and the speed with which it falls— consider, for example, the fact that hailstones may vary considerably in size and weight and yet seem to fall at more or less uniform speed.

Galileo began to devise tests. He dropped objects of varying weights from a given height to see if they behaved as Aristotle had claimed. He rolled objects down inclines of varying angles and recorded the results. He found that for any inclination at a given height, the distances traversed by the falling objects were proportional to the squares of the times.

Philosophy, he concludes,

> is written in that great book ... which lies ever before our eyes ... the universe, ... but we cannot understand it if we do not first learn the language and grasp the symbols in which it is written. This book is written in the mathematical language, and the symbols are triangles, circles, and other geometrical figures, without whose help it is impossible to comprehend a single word of it.[9]

The scientific developments of the fifteenth and sixteenth centuries were exciting ones, and they created an optimism with respect to what human beings might learn about the world that they inhabited. If the universe operated as Galileo imagined, then it lay open, in principle, to rational investigation, and all of its secrets might one day be unlocked.

And yet again, as some writers observe, this progress had a side effect that could be called anything but optimistic. For although it contained the prospect of scientific advances yet unimagined, it created at the same time a very different experience for the average individual. In medieval man there was no great tension between the view of the world revealed in the scriptures and that given by the current science. But new developments in the sciences, as Tilghman explains, were demolishing the old worldview. In so doing, he writes, they knocked the props out from under the religious perspective that was accommodated to it.

> If the earth moves just like the other planets, then it cannot be the center of anything and there may be no reason for believing that humankind occupies the center of any stage or that we are playing out a drama of any sort. We can no longer say that heaven is above our heads beyond the sphere of the stars. If the universe is infinite, then there is no beyond and no place for heaven to be located. In that case hell is probably not in the middle of the earth either. If notions of heaven and hell were to be retained, they would have to be completely rethought.[10]

For this reason, the world inhabited by St. Augustine, writes William Barrett, "was the Neo-Platonic cosmos, a luminous crystal palace with the superessential Good fixed on its highest point, radiating outward like a beacon and diminishing in brilliance as it shone down through the rest of the perfect structure."[11] And Pascal's world, by contrast, "was the desolate and desiccated world of modern science, where at night the sage hears not the music of the shining heavenly bodies but only the soundless emptiness of space." It was a world of frightful and empty space, writes Barrett, in which man was homeless. The universe no longer had warmth, and faith involved now a more daring, more desperate personal leap.

The science of the seventeenth century has two characteristics that set it apart from its ancestors. First, it demands that a given theory be empirically testable and that it likewise be able to explain certain phenomena. Why, for example, do falling projectiles take the path of a parabola, and why do the planets travel in ellipses? The second and related characteristic is its mathematical nature. Its laws and theories have to be stated in terms of mathematical relations between various features of the world that can be quantified.

The upshot of this development is that God can have no part in the explanation of the events under investigation. One can suppose, if one likes, that God is ultimately responsible for the world and all that it contains. But God, as an explanatory principle, becomes superfluous. If everything is the will of God, then it adds nothing to the empirical description of a phenomenon to say that it happens because God wills it this way. And if one can derive the formula, say, for the speed of a falling object, then one has, for all practical purposes, a complete account of the phenomenon.

A prominent theme of Galileo's investigation is the disparity between reality and what appears to the unaided senses. He believes that the key to truth lies in the willingness of investigators to transcend their immediate experience in favor of reason. This outlook is evidenced by the following statement: "I cannot sufficiently admire the eminence of those men's wits, that have received and held it to be true, and with the sprightliness of their judgments offered such violence to their own senses, as that they have been able to prefer that which their reason dictated to them, to that which sensible experiments represented most manifestly to the contrary."[12]

It does not seem, after all, as if the earth is in constant motion and revolving around the sun, as Copernican astronomy would have it. Nor does it seem as if the texture of sense experience—sounds, colors, warmth and cold, and the like, are actually absent from the world as it is in itself. But this divorce of reason from experience is a vital part of the new story. The logical result of this event is the view that mathematical properties are the only real ones. For properties of this kind can be consistently ascribed to the world outside of ourselves. But what would it mean to say that there exists a given sound or color that is independent of the consciousness that perceives it? A given piece of matter, thinks Galileo, is itself shaped in one way or another; it is large or small in relation to others; it has a given place and is either in motion or at rest; "but that it must be white or red, bitter or sweet, sounding or mute, of a pleasant or unpleasant odor," he finds absurd. Such things as tastes and colors thus "hold their residence solely in the sensitive body, so that if the animal were removed, every such quality would be abolished and annihilated."

The effective result of this progress, thinks Edwin Burtt, is a gradual "banishing of man from the great world of nature" and thus, too, a sadly altered human condition. Until the time of Galileo, Burtt maintains, it was taken for granted that man and nature were "integral parts of a larger whole." This subordination of so-called secondary qualities to the level of a derivative and lesser reality was *the reading of man quite out of the real and primary realm.*[13] For man did not seem to himself to be a creature of mathematics. His was a life, Burtt writes, "of colors and sounds, of pleasures, of griefs, of passionate loves, of ambitions, and strivings." The world of science, it seemed, was a world quite alien to his own nature. And with the exaltation of this activity, thinks Burtt, comes a corresponding diminution of man himself. Those "secondary" and unimportant features of the world, those grounded in the deceitfulness of sense, are the very features most intense within human experience. The result, believes Burtt, is a thoroughgoing estrangement of modern man from the reality in which he finds himself.

In a similar vein, Richard Tarnas describes the rift between old and new worldviews in *The Passion of the Western Mind.* The celestial bodies of the modern universe, writes Tarnas, "possessed no numinous or symbolic significance; they did not exist for man, to light his way or give meaning to his life. The universe was now impersonal. Its laws were natural, and had no special connection of any kind with human beings." And yet on the upside, he observes, there emerges a new confidence in the ability of human beings to understand the world in which they live. Between the fifteenth and seventeenth centuries, says Tarnas, there emerges

> a newly self-conscious and autonomous human being, . . . curious about the world, confident in his own judgments, skeptical of orthodoxies, rebellious against authority, responsible for his own beliefs and actions, enamored of the classical past but even more committed to a greater future, proud of his humanity, conscious of his distinctness from nature, aware of his artistic powers as individual creator, assured of his intellectual capacity to comprehend and control nature, and altogether less dependent on an omnipotent God.[14]

Reductionism: Religion as a By-Product of the Natural World

The progress of the natural sciences encouraged a tendency to think of human beings as well in natural terms. Science, thought some, could in principle explain everything, including the vast and varied phenomena of human experience. There developed a number of theories to account for man's religious life as a by-product of the mechanics of the natural world.

Among these theorists is Auguste Comte (1798–1857), who sees both religion and metaphysics as mere remnants of an age prior to the development of genuine science.[15] Every branch of knowledge, maintains Comte, evolves through three distinct phases of maturity. In the first, or *theological*, phase, natural phenomena are explained in terms of volition. (Thus thunder, for example, may be explained as Zeus's expression of his anger; the harvest yield as a gift of Demeter.) At the second, or *metaphysical*, phase, this anthropomorphism is replaced by an explanation in terms of abstract principle—such things as entelechies and vital forces, for example, that make an object seek out the center of the earth or make acorns grow into oaks. The third and final phase is the *scientific*. It is reached when the misguided effort to *explain* phenomena is abandoned in favor of the effort to *describe* them.

A related effort to account for man's religious experience is provided by Karl Marx (1818–1883), who views religious belief as a pathetic substitute for the conditions that might make life in this world more bearable. Religion and philosophy in general, Marx contends, are the product of the economic forces in every age that gives rise to them. Reality is material, and the material conditions of life are what give rise to the various ideologies—political, religious, aesthetic, and philosophical—that appear historically throughout the ages.

Religion, on this view, is man-made. It is, in Marx's famous phrase, an opium of the people, who require a fantastic "other" world that will compensate them for their misery in this one. Man's real salvation, by contrast, Marx believes, lies not in some higher reality, but in transforming the social and economic conditions here and now.[16]

The advances of science have had serious implications for the general way in which persons look upon, not only the natural world, but reality as a whole. These advances have likewise had impact upon religious thought. Perhaps the most provocative development of all began in the year 1832, when a young Cambridge theology student named Charles Darwin (1809–1882) took a position as a naturalist on a Royal Navy ship setting out upon a five-year voyage of scientific exploration. The result of this voyage was a new theory of how life develops, presented in a book by Darwin called *The Origin of Species*. According to the central thesis of this book, which ran flatly contrary to the view of religious tradition, the various species of plants and animals were not specially created at any given time but developed naturally and in biological response to the various demands of the environment.

By no means was this idea brand-new. The spirit of revolution had been in the air for some time prior to Darwin's publication of *The Origin of Species*. Not long before Darwin's voyage, Charles Lyell had published *The Principles of Geology*, which aimed to free that science "from the spell of Moses." This book was to have a powerful shaping influence on Darwin's own thought. The gist of Lyell's thesis is summarized by Anthony Alioto in *A History of Western Science*. Lyell, writes Alioto:

> insisted upon the uniformity of natural law. . . . Extraordinary agents have no place in science. . . . All changes in the geological record, both inorganic and or-

ganic, are governed by laws that are now in operation. Geology is a slow and steady balance of steady and creative forces, operating now before our eyes, the summing of which in almost endless time appears to render immense effects.[17]

Lyell was by no means himself an evolutionist, as the term is understood today. Although he allowed individual species of life some means of variation, he believed that when conditions in the environment outstripped that range, the result was simply extinction. He had no conception of how one species might actually develop out of another. Yet it was Lyell, writes Alioto, who taught Darwin "how to think in terms of slow, continuous change, and how to look at present geological formations and project their history."[18]

Darwin's main thesis, as W. T. Jones[19] points out, is actually quite simple. It is, in fact, a general version of a principle that has been familiar to breeders of animals from ancient times, namely, that certain strains of animals will develop according to given patterns of breeding. If, say, an owner of collies fancies those specimens with longer and narrower skulls, he need only eliminate from each litter the puppies with shorter and broader skulls and mate the ones with longer and narrower ones. If this characteristic catches the public eye, then economic forces enter into the process, as breeders are then motivated to continue the process. Perhaps several other features—long coat, bushy tail, or whatever—may be selected in the same way, and a whole new kind of dog will emerge. Out of the crossing of a few aboriginal species may thus come an enormous new variety.

If this process occurs in the case of domestic animals, why not in nature as well? Perhaps, thinks Darwin, there exists a process of *natural* selection, analogous to that involved in artificial breeding, whereby certain characteristics of plant and animal life are likewise perpetuated and eliminated. No one, says Darwin, would seriously think that all the peculiar types of dog that one sees in domestication, which bear little resemblance to dogs in the wild, actually existed in the state of nature. Perhaps, then, the many varieties of other animals now in existence have also come from some other basic ancestral type.

How might this process have occurred? It is important to see, says Darwin, that nature is really a universal *struggle for existence*. We behold, he writes, "the face of nature right with gladness"; we see often the superabundance of food. We are apt to forget that the birds singing idly around us are constantly destroying life for their own survival, and that they and their offspring are being destroyed constantly in turn. The food that is plentiful today may be scarce in time. This struggle, he explains, follows inevitably from the high rate at which all life tends to increase. Since more individuals are produced than can possibly survive, there is a competition either within a species between its members or between that species and some other. It is the doctrine of Malthus,[20] he writes, applied to the whole arena of plant and animal life. In this competition, any particular difference that makes an animal or a species more fitted to the struggle will tend to be perpetuated. Such an organism will tend, on average, to live longer and to enjoy greater reproductive success during its lifetime. Organisms lacking this advantage will tend over time to fall by the wayside.

In the course of time, explains Jones, "a variant of the species will emerge characterized by the property that was originally an individual difference in an occasional member of that species." When enough of these variants are produced, there is an entire new species. The struggle for survival thus operates in a way that parallels domestic breeding. Suppose, says Darwin, that a group of wolves thrives in the wild, preying upon various animals, and securing some of them by craft, some by strength, and some by fleetness. Let us imagine that the fleeter prey, such as deer, have for some reason increased in number, whereas other prey have decreased during the time that the wolves are hardest pressed for food. Under these circumstances, reasons Darwin, the slimmest and swiftest wolves, on average, will tend to fare best, and this fact will manifest itself over time in the appearance of the group. This scenario, he notes, finds confirmation in a report that two varieties of wolf are found in the Catskills, one a sleek greyhound type that pursues deer, and the other a bulkier type that tends to attack the shepherd's flocks.

Darwin's general theory is supported by a huge amount of evidence, involving both natural observation and experiments of his own. It is summarized in his *Origin of Species,* writes Jones, by the description of the Tree of Life. Jones explains that according to this model, species are not, as religious tradition would have it, "separate classes frozen in eternal independence," connected only by the will of God who made them. The green and budding twigs, writes Darwin, represent existing species, and those produced in former years represent species now extinct. The greater branches were once twigs themselves and represent the lineage of those species that have since developed. Of the many twigs that flourished when the tree was very young, only a few have survived to become branches. Many a limb and branch has dropped off, and these represent whole orders, families, and genera that have no living descendants and are known to us only in their fossil state.

Darwin, of course, did not have access to the science that has since developed and was not aware of the various means, such as genetic mutation, by which new life actually develops. Variations are not, as he supposed, always slight, and the development may proceed, in some cases, more quickly than he imagined. Nevertheless his influence was enormous, and his discoveries inspired a new way of understanding the science of life as a whole. His work also affected the way that science looked upon the human being.

More important than the details of Darwin's explanations, writes Jones, is the fact that he saw species as having an empirical, rather than divine, origin—an origin that can be investigated and understood within the activity of science. Darwin's "Tree" image inspired biologists to see their subject as being a unified field of study. His example gave them the courage to think about it in neutral terms, "untrammeled by extrascientific conceptions."[21]

Darwin's contribution had an impact not only upon the field of biology but also upon the whole broad conception of human nature and its origin. Since his time, it has become common sense that human beings must know something of their past if they are to understand who and what they are. This new approach means, as Jones points out, not merely "taking an interest" in history, but pursuing the inquiry in a different frame of mind and with a new methodological orientation. Things are to be explained genetically, which is to say, in terms of their natural origin and development. Events do not merely *happen* but instead *develop* as part of a natural and witnessable process over the course of time.

Darwinism had its first impact on the public in terms of the controversy between science and religion. If the theory is true, then all of life is descended from a few progenitors, and ultimately, perhaps, "from some one primordial form." Human beings, then, have no special creation of the kind depicted in Genesis, and they are the blood kin of other animals of their general kind, such as apes and monkeys.

Darwin himself, it might be worth adding, did not view his discoveries as being necessarily antagonistic to religious belief. A deity, he thought, that could create a few original life-forms capable of self-development was just as noble in its conception as one that relied each time upon fresh acts of creation. But Darwin's own view of the deity made little difference to those religious types for whom faith meant perfect and literalistic trust in the veracity of the scriptures.

Philosophers of science differed in their reactions to the new theory. Some believed that the evolutionary doctrine was grounds for a thoroughgoing materialism. Ernst Haeckel,[22] for one, holds that man was "but a tiny grain of protoplasm in the perishable framework of organic nature." There is thus no special problem, he believes, in accounting for the origins of life or in explaining the nature of sentient experience. Every such problem can be solved in terms of the evolutionary development of material substance. Scientific fact, thinks Haeckel, shows that traditional beliefs about God, free will, and personal immortality are all a fiction. The new science makes it clear, he asserts, "that the same eternal iron laws that rule in the inorganic world" are valid, as well, in the world of organic life.

Against this effort to reduce life to the mechanics of chemistry and physics arose the theory of *vitalism*. The biologist and philosopher Hans Driesch[23] argued that mechanism was insufficient to explain the phenomenon of life, and that an organism differs from a machine in the wholeness and individuality of its operation. The issue soon faded from the scene, owing in part to the fact that neither concept was ever given a precise enough meaning to allow for a resolution of the difference. Was this vital quality a fluid of some kind? Was it a force? And how exactly did the concept of *force* figure into a comprehensive scientific picture of the world? As a result of this unclarity, the positivistic attitude came to dominate the spirit of science for the coming decades. Its thesis was that metaphysical knowledge is impossible, and that therefore science has no use for debates concerning the "ultimate" nature of reality, of which the preceding debate was an example. Nor, likewise, had the scientific method any use for religious ideas.

The twentieth century has generated a great deal of antireligious thought. Religious belief, think many philosophers, is outmoded in the face of what we now know about the world by way of scientific investigation. Any purported vision of some higher reality, they imagine, is diagnosable as an illusion of one kind or another. The real understanding of human experience, they believe, lies wholly within the sphere of the sciences.

It has been claimed in some quarters that man's religious life owes at bottom to nothing more than some deep mechanism of his own psychology. The classic expression of this view is that of Sigmund Freud, whose pioneer investigation of the mind remains a staple of the science.

Freud's approach to human experience is basically that of a pathologist. A scientist and not a metaphysician, he has little use for notions of higher, or transcendent, realities of the kind entertained in certain areas of traditional philosophy. Conscience, thinks Freud, is not a revelation of some eternal truth; rather it is the natural result of forces present within the mind, which is itself grounded in the events of the nervous system. Religion he likewise believes to be a product of the psyche and to be essentially the stuff of fantasy.

The single best summary of Freud's view of religion is in *The Future of an Illusion,* where he lays out succinctly his interpretation of the general phenomenon of religious experience. Man's helplessness against the forces of nature, thinks Freud, gives rise to a need to reconcile his position in relation to them. Thus there first comes, from deep within the psyche, the personalization of those forces as gods and spirits. The idea of a watchful Providence, he imagines, is born out of a need to make this helplessness tolerable. The result of this process is a view of reality wherein life in this world serves a higher purpose; it is a view wherein all that happens

is an expression of the intentions of an intelligence superior to us, which in the end, though its ways and byways are difficult to follow, orders everything for the best—that is, to make it enjoyable to us. Over each one of us there watches a benevolent providence which is only seemingly stern and which will not suffer us to become a plaything of the over-mighty and pitiless forces of nature. Death itself is not extinction . . . but the beginning of a new kind of existence which lies on the path of development to something higher. And, looking in the other direction, this view announces that the same moral laws which our civilizations set up govern the whole universe as well, except that they are maintained by a supreme court of justice with incomparably more power and consistency. In the end all good is rewarded and all evil punished, if not actually in this form of life then in the later existences that begin after death.[24]

In this way, explains Freud, all the terrors, all the believer's sufferings, all his hardships, are destined to be obliterated. The universe is ruled over by a Father with whom one may have a relationship as his child. Religious ideas, in short, "have arisen from the same need as have all the other achievements of civilization: from the necessity of defending oneself against the crushingly superior forces of nature."[25] As an individual grows and finds that he is destined always to stand as a child in relation to such forces, "he lends those powers the features belonging to the figure of his father; he creates for himself the gods whom he dreads, whom he seeks to propitiate, and whom he nevertheless entrusts with his own protection."[26]

The real, objective support of these ideas, thinks Freud, is nonexistent. To defend them, we rely on the fact that our ancestors believed them; or again, that we have proofs (invariably defective, he believes) handed down from those same primeval times; or once more (and conversely) that we are not supposed to raise the issue of their basis in the first place. Of all the information provided by our culture, he writes, it is just those elements that might be of the greatest importance to us that are the least well authenticated of any. Matters of less concern ("the fact that whales bear young instead of laying eggs") would never gain our acceptance were they as badly founded. The ideas of religion, he imagines, are thus "illusions, fulfillments of the oldest, strongest and most urgent wishes of mankind."[27] The secret of their strength lies in the strength of these wishes.

In calling these ideas illusions, Freud does not mean to say that they must be false—merely that they lack objective support. It could turn out, for all we know, that there exists a god, but that would be entirely a matter of coincidence. Seen from the outside, thinks Freud, religion bears a conspicuous relationship to certain principles of human psychology. We know, he explains, at what periods and by what kinds of people religious doctrines were created. From this new and informed vantage point these doctrines look very different from how they have looked in the past. Seeing them in perspective, he concludes:

> We shall tell ourselves that it would be very nice if there were a God who created the world and was a benevolent providence, and if there were a moral order in the universe and an afterlife; but it is a very striking fact that all this is exactly as we are bound to wish it to be. And it would be more remarkable still if our wretched, ignorant and downtrodden ancestors had succeeded in solving all these difficult riddles of the universe.[28]

Religious skepticism reaches perhaps its most eloquent expression in the writings of Bertrand Russell, who sees religion not only as an illusion but also as a real and active hindrance to human progress. Science, explains Russell, is "the attempt to discover, by means of observation, and reasoning based upon it, first, particular facts about the world, and then laws connecting facts with one another and . . . making it possible to predict future occurrences."[29] Thus it is "tentative," ever ready to admit its own errors and expectant of modifications in its going view of the world. It begins, not from large assumptions, but from particular facts gathered from observation and controlled experiment. From a large number of such facts, a general rule is arrived at, not as a certainty, but merely as a working hypothesis. If contrary facts are observed, the hypothesis is discarded. If evidence mounts in its favor, it gains the status of a theory. In every case the basis for such theory building is *evidence*, not mere tradition or popularity or the comfort that it may give to those who accept it. A religious creed, by contrast, purports to embody "eternal and absolutely certain truth" and cannot entertain doubt as to its own veracity.[30] In place of observation it offers authority.

Religion and science, thinks Russell, are for this reason natural enemies, with science providing an understanding of the world and religion standing with dogmatic stubbornness in the way. Religion is essentially superstition, a manufactured and illusory substitute for the hard-won knowledge provided by disciplined rational inquiry. It was, Russell reminds us, the church that insisted Copernicus was wrong in his claim that the earth moved round the sun. This same institution nearly executed no less a man than Galileo for his scandalous claims that there were (undetected by natural sight) mountains on the moon and satellites orbiting Jupiter. The church also made a serious practice of demonology. And it resisted the theory of evolution, when all evidence and good sense argued for it. Science and religion, all told, are thus like the forces of light and darkness, aligned respectively with reason and irrationality.

And what truth does real investigation disclose? A reality, answers Russell,[31] that is purposeless and void of meaning. On this view, the real stuff of the universe is the undirected dance of atoms, and nothing more. The notion of value or objective purpose is but the passive and fanciful by-product of this mad and meaningless dance. The thought that life has a purpose or that we may have, above this happenstance, some cosmic ally is likewise delusory.

Yet another effort to understand religion in terms of events in the natural world is found in *verificationism*, an outgrowth of the earlier positivistic philosophy of the nineteenth century. The basic tenet of this "logical positivism," as noted earlier, is that language itself can only apply meaningfully within the realm of possible sense experience. Those statements that purport to go outside of this realm—the statements, as it were, of metaphysics—are in fact not statements at all, but merely collections of words without literal content. The meaninglessness of theology, thinks A. J. Ayer,[32] follows as a corollary from the general impossibility of metaphysics.

It is generally agreed, Ayer observes, that the god of mainstream Western tradition cannot be proved to exist. For what, after all, are the premises from which the existence of such a being might be deduced? If the conclusion of the argument is to be demonstratively certain, then the premises must be certain as well. But no empirical proposition is ever more than probable. Only a priori statements, says Ayer, are certain. And such propositions, he believes, are always tautologies—statements, that is, that are circularly true (that $7 = 7$, that all bachelors are unmarried, that a green thing must be colored, and so on). Yet from tautologies one can only deduce other tautologies. And since the proposition in question (God exists) does not seem to be a tautology, it follows, says Ayer, that there is no possibility of demonstrating that a god exists.

What is less generally recognized, Ayer continues, is that there can be no way of showing that the existence of this god is even probable. For if the existence of this being were an empirical proposition, it would be possible to deduce from it, together with other such propositions, certain facts of experience—certain features of the sensible world that one could not deduce from those other propositions by themselves. But the hypothesis of theism offers us no such information.

It has been said, Ayer notes, that the seeming regularity of the universe gives us rational evidence that a god exists. But if "God exists" entails only that there is order in nature, then this assertion is really only a claim about nature, which is surely not all that religious types mean it to be. They wish to say, after all, not just that the universe has order, but that it has a creator, and that this creator is a transcendent being who may be known, in some measure, by these outward manifestations, yet who cannot be defined in terms of them. Therefore, this transcendent being is beyond the range of sight and sound. It lies outside the bounds of any sort of logical or sensory investigation, which is to say, it is metaphysical and so, by verificationist doctrine, is really nothing at all.

This analysis, Ayer believes, applies to all those religious beliefs that involve the notion of a being that exists over and above the empirical world. In the developed religions, this being is a divine person, of sorts, who reigns over the natural world and is not himself located within it; he is supposed to be superior to the world, to be outside of it, and to be endowed with "super-empirical attributes." But the notion of a *person*, insists Ayer, "whose essential attributes are non-empirical is not an intelligible notion at all." Whereas popular use of the word 'God' inclines people to think that there is, or might be, such a being, the analysis of the word indicates that the sentences in which it is used are not capable of empirical verification. Hence the word, and the sentences containing it, have no real content.

This view is not to be confused, Ayer emphasizes, with that of the atheist or the agnostic. An atheist, after all, *dis*believes in God. An agnostic is undecided. But each of these positions assumes that the proposition in question—that of God's existence—actually has some content that can be affirmed or denied. Yet all utterances about the nature of God turn out on examination to be nonsensical. One cannot deny, any more than one can affirm, something that is cognitively empty. Nor, reasons Ayer, can one meaningfully entertain doubt about it.

The same kind of analysis, thinks Ayer, will show that belief in a soul, as something imperceptible and constituting man's "real" self, is similarly vacuous. And likewise with alleged "mystical" experience. To say that there exist depths of apprehension that cannot be described means only that the mystic speaks nonsense when he himself tries to describe them. Mysticism, thinks Ayer, may involve certain peculiar states of mind and may thus have a place within the field of psychology. But the claim that such an experience has furthermore *an object,* such as a divine being, falls once more into the category of the unverifiable.

The broad notion of a truth beyond the realm of empirical investigation is generally out of style in most twentieth century thought, and even nominally "religious" thinkers seem to have little use for it. Thus D. Z. Phillips,[33] for example, rejects as empty any notion of God or personal life hereafter. Charles Hartshorne[34] develops the notion of an afterlife in terms, not of individual conscious survival, but of an individual's life history being somehow eternally stored within the divine omniscience as a part of the story of the universe. A short paper published in 1950 by Antony Flew[35] offers a clearly positivistic challenge to religious believers; the piece has been discussed and reprinted many times since.

What, asks Flew, do religious persons *deny* when they say things like "God exists," "God has a plan," or "God loves us as a father loves his children"? We hear these statements from people all the time, and at first they sound very much like assertions, "vast cosmological assertions" that tell us something about the universe in which we live. But on close examination, they raise doubts whether they assert anything at all.

To assert that something is the case, writes Flew, is equivalent to denying that this same thing is not the case. If we are in doubt as to what someone is saying, one way to find out is to see what he would regard as counting against the truth of his claim. That would enable us to know (in part, at least) what he is denying, and thus also what he is claiming to be true. To know what a statement denies, Flew reasons, is to know by way of logic what it asserts. Therefore, if there is nothing that a putative statement denies, there is nothing that it asserts either.

It often seems to people who are not religious, says Flew, as if there is no conceivable event in all the world that would make religious believers give up their faith. It seems as if there is nothing, in other words, that they would count as reason to say, "There wasn't a God after all," or "God does not really love us then." What, then, are religious claims actually denying? And what, in turn, are they asserting?

We hear, says Flew, that God loves us as a father loves his children. We are reassured. But then, he notes, we see a child dying of inoperable cancer of the throat. His earthly father is driven frantic in his efforts to help. But his Heavenly Father shows no obvious sign of concern. Some qualification is made—God's love is "not a merely human love" or is an "inscrutable" love, perhaps. And we may be reassured again. But at some point we may be led to ask, "What is this answer of God's (appropriately qualified) love worth? What is this apparent guarantee really a guarantee against?" What, in short, will logically entitle us to say that God does not exist?

Flew's challenge is a formidable one, and it has not been easy for succeeding writers to find an effective reply. The direction of these efforts has varied. R. M. Hare,[36] for one, maintains that there does exist a difference between believers and nonbelievers, despite the fact that no event ever serves to refute the believer's position. Religious believers, says Hare, read their entire experience in a way that is fundamentally different from that of nonbelievers. Believers have, as he puts it, a different *blik*, a different basic *view*, from those who do not believe. The whole of their experience, good and bad, is thus filtered through this interpretive structure. They see life as an event that is watched over by a benevolent presence, one who (presumably) has his reasons for the world as it exists in its present condition.

A reply of this kind, however, has its limits. It fails to explain what is the logical difference between the two outlooks—the difference, that is, in the real content in the minds of believer and nonbeliever. It may be, as Hare suggests, that an individual can live his life with a sense, at times, of being watched over by a creator who looks down upon him with good intentions. But given the conditions of the world in which he lives, what can it mean for him to actually believe in such a creator? The existence of this loving being, once again, does not rule out any particular injustice or misfortune that may afflict him during the course of his life. This love is consistent with anything that may happen to him and to the world as a whole—it may express itself as famine, pestilence, warfare, and atrocity. Perhaps there exists a psychological difference between this believer and someone who lacks his feeling of being loved. But what exactly is the cognitive difference? It is hard to know that until we have some sense of the content, the cash value, as it were, of this claim that the world rests in the hands of divine benevolence. The believer may be in some way psychologically different from the unbeliever, but how is the former's belief different, in terms of what it predicts about the world in which they both live?

Before leaving this issue, I wish to take note of what is probably the most promising line of reply to Flew's question. It was made by John Hick[37] in an article first published in 1960 and was developed in several of his subsequent books and essays.

The concepts of verification and falsification, Hick observes, are not logically symmetrical. They are not, as it were, two sides of a coin. For a proposition can, he notes, be verifiable in principle even if it is not falsifiable. Consider, for example, the proposition that there exist at some point three consecutive sevens in the decimal approximation of the number *pi*. If this proposition is true, it can be verified, that is, when the calculation is carried out at sufficient length. Yet it cannot, it seems, be falsified, since the decimal runs on without end, and one can never, in finite time, be sure what would lie ahead, were the investigation continued. (Of course, a proposition may be falsifiable in principle and not verifiable—to cite one example, the negation of the proposition just noted.)

The real difference, thinks Hick, between believer and unbeliever lies, not in their particular views of the world around them, but in their conception of the end toward which this world is headed. The two are walking, in effect, down the road of life, each with a different expectation of what is in store. This road will, if the believer is correct, lead to a Celestial City where a greater life is in store. And if the unbeliever is right, no such end exists. The believer interprets the journey—whatever it may contain, for better or worse—as leading to this end. The unbeliever does not. Thus, nothing along the road will decide the case one way or the other. Yet there exists a profound difference in these respective outlooks on reality. As to the reasonableness of the believer's expectation, more will be said in Chapter 6.

In recent years there has been a tendency in some quarters to think of science and religion as pointing in the same direction in their respective claims. One such example is Robert Jastrow,[38] who writes in *God and the Astronomers* that the two enterprises actually make parallel claims with respect to the origins of the universe. Astronomy holds as a basic view that the universe began in sudden and explosive fashion, a "big bang" from which all else has originated. The Bible holds that it began out of nothing when God said, "Let there be light." Hence the scientist, writes Jastrow, who has put his faith in the power of human reason, "has scaled the mountains of ignorance; he is about to conquer the highest peak; as he pulls himself over the final rock, he is greeted by a band of theologians who have been sitting there for centuries."[39] The commonly envisioned enmity of the two camps, Jastrow maintains, is the product of misunderstanding.

Do science and religion really tell us the same things? This view is ridiculed by scientist and science fiction author Isaac Asimov, who takes Jastrow to task for his rather easy conflation of science and scripture. Jastrow, writes Asimov,[40] suggests that painstaking scientific laborers have turned up nothing more for themselves than just what theologians were telling them all along. In response Asimov spells out the real differences between astronomy and theology in terms of both their methods and their respective particular claims about the nature of the world.

What, asks Asimov, does the Bible have to tell us about quasars, about black holes, about whether the universe is open or closed? Any real comparison of what the Bible says and what the scientist thinks, he contends, shows us instantly that the two sources "have virtually nothing in common." The Bible, for example, declares that the heavens and the earth were created at the same time. The consensus of scientists is that the earth is billions of years younger. The Bible says that human beings came onto the scene "on the sixth day"; science tells us that nothing remotely human appeared on the earth for the first four and a half billion years of its duration. The Bible says that the earth was created by the word of God; science maintains that the universe owes its existence to nothing more than "the blind, unchanging laws of nature," which themselves have no need of divine authorship.

Thus the alleged profound agreement of scientists and theologians, concludes Asimov,[41] turns out to be nothing more than the common assertion that the universe had a starting point. Theologians, then, are right about something. But this by itself is no more impressive than a chance prediction (50–50 in its odds) about the outcome of a championship prizefight. The alleged meeting place turns out to be, not a mountain peak, but a crossroads. Science will continue its progress. Theology will not. The meeting, says Asimov, has been brief, and it is unimpressive.

Although Asimov does not deny the existence of God in this discussion, his characterization of the dynamics of the universe as blind suggests that a higher power has no part in the story. A similar view is expressed by Thomas Gourley in the *American Atheist*, who writes that "whatever was 'before' must have been the same as 'now'." Perhaps, writes Gourley, the original stuff was "total energy," perhaps it was "dense matter." But of one thing, he says, he feels certain: "god didn't do it."[42]

It remains to be asked if indeed science renders this verdict. Do the findings, say, of physics, astronomy, or anthropology actually tell us that we are the lost and accidental cosmic orphans that Russell describes? Is it indeed irrational to suppose that life is the spiritual enterprise that believers imagine it to be? This question will be addressed in the next chapter.

Chapter Six

The Viability of Religious Experience

"I mean, what do people usually say?" Svidrigailov murmured, as though to himself, looking to one side and inclining his head slightly. "They say: 'You're ill, so the things you see are just a non-existent hallucination.' But that's wooly thinking, you know. I agree that ghosts are only seen by people who are ill; but I mean, that only proves that ghosts can only be perceived by people who are ill—not that they don't exist."

—Fyodor Dostoevsky, *Crime and Punishment*

Scientific Fact and Religious Vision

In the foregoing chapter I discussed some of the historical relationship between science and religion, and the effort of certain modern thinkers to understand religious experience as a product of events in the natural world. Religion, thinks Russell, is a compromise of intellect and a hindrance to the truth. Freud maintains that religion, in essence, is an illusion produced by the play of forces deep within the individual human psyche. Religious experience, on the whole, such thinkers deem to be an accident of human frailty. A good many people today, it seems, hold to some broad version of this theory—that religion is a "crutch," a "defense," of some dishonest kind, against an ungiving world that has no concern for their welfare.

It remains to be asked whether this skepticism is warranted, and what rational pronouncement, if any, can be made upon religious experience as a whole. In this chapter I discuss the logical relationship between the truth claims of science and those of religion. I then discuss the issue of how, if at all, religious belief can be justified, and I cite examples of the kind of personal experience on which a religious view of life is apt to rest. Afterward I address the issue of whether such experience, generally speaking, is reliable as an indication of the truth.

Is there room for religion of any kind in the modern world? Surely people today are not so religious as were those of a thousand years ago, for indeed a good many elements of our own religious tradition have fallen by the wayside in the past several centuries—few people today, for example, hold to such notions as that the world was created only a few thousand years ago, or that the human race was specially created at that same time and independently of the rest of the life sphere. Few are apt to think that Joshua stopped the sun in its (relative) motion through the sky,[1] or that the creator of all the universe once turned a woman into a pillar of salt.[2] There are rational objections to such beliefs based upon what we know about the world and our place within it.

And yet again, it appears, the religious impulse remains alive. Books continue to flourish upon a wide range of religious and spiritual subjects. A good many people continue to function with a powerful sense of their own spirituality amidst the present culture of space-age science and technology. What, then, is the relationship between science and religious belief?

To answer this question, it may be worthwhile to ask what really is the essence of religious belief and whether it is outmoded in the face of what we know today about the world in which we live. Can a religious attitude toward life be formulated, in this day and age, as any sort of meaningful hypothesis? If so, what is its relationship to the world that is investigated by the sciences?

The writings of Walter Stace[3] contain an important insight into the history and philosophical relationship of the two domains. In his "Man Against Darkness,"[4] Stace talks about what he calls the "essence of the religious vision," as distinguished from particular religious doctrines. In the great transition from medieval to modern worldviews, he says, there has been a mass movement away from religion. And this movement, he admits, has a direct relationship to the rise of the sciences. Yet it came, he contends, not of any necessity, but instead as a result of a subtle change in the way in which human beings began to look at the world.

There is a tendency, says Stace, to think that some particular scientific theory, such as Darwin's account of evolution, or the views of geologists about the age of the earth, or a combination of these, has brought about this change. And it is true that such theories have had an effect on particular church dogmas. Few people, again, would now take seriously the account of human origins that is found in the literal reading of Genesis. But this fact, he says, does not go at all "to the root of the matter." Religion can adapt itself to scientific discoveries of virtually any kind and to the theories that may develop from them. The root cause of the decay of faith, he explains, "has not been any particular discovery of science, but rather the general spirit of science and certain basic assumptions upon which modern science, from the seventeenth century onwards, has proceeded."[5]

The real turning point came when modern scientists turned their backs upon so-called final causes. The final cause of an event is the higher purpose that the event serves in the cosmic order. What lay back of this notion, says Stace, was the presupposition of an intelligent cosmic plan. But such a notion was not essential to scientific progress.

Thus it was that men like Galileo, Kepler, and Newton, quite profoundly religious themselves, took the revolutionary step of expelling the idea of a controlling purpose from the science of nature. "They did this on the ground that inquiry into purposes is useless for what science aims at: namely, the prediction and control of events. To predict an eclipse, what you have to know is not its purpose but its causes. Hence science from the seventeenth century onwards became exclusively an inquiry into causes."[6]

Stace describes this transition of interest from teleology to causal mechanics as being "the greatest revolution in human history," far outweighing in its importance any of the political revolutions that have shaped the course of human civilization. This change takes place during the lifetime of Galileo. At his time, Stace observes, we can draw a sharp line across the history of Europe, dividing it into "two epochs of very unequal length." On one side of the line (dating back even to pagan times), there is the common belief that the world is controlled by plan and purpose. But after Galileo, "European man thinks of it as utterly purposeless."

> It is this which has killed religion. Religion could survive the discoveries that the sun, not the earth, is the center; that men are descended from simian ancestors; that the earth is hundreds of millions of years old. These discoveries may render out of date some of the details of older theological dogmas, may force their restatement in new intellectual frameworks. But they do not touch the essence of the religious vision itself, which is the faith that there is plan and purpose in the world, that the world is a moral order, that in the end all things are for the best.[7]

The *essence* of the religious vision, the real substance of religion, apart from its historical accidents, is a belief in the higher purpose of the world and thus also of the greater end toward which it—and we—are headed. As religious beings we live within this framework, whatever else we may think in scientific terms about the world and our place within it.

This faith may find itself historically expressed within the dogmatic confines of Islam, Hinduism, or Christianity. Yet these particular views (such things, perhaps, as that Mohammed is the last prophet,[8] that Krishna revealed himself to the warrior Arjuna,[9] that the virgin mother ascended bodily into heaven[10]) are incidental to the real substance of this vision. Any or all of these particular items may fall by the wayside within the flow of history without violation of this "essential religious spirit."

But this spirit cannot survive destruction of belief in a plan and purpose of the world. Religion, says Stace, can get on with any sort of biology, geology, physics, or astronomy. But it cannot get on with a universe that has no moral purpose. For in such a world, a human life has no purpose either. In that world a man may still pursue the disconnected ends of money, art, fame, and science, and gain some pleasure from them. But his life is "hollow at the center." Witness, then, the disillusioned spirit of modern man.

Thus it may be that science and religion are not the logical antagonists that some have imagined. It is true that certain beliefs once held and promoted by the church are no longer rationally acceptable in the face of modern evidence. But the more basic religious view, the view that life is indeed a spiritual adventure and that reality, in the end, is fitted to this enterprise may well be compatible with virtually any fact that science may yet turn up. Russell, once again, maintains that science is empirical. As such, he says, it has no use for broad hypotheses, gleaned from scripture or high cosmic pronouncement, and from which subsequent inferences are made. And this position seems to be correct. But what of very broad or basic hypotheses that do not characterize particular features of the world but provide the basis from which we may understand our experiences within it?

What of the view, for example, that life is a spiritual event—that it has a significance that transcends the particular events of its history, that the reality we now experience is but the setting for our own greater personal evolution? It cuts against no scientific fact that I can imagine. Rather it is a view that provides the foundation of a religious person's experience; on the basis of that view he experiences the whole of life. Religious persons are essentially those who experience the world in spiritual terms and who feel themselves therein to be involved in a process of which the present world is merely a setting. The particular nature of this world is an empirical question. As such it is a subject to be investigated by the sciences. But empirical facts like those (the age of the world, the natural origin of human biology, and so on) may not be the whole story. For what is the greater significance of this empirical phenomenon? Perhaps it is not merely an end in itself, but an arena within which is carried out the spiritual quest of those inside of it.

The Logic of Belief and Justification

This basic outlook, as I have just described it, may be theoretically consistent with the data of the sciences. But aside from that, it may be asked, is there reason to accept the religious outlook as being true? We find it easy to accept the reality of the material world, since it is, after all, right here in front of us. But what reason have we to accept the notion of some further reality over and above it? Such an idea may seem to some persons to be without foundation.

Is religious belief justifiable? An insight into its structure and into the structure of belief in general is contained in an essay by Norman Malcolm entitled "The Groundlessness of Belief."[11] In this essay Malcolm tries to show by a series of comparisons that the basic dimension, or "framework," of religion is as legitimate as that of other human enterprises, such as the sciences. At the same time, and in line with this thesis, he expresses a general disregard for attempts to justify religion intellectually, as, for example, by trying to theoretically prove God's existence. Indeed the very notion of justification, he thinks, is misunderstood by persons who are involved in a philosophical project of this sort. To be religious, thinks Malcolm, is not to formulate and defend abstract hypotheses, but to live one's life (at times, at least) within the religious framework. It is to experience life as a spiritual event.

This essay, in turn, is inspired in large part by the philosophy of Ludwig Wittgenstein, especially as it is expressed in his *Philosophical Investigations* and his later work *On Certainty*. Near the end of his life, Wittgenstein became increasingly concerned in his writings with the philosophical problems of knowledge and certainty. In a number of places, he criticizes the notions of evidence and justification as they were handled by some philosophers regarding certain "common-sense" propositions about reality. In particular, he criticizes G. E. Moore's assumption[12] that our knowledge of reality of the external world is supported in some way by rational evidence. Such an assumption, Wittgenstein thinks, stems from a basic misunderstanding of the nature and inherent limits of the justification process.

Repeatedly Wittgenstein stresses the impossibility of justifying certain fundamental propositions that make up the "world picture" within which we carry on our lives. Examples of such propositions are (1) the external world exists; (2) the planet earth has been here for many years past; and (3) our past experiences are in some way relevant to what we can expect in the future. We must understand, thinks Wittgenstein, that the justification process, and likewise the very notions of such things as evidence, proof, argument, and confirmation, all depend upon a certain context, or framework, which itself is presupposed.

Quoting from *On Certainty*, G. H. Von Wright summarizes this point in Wittgenstein's philosophy as follows:

> The core of Wittgenstein's thoughts on these matters could perhaps be paraphrased as follows. In every situation where a claim to knowledge is being established, or doubt settled, or an item of linguistic communication (information, order, question) understood, a bulk of propositions already stand fast, are taken for granted. They form a kind of "system." If this were not so, knowledge and doubt, judging and understanding, error and truth would not "exist," that is, we should not have and handle those concepts in the way we do. "All testing, all confirmation and disconfirmation of a hypothesis takes place already within

a system." And this system is not a more or less arbitrary and doubtful point of departure for all our arguments: no, it belongs to the essence of what we call an argument. This system is not so much the point of departure, as the element in which arguments have their life. (*On Certainty*, #105)[13]

Concerning the problem of the external world, he explains:

The problem of the existence of the external world, one could say, is in fact solved before it *can* be raised—In order to raise the question we must know what our question is about. But in order to acquire the notion of an external world we must first acknowledge a huge number of facts, all of which "entail" (in that Moorean sense) the existence of material objects, that is, of a world external to my mind. I can inquire whether this or that object is in the external world, or is perhaps only an illusion. But whether the result in the individual case is positive or negative, the grounds for the decision will be some facts which stand fast and which entail the existence of an external world. This also explains why there is no procedure for investigating whether or not the external world itself exists. Its existence is, so to speak, the *"logical receptacle"* within which all investigations . . . are conducted.[14]

And he later adds:

Beyond everything we hope or conjecture or think of as true there is a foundation of accepted truth without which there would be no such thing as knowing or conjecturing or thinking things true. But to think of the things, whereof this foundation is made, as known to us or as true is to place them among the things which stand on this very foundation, is to view the receptacle as another object within. This clearly cannot be done. If the foundation is what we have to accept before we say of anything that it is known or true, then it cannot itself be known or true.[15]

The gist of Malcolm's argument is that our beliefs, be they historical, scientific, religious, or mathematical, depend in some way upon other, more general, beliefs, perhaps implicit, from which they derive. At the bedrock of this logical structure are beliefs so basic, so general, that they simply do not admit of justification. Rather they are the things that we must take for granted if we are to believe anything at all.

Malcolm begins by citing Wittgenstein's remark (*On Certainty*, #166) that it is difficult for us "to realize the groundlessness of our believing" and gives a number of examples of how the lives of "educated, sophisticated adults" are formed by groundless beliefs. None of us, for example, would seriously entertain the thought that some given object has disappeared into thin air, and we would refuse to take such an explanation seriously were it offered to us.

Why is that? It is not that the object-vanishing hypothesis is ruled out by evidence, for surely the hypothesis is consistent with our common experience. (After all, we do sometimes lose things that never turn up and whose disappearance is never explained.) Rather our denial of such a thing seems to be implicitly contained in our view, or picture, of the kind of world in which we live. Malcolm makes a similar observation concerning what he calls "the principle of the continuity of nature." As Wittgenstein says:

> Think of chemical investigations. Lavoisier makes experiments with substances in his laboratory and now concludes that this and that takes place when there is burning. He does not say that it might happen otherwise next time. He has got hold of a world-picture—not of course that he invented: he learned it as a child. I say world-picture and not hypothesis, because it is the matter-of-course foundation for his research and as such also goes unmentioned.[16]

Framework principles, says Malcolm, such as the principle of continuity and the assumption that objects do not suddenly and inexplicably cease to exist, belong to what Wittgenstein calls a system. It is the system that "provides the boundaries" within which we ask questions, carry out investigations, and make judgments. They form what Wittgenstein calls "the inherited background against which I distinguish between the true and the false."

Thus hypotheses, says Malcolm,

> are put forth, and challenged, within a system. Verification, justification, and search for evidence, occur within a system. The framework propositions of the system are not put to the test, not backed up by evidence. This is what Wittgenstein means when he says: "Of course there is justification; but justification comes to an end" (*OC*, #192); and when he asks: "Doesn't testing come to an end?" (*OC*, #164); and when he remarks that "whenever we test anything we are already presupposing something that is not tested" (*OC*, #163).[17]

This terminus of explanation, Malcolm stresses, is not a mark of human weakness or limitation. It is not as if we put an end to the justification process because we are too ignorant or too lazy to go any further. It is instead "a conceptual requirement" that our proofs and inquiries stay within boundaries. We could not, after all, carry on the process of justifying a given belief ad infinitum, or we would not have any justification at all! This fact underlies theoretical investigations as well as beliefs and actions of common sense. Consider, for one, our reliance upon memory: If it seems to us that something has happened to us in the past, we have some reason to suppose that such a thing did happen. If it seems to us that the past provides us with some indication of the future, then we have reason, once again, to suppose that this is the case. Yet no amount of reasoning will ever justify in principle the belief that a particular feeling at any given time is a reliable indication that something has happened in the world at a certain time in the past. Nor can we claim (except by way of circularity) that memory has (we seem to remember) proven reliable in the past. Justification, concludes Malcolm, must "come to an end"; it must presuppose something that is itself not tested.

How is all of this relevant to the problem of religious belief? Malcolm contends that religion, like science, is a framework within which we carry on our existence. That is not to say, of course, that we are all equally religious, or that all religious persons have the same beliefs. No doubt there are certain cognitive aspects of an individual's religious outlook that are determined by his cultural surroundings and philosophical development. But the point is that the religious mode of experience is not itself a "view" or "position" to be defended with reasons. In which case,

> religion is groundless; and so is chemistry. Within each of these two systems of thought and action there is controversy and argument. Within each there are advances and recesses of insight into the secrets of nature or the spiritual condition of humankind and the demands of the Creator, Savior, Judge, Source. Within the framework of each system there is criticism, explanation, justification. But we should not expect that there might be some sort of rational justification of the framework itself.[18]

It is very important to understand here that Malcolm is not suggesting that religion is *ir*rational. Nor is he saying that rational considerations are (or should be) irrelevant to the content of religious beliefs. Within the system, as he says, there is controversy, argument, and greater or lesser insight into the truth of religious life. I think he would say, for example, that a particular religious belief ought to be rejected if it turns out to have consequences that are contrary to reason or basic moral sense. But that life itself is religiously significant, that it has a spiritual dimension at all, is something that (whether accepted or not) lies outside the bounds of dispute. The religious life is not purchased with intellectual insight or at the cost of intellectual integrity.

Malcolm's discussion is valuable in several respects. It helps us to understand the nature of the justification process, both in philosophy and in disciplines of other kinds. His discussion also helps us to understand how it is that two persons of comparable intelligence and scholarship can entertain such utterly different views of reality. It enables us to understand as well why philosophical approaches to religion that seek to found religious belief (or disbelief) on mere analysis never go to the heart of the subject and never provide the average philosophy student with anything of value beyond an exercise in ideas.

Is religious belief justified by assigning it a "framework" of the kind that Malcolm has described? It seems to be correct as a point of logic that no belief can be justified without end. It may also be correct that religion, like science, may be considered a basic framework within which we understand our experience. But is that enough? It may be, as Malcolm suggests, that each of our particular beliefs rests upon some basic belief or assumption. But is every possible framework a legitimate one? Consider, for example, the "basic" belief of an individual who interprets the actions of everyone in the world as being part of a conspiracy against him. That, too, might constitute a framework of sorts through which experience might be interpreted. But it would hardly seem like a sane one to those of us outside of it. What, then, should we say about the religious outlook?

Intimations of a Greater Destiny

At this point it may be instructive to look at a few of the experiences that give rise to our sense of spirituality in the first place. In this section I will note, for the sake of illustration, several of these experiences. In the section following I will take up the question of what we might say in philosophical response to them.

As to the particular nature of some of these experiences, I will begin with a much-noted example from the work of James himself:

> I remember the night, and almost the very spot on the hill-top, where my soul opened out, as it were, into the Infinite, and there was a rushing together of the two worlds, the inner and the outer. It was deep calling unto deep. . . . I stood alone with Him who had made me, and all the beauty of the world, and love, and sorrow, and even temptation. I did not see Him, but felt the perfect unison of my spirit with His. The ordinary sense of things around me faded. For the moment nothing but an ineffable joy and exaltation remained. It is impossible fully to describe the experience. It was like the effect of some great orchestra when all the separate notes have melted into one swelling harmony that leaves the listener conscious of nothing save that his soul is being wafted upwards, and almost bursting with its own emotion. The perfect stillness of the night was thrilled by a more solemn silence. The darkness held a presence that was all the more felt because it was not seen. I could not any more have doubted that *He* was there than that I was. Indeed, I felt myself to be, if possible, the less real of the two.[19]

In a similar vein: "God is quite real to me. I talk to him and often get answers. Thoughts sudden and distinct from any I have been entertaining come to my mind after asking God for his direction. . . . God has frequently stepped into my affairs very perceptibly, and I feel that he directs many little details all the time."[20]

And again:

> God is more real to me than any thought or thing or person. I feel his presence positively, and the more as I live in closer harmony with his laws as written in my body and mind. I feel him in the sunshine or rain; and awe mingled with a delicious restfulness most nearly describes my feelings. I talk to him as to a companion in prayer and praise, and our communion is delightful. He answers

me again and again, often in words so clearly spoken that it seems my outer ear must have carried the tone, but generally in strong mental impressions.[21]

Religious experience, as may be apparent, has many varieties. It is not always so forceful as these last examples might suggest. At times it may involve only subtle stirs and inklings. And it may or may not involve a putative encounter with another being. Some varieties of religious experience seem to provide glimpses of our own greater destiny beyond the present life.

"There is," writes Cicero, "in the minds of men, I know not how, a certain presage, as it were, of a future existence." This sense takes root, he observes, "in the greatest geniuses and the most exalted souls." Cicero's observation is noted by John Haynes Holmes in his extraordinary sermon, "Ten Reasons for Believing in Immortality."[22] If immortality is an illusion, writes Holmes, then we have a curious inversion of the usual relationship between truth and intelligence. For throughout history there has existed among the greatest representatives of science, philosophy, poetry, and social movement a rough consensus that life in this world is but a part of something far greater and more momentous. Quoting James Martineau, Holmes notes that if we do not survive, then those who are deceived are not "the mean and groveling," who may be deceived about so many other things, but instead "the great and holy, whom all men revere; the men who have lived for something better than their happiness and spent themselves on the altar of human good." In such a case, then, whom are we to admire? And if our own deepest instincts cannot be trusted, what ought we henceforth to believe about the real nature of the life in which we are engaged?

In a related vein, Holmes takes note of the peculiar "lack of coordination" between the human body and the human mind. If these two things are aspects of a single organism, he asks, adapted only to the conditions of this life, why do they seem to pull so decisively apart in their development over time? With maturity, the body begins to lose its resiliency, to harden, to decay, and at last to dissolve. There exists no such cycle in the life of the soul. The personality of man, says Holmes, is an enduring thing. As the body weakens through the years, "so the soul only grows the stronger and more wonderful. As the body approaches irrevocably to its end, so the soul only mounts to what seems to be a new beginning. We come to death, in other words, only to discover within ourselves exhaustless possibilities."[23]

The aged, he writes, have testified time and again to the fact that "as the body turns to ashes, the spirit mounts as to a flame." Holmes quotes the novelist Victor Hugo, who protests against the waning of his own mortal powers and says: "For half a century I have been writing my thoughts in prose and verse. . . . But I feel that I have not said a thousandth part of what is in me." And Martineau, who exclaims on his eightieth birthday: "How small a part of my plans have I been able to carry out! Nothing is so plain as that life at its fullest on earth is but a fragment."

At times these intimations of a future life involve putative communication between a subject and someone departed. A striking account of such an experience is offered by the Reverend Norman Vincent Peale in his inspirational classic *The Power of Positive Thinking*. Near the end of this book, Peale describes his relationship with his mother, a "great soul"; he writes that "her influence on me will ever stand out in my life as an experience that cannot be surpassed."

Her passing, he says, came as a great loss. Months later Peale felt a longing to be near her, and he traveled to visit at the grave site, where she had once lived as a girl. "All night long on the train," he continues, "I thought sadly of the happy days now gone and how things were utterly changed and would never be the same again."

He then describes walking through the cemetery in cold and dismal weather, under gray skies. Suddenly, he writes:

> the clouds parted and the sun came through. It cast light upon the surrounding Ohio scenery, in gorgeous autumn colors, the hills where I grew up as a boy, which I have always loved so well, where she herself had played as a girl in the long ago. . . . Then all of a sudden I seemed to hear her voice. Now I didn't actually hear her voice, but I seemed to. I am sure I heard it by the inward ear. The message was clear and distinct. It was stated in her beloved old time tone, and this is what she said, "Why seek ye the living among the dead? I am not here. Do you think that I would stay in this dark and dismal place? I am with you and my loved ones always." In a burst of inner light I became wondrously happy. I knew that what I had heard was the truth. The message came to me with all the force of actuality. I could have shouted, and I stood up and put my hand on the tombstone and saw it for what it is, only a place where mortal remains lay. The body was there, to be sure, but it was only a coat that had been laid off because the wearer needed it no longer. But she, that gloriously lovely spirit, she was not there.[24]

Again, we may recall, opinions differ in regard to the proper reading of religious experiences. Some people would subordinate such experiences to forces operating within the world of nature. Others take them more or less at face value, as genuine revelations of truth about life and reality. Can anything be said in favor of one of these broad lines of interpretation over the other?

Of course, for the subject himself in many cases, there is no practical issue involved in the reading of such experience. For it may impress itself upon him with such force that its message cannot be denied. The subject can no more remain neutral about the testimony of such experience than sighted persons can remain neutral about the testimony of their eyes. The force of this experience and the nature of its conceptual scheme give it indeed a supremacy over all other aspects of life. In this vein, David Swenson[25] writes that true religion "does not borrow significance from other forms of human culture," and so does not ask to be supported, for example, by the sciences or by any human activity external to itself. It has instead an innate "aggressiveness" such that it cannot be defended or patronized without suffering betrayal.

But of course, the psychological force of such an experience is one thing, and the theoretical reading of that experience is another. Is there any theoretical reason for someone to prefer the "realist" interpretation of these experiences and others like them over the reductionist one? What can be said about the theoretical merits of either basic reading of such experience?

A Common Error of Materialism

Some people imagine that the reductionist interpretation is the sounder one, on the grounds that it is, in a sense, the more economical. For the data of each experience are consistent, in principle, with either interpretation. Why, then, multiply realities when a single one will suffice? One world, as theories go, is cheaper than two, in terms of what one is required to believe in each case. By dismissing alleged higher "visions" as illusory aspects of the material world, one can maintain a relatively simple theory with respect to the facts. And a simpler theory, it seems, is a logically better one.

Whatever the merits of the religious hypothesis, it is worth noting that there are some people who by their basic inclination are probably incapable of accepting it. For there are, after all, some people who are simply untouched by religious experience of the kind that I have been describing. It is to be expected that such individuals will not share in the excitement that a religious person feels for the notions of some reality beyond the present. They will find it most reasonable to remain within the bounds of what the material senses disclose and they will look to the world of science as a source of truth that is comprehensive. Such mystical and otherworldly encounters as those just noted will be, for them, little more than a feature of human psychology. The real source of these leanings, they will imagine, is the material conditions that "give rise" to them. To go further, they imagine, is to indulge in idle fancy.

Perhaps it is impossible, then, for some people to entertain seriously the notion of a reality beyond this one. But for others, again, it is an entirely different matter. To them life is a spiritual event before it is anything else.

Their feelings, their choices, their encounters with other people—that is all a part of something far greater than the world of material events and objects. These people feel themselves, at times, to be en route to an end that transcends this world. At times they may perceive themselves to be in some form of contact with that other reality, as for example when they feel themselves to be guided or inspired by some power from above. Ask them to describe their lives, day to day, and there wells up out of them a whole systematic vocabulary of such terms as 'trial', 'purging', 'presence', and 'awakening', all of it coming as a reflection of their basic awareness, of what they perceive to be happening within themselves in the process of life.

Owing to this profound difference, it is unlikely, I think, that the question of what is ultimately real and what is credible will ever find a rational consensus. But there remains a question as to what is the philosophically reasonable interpretation of this broadly religious experience. Is a simpler theory of reality an inherently better one? The reductionist view, once again, explains each such experience in terms of events within this world. But suppose that a man feels himself to be addressed by some higher reality. Is it a violation of reason for him to suppose that such a thing is really happening? And what do we ourselves as a philosophical audience say about the situation? This question was addressed by William James in *The Varieties of Religious Experience*.

As James explains at the outset, the inquiry into human religious experience is really an inquiry on two levels and with two different orders of investigation. The two levels, he insists, should not be confused. The first of these, he explains, is the investigation of religion as a psychological phenomenon—what it is like to have religious experience of one kind or another. The second is the assessment of this experience—the determination, as far as we are able, of the significance of such experience over and above its psychological reality.

There exists a popular tendency, James observes, to dismiss religious experience as an accident of the material conditions with which it is associated. One dismisses, for example, a purported vision of God, or a general leaning toward belief in immortality, on the grounds that it owes to a certain event within the brain or to a certain frailty of the nervous system.

Is this strategy sound? James answers as follows:

> In recent books on logic, distinction is made between two orders of inquiry concerning anything. First, what is the nature of it? how did it come about? what is its constitution, origin, and history? And second, What is its importance, meaning, or significance, now that it is once here? The answer to the one question is given in an existential judgment or proposition. The answer to the other is a proposition of value . . . or what we may, if we like, denominate a spiritual judgment. Neither judgment can be deduced immediately from the other.[26]

The proper estimate of religious experience, then, is not derivable from the natural conditions that accompany it. To dismiss a purported revelation as being merely a product of this or that physical circumstance begs the question.

> Perhaps the commonest expression of this assumption that spiritual value is undone if lowly origin be asserted is seen in those comments which unsentimental people so often pass on their more sentimental acquaintances. Alfred believes in immortality so strongly because his temperament is so emotional. Fanny's con-

scientiousness is merely a matter of overinstigated nerves. William's melancholy about the universe is due to bad digestion. . . . Eliza's delight in her church is a symptom of her hysteria.[27]

This quasi-diagnosis, writes James, "finishes up Saint Paul by calling his vision on the road to Damascus a discharging lesion of the occipital cortex, he being an epileptic. It snuffs out Saint Teresa as an hysteric, Saint Francis of Assisi as an hereditary degenerate. George Fox's discontent with the shams of his age, and his pining for spiritual veracity, it treats as a symptom of a disordered colon."[28]

In such fashion, James says, this "medical materialism" supposes that it has undermined the authority of religious experiences. But what, he asks, is the warrant for this method? If one can discount religious perceptions in this manner, then what of other perceptions as well? Would one discount a *scientific* theory on the basis of the constitution of the theorist? And what of religious *dis*belief? Can it be refuted in the same manner? "To plead the organic causation of a religious state of mind, then, in refutation of its claim to possess superior spiritual value, is quite illogical and arbitrary, unless one has already worked out in advance some psycho-physical theory connecting spiritual values in general with determinate sorts of physiological change."[29]

Let us play fair, writes James, with each side. "When we think certain states of mind superior to others, is it ever because of what we know concerning their organic antecedents?" Certainly it is not. When, for example, we speak of "feverish fancies," surely it is not the fever state itself that disqualifies the belief in question. Rather it is the irrationality of the thing fancied. For all we know, "103 or 104 Fahrenheit might be a much more favorable temperature for truths to germinate and sprout in, than the more ordinary blood-heat of 97 or 98 degrees." It would be likewise unthinkable to apply such criteria to any other portion of our experience.

> In the natural sciences and industrial arts it never occurs to anyone to try to refute opinions by showing up their author's neurotic constitution. Opinions here are invariably tested by logic and experiment, no matter what may be their author's neurological type. It should be no otherwise with religious opinions. Their value can only be ascertained by spiritual judgments directly passed on them, judgments based on our own immediate feeling primarily; and secondarily on what we can ascertain of their experiential relations to our moral needs and to the rest of what we hold as true.[30]

That is not to say that we should trust all experience as being informative or should think that the material conditions of perception are irrelevant to its assessment. We would not take seriously, for example, the claim of a delirious man of seeing a mad dog at his bedside, if our senses told us that no such thing was there. But with the case of "higher" visions, James observes, it is different. Suppose that the same man said that he had been visited by an angel. Would we still remain skeptical? Granted, our senses, once again, do not corroborate what the man sees. But then angels are not the kinds of things that are publicly seen, or at least, they are not the kinds of things that need be seen. On what basis, then, can we dismiss this vision as being illusory? Some will say that this vision should be dismissed as hallucinatory, given the man's diseased condition. But what is the principle being invoked in this case? That an angel would not visit a person who is ill? On what basis would one wish to make this claim?

The real criteria, thinks James, are not material, but philosophical. What was the putative content of the vision? What was the effect of this vision upon the subject? Did its message seem rational? Was the subject uplifted by it? We must judge the experience on its own merits, not by the outward conditions that accompanied it. In summary, he writes, "*immediate luminousness,* in short, *philosophical reasonableness,* and *moral helpfulness* are the only available criteria." Thus Saint Teresa, for example, could have had "the constitution of the placidest cow" and it would avail her nothing if her theology could not stand on its own. But if her theology could stand, it would make no difference either, if she were otherwise frail or imbalanced.[31]

The Essential Reliability of Religious Experience

A related discussion of religious experience and its interpretation is offered by Richard Swinburne in his book *The Existence of God.* Swinburne[32] begins by distinguishing between what he calls the "internal" and the "external" descriptions of experience in general. The first of these describes only the conscious state of the subject, whereas the second includes in its scope the purported object of the experience as well. Normally, he says, persons who have religious experiences—those of God, of other worlds, or of some "timeless reality" beyond themselves—mean to describe them in the external fashion.

Religious experience, Swinburne notes, has several forms. There is, for example, the experience of seeing a supernatural object in looking at "a perfectly ordinary non-religious object." Thus one might experience, say, the night sky, not merely as a natural object, but also as the handiwork of its creator. Also there are seeming inward perceptions of the supernatural, as, for instance, nonsensory feelings of the presence or the command of a higher power watching over oneself. For some persons, as Swinburne points out, life on the whole is "one vast religious experience."[33]

How does one read such experiences? Are they mere odd feelings, aberrations, and nothing more, amidst the ordinary stream of consciousness? Or are they genuine revelations of reality and of human destiny? In response,

Swinburne sets forth the general principle, "How things seem to be is good grounds for a belief about how things are."[34]

It is a founding principle of rationality, Swinburne contends, that (in the absence of considerations otherwise) if it truly seems to a subject that X is present, "then probably X is present; what one seems to perceive is probably so." Therefore, "in the absence of special considerations, all religious experiences ought to be taken by their subjects as genuine." This principle of credulity, as Swinburne calls it, is offered both as a general principle of understanding and as a method of interpreting religious experience. Thus on the face of it, according to this principle, religious experience is evidence in favor of whatever truth it purports to reveal.

It is important to understand that Swinburne is not suggesting that all experience is truth-telling, or that it ought to be accepted unconditionally as a reliable indication of what is real. He is only saying that a putative indication that something is real is a reason, in some degree and all things being equal, to suppose that such is the case. The principle is in a way so basic as to be elusive. Put as simply as possible, it holds that experience is to be valued. This assumption is a starting point, thinks Swinburne, for the whole enterprise of human inquiry; without this assumption there could be no such thing as inquiry itself. There may be reason, in a given case, to discount the experience, as, for example, when one seems to "see" a shining pool of water ahead on the freeway on a sunny day. One knows from experience that not all perceptions should be taken at face value. But this knowledge itself is grounded, as all knowledge must be, in a basic reliance upon experience.

Swinburne goes on to note special considerations that may limit the principle in certain cases, and thus may lessen the strength of any such experiential arguments in favor of religious truth. For example, he explains, it is normally thought that an individual's claim to have experienced X is open to some doubt if it can be shown that the experience took place under conditions that diminish its reliability. If it can be shown, say, that a subject was under the influence of a hallucinogenic drug[35] at the time, it would significantly lessen the strength of his claim. But this line of objection does not seem to be available in most cases of religious experience. Second, it might be shown that such experiences themselves are unreliable. But this argument, too, seems inapplicable. For example, a convincing proof of the nonexistence of God does not seem to be available.

Nor, as Swinburne observes, does there appear to be a proof of this unreliability on the grounds that religious claims, owing to their diversity, tend to conflict with one another. It is true that there exist differences in such claims on the surface. But there exist, Swinburne maintains, different levels in the descriptions by which religious objects are identified, such that objects differing at one level may have deeper similarities at another. So, for example, "a Greek's claim to have talked to Poseidon is not necessarily in conflict with a Jew's claim to have talked to the angel who watches over the sea."[36] It is only conflictual if one insists that each claim commits the subject to certain other details that would specifically rule out the claim of the other. (Say, if the Poseidon claim committed its subject to polytheism.)

Nor, tracing out further possible challenges, does it seem to be possible to show that the object of religious experience—that is, God—was not present to be perceived at the time and place in question. For if God by definition is omnipresent, one can show that he was not present only by showing that he does not exist. Finally, says Swinburne, it does not seem possible to write off such an experience as being merely the product of some material cause (say, the condition of the subject's nervous system), since God may be viewed as the ultimate cause of an individual's experiences no matter what other causes (such as brain states) might enter into the situation as well. Swinburne concludes that an individual who has had an experience of God has some reason therein to suppose that God exists. This is especially so, he thinks, if the experience is a forceful one.

The Logic of Transworld Belief

I have offered, to this point, several examples of what may broadly be termed religious experience. I have suggested that such experience is open, in principle, to more than one theoretical interpretation. At the same time, I have maintained (following Swinburne) that we are entitled to a basic trust in these encounters as an extension of the common-sense trust in experience in general. In several of his writings, John Hick provides a relevant insight into our situation with respect to alleged higher realities.

According to Hick,[37] we might look at the various cross-cultural phenomena of world religions as being diverse apprehensions of a single reality. The differences, on this model, between mystical encounters of given persons across different times and places is a product of human differences of attitude, temperament, and philosophical milieu. So, for example, the Buddhist *sunyata*,[38] the *nirguna Brahman*[39] of Vedic Indian tradition, and the Heavenly Father of Christianity might be seen as being different aspects of a single reality. Much like the various shadows cast at different angles by a physical object, these forms of religious apprehension could be viewed as ways in which the religious *noumenon* (the reality as it is "in itself") is made available to human apprehension.

The chief attraction of this model is that it allows us to make some objective sense out of the general phenomenon of mystical experience, while at the same time it avoids the exclusivist view that one such mode of apprehension is "correct" and others are somehow misguided or illusory. But suppose it is said that mystical experience in every case is really no more than a subjective phenomenon. That would mean that mystical states have no object independent of themselves but amount only to alterations (albeit extraordinary) in the consciousness of their subject. What can be said about this hypothesis against its alternative? Each hypothesis, it seems, is consistent with the facts. Which, then, is rationally preferable? On the whole, thinks Hick, the acceptance of mystical encounter as real and veridical is demanded by the facts. "I suggest that it is rational for him to make such a claim, and indeed that it would be irrational on his part not to. We have to trust our own experience for otherwise we have no basis on which to believe anything about the nature of the universe in which we find ourselves."[40]

Of course, we know that some parts of our experience are delusory; thus experience is not always to be taken at its face value. But we only know this, says Hick, on the basis of some general trust in the veracity of our experience otherwise. And this basis indeed seems to be true, for there would be no grounds for judging certain parts of our experience to be delusory unless we believed that experience is at least sometimes reliable. To judge one such part as being delusory requires that we trust another.

But we cannot, Hick says, go beyond experience as a whole. For there is no "beyond" left over, since any further data, once acquired, become part of the whole again. And if some part of that whole is "sufficiently intrusive and persistent," we have no choice but to accept it, unless we wish to doubt our own sanity. But such doubt would mean an act of "cognitive suicide," which is self-defeating and is itself, in that case, presumably groundless!

Thus, for example, one who has "a powerful and continuous sense of existing in the presence of God" has no rational choice but to trust this experience as revealing to him an objective fact, that is, the fact that God exists. By way of analogy, Hick says that this individual

> is as entitled to make this claim as he and the rest of us are to claim to know that the physical world exists and that other people exist. In each case doubt is theoretically possible: a solipsism which reduces the world, or other minds, or God to a modification of one's own private consciousness remains a logical possibility. But we are so made that we live, and can only live, on the basis of our experience and on the assumption that it is generally cognitive of reality transcending our own consciousness.[41]

The analogy with solipsism is instructive. Consider the difference between two persons, one who accepts the testimony of the senses and takes the external world to be real, and one who supposes that there is no world outside of his own experience. What might each say in defense of his own view? The common-sense advocate simply says that it seems as if there is a world "out there," and so assumes it to be the case that such a world does exist. The other may say that he has no conclusive reason to think that any such world exists—for all that he has, he may say, is his own experience, and that can be accounted for just as well on his own hypothesis. Which of these two cosmic outlooks is the sounder one? The solipsistic view, although it is surely at odds with ordinary belief, is actually the simpler. For the solipsist entertains only the reality of one world, whereas the externalist entertains two, namely, the world of his own immediate experience and the greater world of which that experience is (he supposes) a part. Is the solipsist's outlook therefore superior? It does not seem to be. It seems rather that credulity is an advantage in this case, and that a basic trust in one's perceptions is in keeping with the demand of rationality.

What, then, of the difference between a religious individual and an individual who supposes that alleged other worlds are reducible to the world of nature? The former accepts the testimony of his experience as being a valid indication of an external reality to which this experience corresponds. The latter maintains that such experience can be accounted for just as easily by supposing it to be an illusion. Which of these positions is the sounder?

The religious person takes his own otherworldly experience to be an indication of reality. In so doing he, too, like the externalist, multiplies worlds beyond logical necessity. Is that an error? Multiplication did not seem to be an error with regard to the external world. It is hard to imagine anyone thinking that the acceptance of such a world is somehow rationally inferior to the alternative. One can, it is true, entertain a theoretical doubt as to the existence of this world. Our sensory faculties, after all, could be misleading. One can also entertain such doubt about the existence of the world that is revealed by the faculty of the spirit. But if there is indication, in either case, that such a world exists, what possible reason does one have to remain a skeptic?

Recalling the principle of credulity, if it seems that there is an external world of objects and events independent of experience, then there is reason to suppose that there is. And this principle seems no less sound with respect to visions that extend yet further beyond the material world itself. Suppose that it seems to a man as if another whole level of reality, beyond the ordinary one, occasionally breaks in, as it were, upon that one and supersedes it. What is the rational response? If it seems that there is a world outside of the material world, then is there not some reason to suppose that such a world exists?

Similarly, I think, with other kinds of purported revelations, and with experiences generally that give us a sense of our own spirituality. These experiences do not constitute proof of our spirituality or of the truth of the religious hypothesis. But if we feel ultimately that life is a spiritual adventure, we have no rational choice but to act and believe accordingly. We do not have proof, in that we cannot somehow stand outside of ourselves and assess our own experience in its entirety. But if we experience life as a spiritual event, then we have no basis on which to treat it in any different manner.

In conclusion, I should perhaps reiterate that I do not think that religious experience constitutes a theoretical proof of what it conveys to the subject. The fact that there are mystics in the world does not prove the existence of what they claim to apprehend. The fact that a man seems to hear his mother's voice from beyond the grave does not prove the reality of postmortem survival; indeed it may only show us that the grieving process and related stimulus may trigger hallucinations of a certain peculiar kind. In each such experiential case, I believe, one may entertain the possibility that the experience in question is merely a product of the natural order and has no object outside itself. Nor does it seem that we can ever know, in our present condition, that this is not the case.

But this fact, I think, does not forbid a man from interpreting his own experience religiously in the absence of reasons to treat it otherwise. If an inward voice presents itself to his consciousness as being genuine—that is, as being independent of himself—then he has prima facie a logical right to so treat it. Similarly, I believe, for we ourselves who view the event "once removed." For if (as presumably one giving testimony hopes) it touches upon our own higher sensibilities, then we, too, have the right to so treat it, though its impact may diminish with the experiential distance.

The real truth or falsity of such experience, when all is said and done, lies outside the range of what can be affirmed or denied with rational certainty. It is, I must think, just what a good many religious types would make of it— the most obvious and most elusive thing in our lives. We cannot know, as we know a truth of arithmetic, that we are spiritual creatures. We cannot know otherwise. Somewhere in the middle lies the possibility of religious life. It is a life that gives no guarantees, yet still a life that may give to us on occasion some glimpse of the destiny for which we were created. Herein lies the possibility of religious knowledge—of the revelation that is given to us in daily experience of our uncertain and undeniable spirituality.

Chapter Seven

Conclusions: The Worldview Encouraged

It feels like a real fight . . . as if there were something really wild in the universe, which we, with all our idealities and faithfulnesses, are needed to redeem.
—William James, "Is Life Worth Living?"

To this point I have examined and criticized materialism with respect to several of the key issues of philosophy. What sort of beings are we? What is the real nature of moral value? And what sense can we make of alleged "visions" of worlds beyond this one? I have suggested that any satisfactory approach to questions like these must incorporate some notion of the immaterial as a real and basic element in our conception of reality. In this chapter I wish to summarize the conclusions of the previous chapters and to discuss their relationship to a general philosophy of life.

Absurdity and Life-Meaning

Some of the conclusions reached in previous chapters have relevance to one particular problem that has figured prominently in a great deal of philosophy and literature of the past century, namely, that of the ultimate meaning of human existence. Some philosophers contend that life actually has no meaning apart from the one that we choose to give it. A prime example of such thinking is Sartre, who insists in much of his writing upon life's absurdity.

A central theme of Sartre's philosophy is the cosmic abandonment of the human race to a freedom without guidelines, and to an existence with no pregiven formula for action. What convictions we may come to have about meaning, about purpose, about righteousness, thinks Sartre, have no congruence with the universe in which we live. This universe does not share our ideals, and it will likely as not mock them, by its outcome, with indifference.

Even our efforts to maintain a dignity in the face of this fact, he believes, might well be rendered as a play of dark humor. We sometimes imagine ourselves, Sartre says, awaiting our deaths in a figurative prison cell, with the thought of facing the end with heads held high against the fates. But in reality, he observes, life is apt to grant no such opportunity. It is as if we are taken in our cells by an epidemic that arrives unannounced before any such grand show of strength can be enacted. Our sentimental notions of a universe that is divinely ruled, about lives that have some rational purpose and place in the scheme of things, are illusions. The universe does not reward heroism, and it does not respect our convictions.

Something of this idea is expressed in Sartre's short story "The Wall,"[1] which he writes from the point of view of a Spanish revolutionary named Pablo Ibbieta who is imprisoned and awaits execution in the morning. Like much of Sartre's other fiction, the story abounds in fleshly images; it is rich and alive, even in its darkness, with the portrayal of human will set grimly against the material conditions that beset it.

Pablo faces his waning hours in the hopes that he will meet death with honor. His two cell mates, lacking any sense of such things, do not have the strength to face the end with dignity. They are a source of disgust to Pablo, who does what he can to avoid any show of weakness in front of them. The hours pass, and he feels the crush of an invisible weight. His cheeks burn and his head aches. He describes the ordeal: "I shook myself and looked at my two friends. Tom had hidden his face in his hands. I could only see the fat white nape of his neck. Little Juan was the worst, his mouth was open and his nostrils trembled. The doctor went to him and put his hand on his shoulder to comfort him: but his eyes stayed cold."[2]

Juan wonders if it hurts when the shots strike home. Tom tries to envision the sensation of his back against the unyielding wall and the bullets tearing into his face. He is fat, notices Pablo, and he has begun to stink of urine. Soon that soft body will be impaled as if it were butter. Tom, says Pablo:

> didn't realize the situation and I could tell he didn't want to realize it. I hadn't quite realized it myself, I wondered if it hurt much, I thought of bullets, I imagined their burning hail through my body. All that was beside the real question; but I was calm: we had all night to understand. After a while Tom stopped talking and I watched him out of the corner of my eye; I saw he too has turned grey and he looked rotten; I told myself "Now it starts."[3]

The story is an allegory of the human condition. We all face execution, and once admitting this fact, we take a grim view of what life is left to us. Even were the guards to grant Pablo a full reprieve, at this point, he would be "left cold." Several hours or several years of waiting is the same, he decides, "when you have lost the illusion of being eternal." He resolves to do the one thing that still matters to him—to "die cleanly."

His two comrades are led away. One must be carried beneath the armpits. Then come the sounds: "I heard shots at almost regular intervals; I shook with each one of them. I wanted to scream and tear out my hair. But I gritted my teeth and pushed my hands in my pockets because I wanted to stay clean."[4]

Expecting to be next, Pablo is taken to a room where instead he is offered his own life in return for his betrayal of activist leader Ramon Gris. He first refuses, then later, in what is intended as one last act of defiance, sends them on a farcical hunt for the revolutionary leader in the cemetery. By a wild coincidence, they find Gris in that place and Pablo is freed. "Everything," the story concludes, "began to spin and I found myself sitting on the ground: I laughed so hard I cried."

The malaise expressed in this story is certainly not unique. One can find other examples of it in the literature of philosophy and various works of theater and fiction. The lesson of "The Wall," it seems, is that life is absurd because the universe is indifferent to our ideals. This incongruence of self and world, Sartre seems to believe, is a verdict upon us, a measure of our worth in the universe. We may imagine our lives to be of value and to have some meaning, yet that is merely a subjective fantasy. Looking at our lives from the outside, we see that reality itself harbors no such concern. Thus abandoned, we must find our purpose in life by our own free choosing, without the benefit of any absolute guidelines.

Sartre is not the only philosopher who has asserted that reality is in some basic way out of accord with our own ideals and inclinations. This notion of an incongruity of self and world is discussed by Thomas Nagel in a very perceptive essay entitled "The Absurd."

We occasionally hear it said, Nagel observes, that life is somehow absurd. This absurdity, he argues, owes not to any of the things that are normally adduced as reason for it. It is not, he says, that our lives are too short, or that we occupy too little space in the universe, or that the reasons for our daily endeavors "come to an end." What makes life seem absurd, says Nagel, is our peculiarly self-transcending ability to view our own lives both in the usual manner ("from within") and yet again from an altogether higher vantage point, from which these same lives seem minuscule and trifling.

We live our lives in the usual way, taking them to be important and serious things, while at the same time we are able to see them, in mind's eye, from this other and seemingly more realistic point of view, from which they are of no real importance whatsoever. And neither point of view can be relinquished. Thus a man functions, on a practical level, with strong and constant worry about whether he is maintaining respectability as regards "his appearance, his health, his sex life, his emotional honesty, his social utility, his self-knowledge, the quality of his ties with family, colleagues, and friends, how well he does his job, whether he understands the world and what is going on in it."[5]

But this same individual and others like him, says Nagel:

> have the special capacity to step back and survey themselves, and the lives to which they are committed, with that detachment that comes from watching an ant struggle up a heap of sand. Without developing the illusion that they are able to escape from their highly specific and idiosyncratic position they can view it sub specie aeternitatis—and the view is at once sobering and comical.[6]

As Nagel later explains, "philosophical perception of the absurd resembles epistemological skepticism."[7] Such skepticism begins when we adopt an imaginable point of view from outside ourselves in order to look critically at the ordinary, subjective point of view that is our own. We then realize that we may be quite deluded in our notion of what the world is really like.

> Reference to our small size and short lifespan and to the fact that all mankind will eventually vanish without a trace are metaphors for the backward step which permits us to regard ourselves from without and to find the particular form of our lives curious and slightly surprising. By feigning a nebula's eye view, we illustrate the capacity to see ourselves without presuppositions, as arbitrary, idiosyncratic, highly specific occupants of the world, one of countless possible forms of life.[8]

What Nagel seems to have in mind is that the final basis on which we live our lives—the reasons for our choice of actions, lifestyle, and ideology, and the things that we regard as being ultimately important—is itself grounded in our subjectivity. We cannot cease to take our lives seriously, of course, for no other attitude is (for us) psychologically possible. At the same time, we can look at these same lives from the outside and can view ourselves as we view the ant—that is, as something that has no objective importance. Thus we can view as trivial the very things that still concern us; this seems to involve a contradiction that cannot be escaped, hence life, it is thought, is riddled with a basic irrationality. We live for purposes that (looked at objectively) do not merit the concern that we give them. Whether it be, say, my hairstyle, or my next automobile, or even my concern over my own pain, all of it, from the outside, thinks Nagel, seems to be peculiar and arbitrary.

Do considerations of this kind suffice to show that life is ultimately without meaning? It is true, I think, that some of our concerns may well seem trivial when we look upon them with detachment. But are all of our concerns like this? Granted, I may be, in my present and largely self-bound condition, excessively worried about my appearance, or about securing creature comforts, or about keeping pace with the material lifestyle of my neighbors. But what of other concerns? Consider, for example, my desire to develop in a positive fashion as a human being, and to see persons in my acquaintance become interested in the same kind of enterprise. Is this concern objectively trivial? It does not seem so to me, nor can I see why the same concerns entertained by some other individual far removed from me might not be just as important. If there is another person at the far end of the galaxy, or at some other time, who has this concern for himself and for his fellows, it seems perfectly rational to me even if (given the limits of the situation) I cannot share it with him. And if someone watches it all from above, I must think that this being as well can see value in his enterprise.

Some events are important, I believe, from every point of view. Moral choices come to mind as a primary example. From what point of view are they peculiar or trifling? As for myself, I cannot think that a striving for justice, for example, be it made in another part of the universe, or at a remote time, or in some infinitesimal world beneath that of the electron, would be any less important than one committed before my own eyes. That is not to say that I myself can have a personal concern with such events—I cannot, since they are beyond the reach of my knowledge and influence. But this limitation is a fact of psychology, not one of value.

Perhaps Kant's earlier-cited discussion[9] is worth recalling. My place in the material universe, Kant writes, makes me seem as nothing. Yet the moral law provides me with a source of value that all of the universe cannot diminish. My own particular moral choices, it is true, are embedded, as Nagel observes, in a set of life circumstances that are odd and idiosyncratic. Looked at in this manner, this life is an odd, gratuitous thing, perhaps even astonishing in its sheer peculiarity. But I fail to see how that makes the moral drama within it any less crucial, either from my own immediate vantage point or under the aspect of eternity. Were someone to say that such choices are meaningless, I would wonder what further kind of meaning was being sought.

Similarly, the fact that the world does not seem to share my ideals is not a reason to think that these ideals in themselves are worthless. For it is just in a world of this kind—an objective environment in which the best-laid plans may indeed go awry, and in which the better cause may not be victorious— that a real test of integrity is made possible. If the world is in fact a place where I am to make progress, it must be a place that is (as far as appearances are concerned) indifferent to that cause, and that offers no guarantee of a positive outcome.[10]

Whether an individual life is a consequential part of reality does not, as Nagel himself agrees, depend upon how large a place that individual occupies in the space and time of all the universe. It may be, as some religious types would have it, that the universe is intended to serve some purpose for consciousness. It may serve the purpose of what some have called a "soul-making" enterprise, wherein human beings evolve spiritually through their contact with it. This way of looking at the world suffers, as best I can tell, from no inconsistency within itself and contradicts no observable fact about the world itself. Nor, I think, is it made any less probable by the size of the universe or by the relative smallness of the space and time that we now occupy within it. I see no reason to think, for example, that human life would be any more precious or human actions any more significant were the human organism any larger, or any less precious, were it smaller. Nor, I think, does the issue of meaning depend upon how peculiar the human organism and his concerns may look from the "objective" point of view. For the real issue is not how odd he may look (even to himself) from the outside, but rather the principle in which his life is grounded. If a man lives only for his own sensual gratification, he might have reason to think his life objectively trivial. But if instead he perceives himself subject to a law that summons him, as Hick has said, to rightful obedience, he can hardly think his life to be lacking in meaning.

I have said that some aspects of our lives may indeed seem trivial when looked at from an outside point of view. It may not matter, in the scheme of things, whether I profit materially from the sale of this book, or whether I continue my current hitting streak in games with the city softball league. Thus my ordinary train of thought does at times seem silly to me if I look at it from the outside. But what is the moral of this story? Is it that life is meaningless, or merely instead that I am prone to a habitual falsification of values in my usual (and self-preoccupied) frame of mind?

This issue of life-meaning, I believe, is logically related to the issue of materialism. Perhaps the case of the Russian author Leo Tolstoy is instructive. There came a time, Tolstoy[11] writes in his autobiography, when he began to ask the reason for his own existence, for his continued efforts to persevere with life as he knew it. This need for justification, he explains, had nothing to do with any shortage of wealth or comfort, or with desire for greater reputation. Tolstoy had by this time already become quite successful and was growing more affluent with little effort in that direction. His writing had become well known, and he had (outwardly, at least) the kind of life for which a great many persons strive.

And yet it was not enough. Something was lacking. The first moments of doubt, Tolstoy recalls, were like single drops of ink on a sheet of white paper. They passed, and life went on as before. But the moments of doubt continued and became more frequent. In time it was as if this page—his life—had turned black with the stain.

He sought an answer to his problem in the world's great literature—texts of science, history, psychology. But nowhere, he explains, amidst this "forest" of fact and figure was there a place for a home. No amount of reading, of intellectual discovery, of information about the structure of the world, provided an answer to his need for a life-purpose.

Tolstoy, as it turned out, found his solution in an embrace of the Russian Orthodox religion. It was in the plain faith of the common folk, he writes, that he found meaning, reason to continue with life—a dimension of truth, he maintains, unfathomed by the sophisticates of his day. The answer to his quest was found in terms of his own spirituality. Real meaning could only be found in transcending the natural world, in acknowledging the fact that his own true nature was not contained within it. It was found, not in some value of his own personal creation, but in his relation to something absolute and infinite that awaited his response.

I am not especially concerned, for present purposes, with the details of Tolstoy's particular solution. Another person in another place, I must think, might reach out to Catholicism, or Islam, or Buddhism, and with much the same result. Nor do I imagine that every person undergoes this same crisis, at least not in this present life. Asked for a justification of his existence, one man may say that he enjoys life; another may say that he has a responsibility to his family; and another may point to some social cause of which he is a part. And this answer or some other might well suffice for the duration of his natural life. The point I wish to stress is that nothing in the natural world can provide a solution to a crisis of the kind that Tolstoy describes. The reason (recalling a kindred discussion in Chapter 4) is that this world itself cannot provide the answer to the question of how we should relate ourselves to it. No knowledge, on our part, of fact, of number, of details concerning the arrangement of matter in space, can resolve the issue. The world presents us with a given set of circumstances. It tells us, within probable limits, what will happen if we choose in this direction or that. But it can do no more than that. It can provide us with a set of facts. But it cannot provide us with a sense of direction. For the question always remains: What ought we to do with these facts? How must we respond to them? It is only when we go beyond the world, when we lift our gaze above this collection of fact and circumstance and address our inward condition—address the situation, in other words, in spiritual terms—that we find the prospect of an answer. Those individuals who see no guiding purpose, no higher source of truth or value that makes a claim upon them, may well feel cast adrift when they reflect upon their lives from the outside. If we cannot find meaning within the world, we must transcend it. Whether any such purpose exists, I believe, is a question that lies beyond the realm of theoretical investigation. But in searching ourselves, perhaps we will find an answer.

The Limits of Rational Inquiry

"And is this going to be some kind of . . . dualism?" This question was asked, somewhat warily, by a colleague whom I was consulting about some of the material that would be of use in one of the chapters of this book. My conception of human identity is in a sense dualistic, in that I believe we are something quite different from the bodies with which we are commonly identified. And I do not wish to minimize the difficulties that attach themselves to a view of this kind. Even so, I am inclined to think that the term 'dualism' is a bit of a misnomer. For this notion of *duality* has in it the sound of something that is inherently implausible, namely, that human individuals are in fact a kind of ontological sandwich of two things utterly different from each other.[12] In truth, I am inclined to think that people are not any such combination, but one thing only—and that is spirit. The material vehicle of this spirit, I believe, is neither lasting nor essential. The matter making up my body, I suspect, no more constitutes me now than it did (in whatever was its arrangement) a million years ago. A human being does indeed, as Plato supposed, stand in relation to the body as a pilot to a ship. It is this conception of things that fits best, I believe, with the rest of what we seem to believe about ourselves and the demands of the life in which we find ourselves.

Philosophy, say some, begins in wonder. I am inclined to think that it ends the same way. It does not seem to me that consciousness can be reduced to any set of facts about the natural world; and I do not think that our moral experience can be explained in any such terms either. Recalling C. S. Lewis's discussion cited in Chapter 4, I do not believe that we can rest comfortably with any naturalistic account of values if indeed we wish to continue to take our moral experience as seriously as conscience demands. We must suppose that it has a reality that is outside the world of scientific investigation.

The *Tao*, writes Lewis, is beyond all predicates. Does that mean that we cannot know what it is? What is the relationship between this rather elusive entity and the moral system, say, of a Kant or a Mill? The answer, I believe, is that we can know the *Tao* in a limited and relative fashion even if we cannot have an intellectual account of its inherent nature. We can know its nature in relation to ourselves. We can know, for example, that kindness is better than cruelty, that self-sacrifice on the field of battle is a thing to admire; we can know that it is somehow incumbent on us to do certain things (to tell the truth, to honor a promise, or whatever) in given situations, and that we are better persons for meeting such obligations. We can know that justice is a thing worthy of our effort.

As to the relationship between the *Tao* and various particular moral doctrines, several things may be said. First, the *Tao* is probably not captured by any single view of ethics. This is consistent with the fact that no single theory of ethics ever seems to intuitively satisfy all of those who study it. Most of the classic moral doctrines seem to have in them something of worth, yet they seem also to have problems. Kant seems to be right, for example, in saying that honesty is a good thing. But is every act of honesty good and every act of dishonesty immoral? Mill seems to be correct in his view that one ought to bear in mind the consequences of one's actions in terms of the happiness and unhappiness that will result from it. But is utility the only thing that ever matters?

Standard texts of moral philosophy, as many readers know, often take the approach of first summarizing the views of Kant, Mill, and others and then running down a standard list of the "problems" with each of them. Often the matter is left at that, and the reader is left to marvel at the "enduring" nature of philosophical questions. Small wonder that so many undergraduates are discouraged by their first encounters with the subject. Perhaps it would be better, perhaps more constructive, to place emphasis upon what is right with certain views of morality—to see them, whatever their limitations, as each capturing some aspect of the truth, even if it does not capture all of the truth. There is a reason, I believe, why Plato's story of the cave has fired the imagination of readers for the past two and a half thousand years. The reason is not, as many will say, that it is merely "haunting" or "picturesque," but that it echoes our own deepest instincts as to what is ultimately real. Contained in this imagery is the apprehension of a truth that lies at the heart of the enterprise of life. Granted, no single account of the truth may be complete. But this admission does not require us to think that no such account has any truth in it.

Indeed there may be room for whole new explorations of the *Tao*. Thus Harvard psychologist Carol Gilligan,[13] for example, makes the claim that the whole moral tradition of the Western mainstream suffers from an imbalance owing in large part to its exclusion of female voices from its literature. Gilligan claims that this tradition has emphasized such notions as those of rights and justice with relatively little emphasis on that of care. A better moral theory and a better society, she believes, may result from an integration of male and female perspectives into the discipline.

This suggestion that moral philosophy may be in need of some radical amendment does not mean that the discipline has no truth. Rather it means that the truth as yet has not been fully revealed. The neglect of a female perspective is presumably an objective defect, which must be addressed for the sake of arriving at the truth that presumably exists. And this truth, I think, is not obscured by appealing to an immaterial and indeed otherworldly source as a means of its explanation. What this *Tao* is in itself we may never know, not, at least, in our present condition. But what it is in relation to ourselves we can know perhaps a good deal. It is the source of what is true in every attempt to explain what is involved in the difference between good and evil. It is likewise what gives value to every moral theory, to the extent that the theory reflects the truth. The *Tao* cannot be spoken, but it can be lived. It is the truth in which a life must be grounded if that life is to be sound.

My approach to philosophy will not sit well with some philosophers. They may find it mystical, in some pejorative sense, and too much given to what is subtle and hidden. My willingness to incorporate into philosophy such things as mystery, the timeless, and the intangible will strike some readers as being an ignoble way to handle the great questions of philosophy. They will say that it is the business of the discipline, after all, to grasp the issues, to comprehend them intellectually, and thus that my own approach is less than wholly faithful to this grand enterprise. In reply I say that my approach, whatever its faults or its merits, does not issue from any basic intellectual pessimism or from a wish to obscure. If someday I come across, say, a naturalistic account of consciousness or of value that comes within a light-year of satisfying my own instincts or that I can square with the convictions of common sense, perhaps I will think otherwise. Until that time, I must continue to believe that the soundest approach to philosophy is the one that I have chosen—one that sees human existence as being grounded in a reality that cannot be seen, heard, touched, or even fully comprehended.

This notion of mystery is itself an issue that occasionally receives comment in the literature of philosophy. Mystery, some say, is really not a thing in itself: In calling something a mystery, we mean only that we do not (as yet) understand it. But a mystery is not, they will maintain, a thing to be treated as being objectively real or as being the end point of an investigation. A sentiment of this kind is expressed by Peter Van Inwagen in his book *Metaphysics,* when he reminds his readers: "The mysteries that metaphysics uncovers are, of course, mysteries relative to ourselves and to our ability to understand things. Nothing is a mystery in itself, whatever that might mean. Everything is as it is; everything has a certain set of properties and these properties must be consistent."[14]

Thus all truths, it is imagined, lie naked in themselves, behind whatever conditions (principally, it seems, our own intellectual limitations) may obscure them for the time being. The obscurity is incidental. All truths are in themselves just what they are and nothing more. Every fact is transparent to the mind that can grasp it.

It seems to me that Van Inwagen is right in saying that mystery is relative to the limits of apprehension. But I must still wonder if the world is as thinker-friendly as the standard enterprise of philosophy currently takes it to be. It may be that all truths, in principle, lie open to understanding of some kind. But it is another question whether we ourselves are equipped to understand them in our present condition. Consider, for example, the element of spatial dimension. We know more or less what it is, even if perhaps it is too basic to admit of an easy definition. We commonly suppose that three dimensions exist. Might there exist others? The notion of a fourth dimension contains within itself, as best I can tell, no contradiction—if, after all, there can be three, then why not four, or ten, or a myriad?—and perhaps there are beings who inhabit such worlds and find those environments as natural as we find ours. But that does not mean that I myself or any creature like me can have a concrete understanding of what such a world is like or of what it would be like to be a part of it.

As we look around, we may find that certain aspects of our own world as well seem to resist rational description; consider, for one, the problem of understanding certain events at the subatomic level. They are, by some serious accounts, strange enough to call into question even the foundations of logic itself.[15] Nonetheless, they make up a part of our view of reality. And regardless of how the science continues to develop, how can we ever think that physics is founded upon anything other than mystery? Why, after all, *these* laws and not some others? The bare fact that there is something rather than nothing is a contingent fact. And why *this* something rather than another?

Consider also what has been said about religious experience by those who have endeavored to describe it. Rudolph Otto's *The Idea of the Holy* is subtitled "an inquiry into the non-rational factor in the idea of the divine and its relation to the rational." The book abounds in references to what is holy, in contrast to what is merely profane; to what is awesome, numinous, and wholly other. What lies in this realm, we are told, is sheerly and irreducibly *uncanny.* Are we to think that such elements as those would be available to us in rational terms if we were to think on them a little longer? It appears that the consensus, among those who have investigated such things in depth, is negative. If we put any stock in their competence and in our own instincts, we will content ourselves with the fact that the enterprise of analysis is limited.

The element of mystery is not completely gone from the contemporary literature of philosophical inquiry. In 1995 a weekly news magazine[16] dealt with efforts to "unravel" the various secrets of the human brain and its relationship to conscious experience. Science, reports this cover story, is now peering into the brain "looking for that evanescent thing called consciousness" and is solving the age-old problem.

"What, precisely," asks the author, "is the mind, the elusive entity where intelligence, decision-making, perception, awareness and sense of self reside?" The thesis of this article is that new and more powerful technologies of observation are providing us with answers to questions of this kind some two and a half millennia after they were first raised by the Greeks. The employment of such refined techniques as magnetic resonance imaging and positron emission tomography is providing a window, as it were, on the brain, wherein scientists can watch a thought taking place and can see the red glow of fear erupting from the amygdala. "A memory," it is announced, "is nothing more than a few thousand brain cells firing in a particular, established pattern." Consciousness, as it turns out, is much more complex, yet also more amenable to scientific investigation, than was expected.

Against common sense and contrary to what seems to be the case in introspection, consciousness may be "nothing more than an evanescent by-product of more mundane, wholly physical processes—much as a rainbow is the result of the interplay of light and raindrops." By implication, it appears, the various mental processes of memory, learning, vision, recognition, decision-making, and others are likewise grounded in the respective neural events with which they are associated. Whatever else consciousness is, we are told, there is one thing it is not: "some entity deep inside the brain that corresponds to the 'self,' some kernel of awareness that runs the show, as the 'man behind the curtain' manipulating the illusion of a powerful magician in *The Wizard of Oz.*"

This discussion, of course, is informative. And it is interesting. It relays up-to-the-minute information about brain research and the inferences being drawn from the findings. As such it represents the absolute forefront of thought (in scientific circles, at least) concerning the mind and its relationship to the events of neurophysiology. It expresses, too, a serious appreciation of the massiveness of the project that is being undertaken. Moreover, it abounds in words like 'elusive' and 'intriguing', and the word 'mystery' appears more than once.

But mystery in this context, it appears, has to do only with the brain's material *complexity*. The real mystery, I think, involves more than that. Brain activity itself is an empirical phenomenon. As such it is not so much a mystery as a problem, albeit a fantastically complicated one. What is genuinely mysterious, I believe, is not so much the neural activity to which the *Time* article alludes, but the fact that this activity, a material event, can be associated with a whole theater of events—of feelings, sensations, recollections, and deliberate conscious action—that seem to resist description in terms of material reality.[17]

It is apparently correct to say that brain research has not turned up "some entity deep inside the brain" that constitutes a self. But that, I believe, does not discourage us from thinking of the self as being an enduring and substantial thing just the same. It is hard to imagine just what investigators had in mind when they hoped to find a self residing somehow at the core of the brain and underlying all the rest of the conscious events related to it. I myself do not know what this exposed wizard, this core element of "me," as it were, would look like when an electrode impinged upon it, or what this investigation of neural episodes could ever produce except particular experiences, of one kind or another, for the subject whose brain was being prodded. But again, and recalling our discussion of James,[18] that is not an obstacle to thinking that the self is indeed a unity. Rather than viewing consciousness as being the product of the brain, perhaps we might see it instead as being an agency that works through the brain, a real and viable entity that stands in relation to that mechanism as an owner to an object or, again, as an operator to a piece of machinery. This way of thinking about the mind-body relation, as far as I am aware, is perfectly consistent with any research available on the subject of brain activity and allows us to maintain the idea (as discussed in Chapter 2) that selfhood is something more than a by-product of material events.

Spirit and Philosophy:
A Summary of Conclusions

What general view of life is encouraged by our view of ourselves as rational and decision-making agents within our present circumstances? Reflection upon our daily experience and upon the assumptions with which we commonly operate leads us, I believe, to a worldview that is spiritualistic at its heart. What emerges, it seems to me, from our common-sense beliefs about ourselves and the world around us is a view of life as a spiritual enterprise, transworldly and ongoing, and a view of ourselves, likewise, as spiritual beings involved in an enterprise of growth and development that extends beyond the limits of the material world. The conception of human nature, I contend, that best accords with our ordinary beliefs about who we are and what we are doing is that of an immaterial agent, rational and autonomous, working through the challenges of a material world.

The conclusions reached in this book encourage an outlook that is broadly religious in its basis. Man, we are told in Genesis,[19] is made in the image of God. We are made by God, writes Augustine,[20] with a tendency toward him, and we cannot find rest except in finding him. Our real nature, say the Vedic scriptures,[21] runs deeper and involves more than we ordinarily suppose. The general direction of these claims, I believe, is similar and implies that our nature and final good lie beyond the world of immediate appearances. I believe also that this basic conception of life grows naturally out of the investigation of such things as freedom, value, and rationality.

This inquiry has been divided principally into three parts. The first of these parts involved questions about the nature of consciousness and the attempt to reduce consciousness to facts about the material world.

Our own consciousness reveals to us a reality that is very different from the reality that we observe in the world around us. This inner world, that of conscious experience, is one of will, of mood, of passion, love, and reason— things whose nature cannot, except arbitrarily, be equated with material events of any kind whatsoever. If we believe furthermore that we are rational creatures, we must believe that we are able to comprehend truth and to respect it and to abide by its dictates. But that requires that we are able, in some way, to transcend the world of inanimate nature, which presumably has no allegiance to such things as truth, or goodness, or rationality. And yet again, if the reductionist thesis is true, our consciousness is determined in the end by material events that go their way without regard for what is true, or good, or reasonable. Thus if we believe ourselves to be rational, we must believe that there is more to us than this thesis would maintain.

Similarly, if we believe that our moral judgments are true—that they are real and objectively valid and worth taking into account—then we must believe that they are more than reports or expressions of our own psychology, and that they have to do with more than just the going attitudes of the cultural settings in which they occur. We must likewise believe that we are able to act upon their truth, and thus to shape the world (or not) in the direction that they command. We must then also believe that our actions are truly chosen, at times, on the basis of value and are not inexorably determined by the material forces that rule the course of inanimate nature.

An interesting reflection upon the nature of moral experience is contained in William Barrett's *The Death of the Soul.* The fundamental question of ethics, writes Barrett, "is that of the individual asking himself 'What *ought* I to do?'" This *ought*, he explains (recalling Hume), can never be accounted for in terms of an *is*. And this aspect of our lives cannot be translated into any fact about mere thought or feeling.[22]

The singular nature of the moral element, thinks Barrett, is well illustrated by the example of lying. One has ordinarily, it seems, an obligation not to lie. But at times, notes Barrett, the complications of social life may nevertheless drag us into acts of dishonesty. When this happens, he explains, we are still uneasy about it, and we are apt to be "dreadfully ashamed" when the lie is exposed—even if that lie happens to be a trivial one.

A lie, insists Barrett, is more than a breach of rationality. If it were merely a formal contradiction, an error of logic, we could hardly account for the peculiar guilt we feel in being caught in one. Think, for a moment, of the embarrassment that one might feel in being caught in a slip of logic. It would not compare in degree or kind with what one feels in being caught instead in a lie. Barrett recalls the scene at a small party when, late in the evening, conversation turned to the subject of lies and the guilt associated with them: "'My lies,' one lady exclaimed, 'when they come back to find me, are like sticky little worms crawling over me.' The lie, in short, provokes a kind of intimacy of disgust, as if one's whole person—body and soul—had been contaminated. Hardly the feeling that logical form had been violated!"[23]

The majority of those who read this description will read it, I suspect, with recognition. They may not be liars as a matter of habit, but they will understand the feeling that this woman describes. It remains to be asked what philosophical account of the phenomenon best accords with the fact. If this feeling of repugnance at oneself is merely, as reductionist accounts would have it, an accident of human psychology, then it signifies nothing outside itself. It informs us of nothing as to the objective worth of lying, but merely occurs within the flow of natural events that constitute human consciousness. If that is the case, then we should admit that we have no reason in principle to be ashamed of lying.

Indeed we might be better off without this shame. If we could take a pill, say, that would erase such a feeling, we might be able to lie without paying afterward the price that conscience extracts. Once rid of this burden, we could lie when the situation seemed to allow it, without the price of this moral hangover.

Yet how many of us would choose to alter our experience in this manner? Few, I will wager, if any. The reason, I believe, is that most of us, when it comes down to it, believe that our moral consciousness is not merely a feeling but a revelation. The philosopher who thinks that his own conscience is fundamentally a mere accident of his biological development ought to ask himself whether he would be willing to rid himself of this feature of his own consciousness, and indeed why he bothers to concern himself with it at present in the course of his daily life.

A related discussion appears in Hywel Lewis's *The Elusive Self.* Early in the book, Lewis describes his experience with a young colleague who became an ardent Communist. This colleague left his country and spent a number of years in the Soviet Union, after which he returned to make a lecture tour. Lewis attended two of the lectures. The first of these was a praise of all the improvements this man had witnessed in the Soviet Union—better housing, education, arts and theater, and so on. The second was a statement of the "outright materialism" of the Marxian doctrine, as he understood it.

"I still remember," writes Lewis, "the bewilderment of his audiences as they sought to reconcile the themes and spirit of the two lectures. Assuming that the first could be accepted without qualification, what importance could it have if the second was sound? What does better education, or better housing, or better theater mean if we are dealing with strictly material reality?"[24]

Inanimate matter, Lewis notes, does not require itself to be properly housed, and it cannot appreciate good art or humor. It is only at the level of sentience that questions can arise as to worth or significance, and herein, he writes, "we seem compelled to recognize some reality which cannot itself be described in strictly physical terms."

I am not sure whether Lewis means to say, by way of this argument, that sentience must be more than material, or that materialism cannot provide a satisfying account of the nature of good and evil. A good many philosophers, as noted in Chapter 1, have maintained that matter can in some way give rise to consciousness, though I am not one of them. It seems to me, in any case, that whatever we think about the mind-body problem, we must suppose that value judgments transcend the material world.

In order to understand this position, it may be helpful to consider, once again, the thesis of materialism against certain moral claims that we are apt to make in the course of our lives. Take, for one, a man's decision to remain faithful to his spouse. In making this decision, he presumably is able to entertain two scenarios, one wherein he becomes involved with another woman and one wherein he does not. If he says that the latter choice is morally preferable, he means to say that this latter state of affairs is somehow better than the other. But how does he justify any such statement on the materialist hypothesis? Reality, if that hypothesis is correct, is a great ocean of particles moving through space in accord with whatever laws may ultimately govern their behavior. Each state of affairs that he envisions is thus itself made up entirely of a collection of such particles in some given arrangement. If the whole reality involved in each of these scenarios is but a certain set of particles, on what objective basis can one prefer either? Which swirl, which configuration, is the better one? If the only reality, in each case, is particles, then what is the objective content of the claim that one state of affairs is better than another?

An individual can say, perhaps, that he *prefers* one to the other in that he finds that one to be in some way more pleasant or more profitable. But what *ideal* quality can he attribute to it? If reality, at bottom, is material, then he must describe it in terms of its material characteristics. How, then, can any ideal description of reality ever arise?

And how can an individual think (with respect to the two scenarios) that a single collection of particles has in it any more than one potentiality? If matter is all that is involved, the choice must presumably itself follow (in whichever direction) that course necessitated by whatever material energies are present therein. Material descriptions, it seems, do not capture what we have in mind when we speak of such things as good and evil, or our freedom to choose between them.[25]

Our notions, likewise, of virtue and of duty imply that there is more to reality than can be revealed by any investigation into the natural world. Our sense of obligation requires us, I believe, to think of ourselves as being not only genuine moral agents, but as being engaged moreover in a moral quest that extends in its duration beyond the course of the present life. As Kant[26] observed, it is only on the assumption of a continued existence that we can understand our relation to the moral law. For this law holds out to us the ideal of *holiness*, a perfect congruence of the will to the moral demand. It is not something that is achieved within this lifetime, yet it is something that we are in the process of achieving. Indeed it is something that we must achieve, for if not, we are not fully in accord with the law that requires our assent. The notion, then, that we are here to strive, with utter seriousness, toward this goal, to reach it in some fractional measure, only to meet annihilation, and so to abandon this progress at life's end, Kant believed to be absurd. If we take the moral law seriously, it seems, we must suppose ourselves to be involved in something more than a partial fulfillment of the goal.

A third issue addressed in this book was that of religious experience and its interpretation. Perhaps the most basic element in common sense is a simple trust in the veracity of our experience. But experience is not, on the face of it, experience of only one world. In varying degrees we (some of us, at least) have intimations of a truth and a destiny that extend past the world that greets our senses. And if we read our experience without bias, we should admit that we have some reason to believe that reality extends beyond the one that immediately surrounds us. If this sense of the "beyond" is sufficiently strong, then we are acting squarely contrary to the standards of rationality if we do not heed it.

Once again, as in previous cases, the materialist answer is a theoretical possibility. We cannot, on logical grounds, know that our religious impulses are anything more than by-products of the material world in roughly the way that thinkers like Russell have imagined. Here again, I do not insist that the reductionist view must be mistaken, or that it suffers from some inconsistency within itself. I have addressed the question instead of whether we are compelled by some consideration of evidence or rationality to accept it. I have argued that we are not.

Life's Ultimate Direction

What philosophy of life best accords with the conclusions that have been offered to this point? What values, what lifestyle, are encouraged by the discussion to this point? This book, in some measure, has encouraged an "otherworldly" outlook, one that views reality as being fundamentally removed from the world around us. As such the discussion herein might be viewed as being in some general way religious, though I have made no attempt to argue herein for any particular religious outlook or doctrine.

"Shall the seen world or the unseen world," asks James, "be our chief sphere of adaptation?"[27] What kinds of persons ought we to be? The sort of ideal we shall have and the life we shall lead will depend in large part on which world seems to us to be the more real. James contrasts in his lecture two different ideals of humanity, one the *warrior* before whom the ordinary man may grovel in physical admiration, and the other the *saint* who, when judged by this same worldly standard, is "tame" and "herbivorous." Yet the saint, again, he observes, appeals to "a different faculty." His victory lies in a different sphere.

For most of us, of course, the choice is wider. We will not aspire, in our present condition, to be either Attila or Saint Francis. Nor will we insist necessarily that the pacifistic and self-mortifying types described as saints in James's discussion must represent the highest types of humanity. But nonetheless, the question of saint or warrior reflects a practical question with respect to the choices we shall make on a daily basis. In which general direction ought our development to proceed? Few of us, I believe, will be capable of forsaking this world altogether for some other. Yet we are faced all the time with dilemmas that require a choice with respect to our basic allegiance. Suppose, for example, that I am presented with an option that will make me more wealthy at the cost of my integrity. Which choice is the wiser?

The consistent direction of this book has been away from materialism as a solution to various theoretical issues of philosophy. I have said that we remain truest to our ideals and to our daily common-sense assumptions when we conceive of ourselves as being something other than the collections of organic matter with which we are commonly identified. I have argued likewise that we have reason to trust our intimations of other and higher worlds as a basic principle of rationality. Therein, I have claimed, we have reason to think of ourselves as creatures whose destiny extends far beyond the present life. A corollary of this outlook, it seems to me, is that we ought to look beyond our material condition for the things in life that are ultimately valuable.

In saying that, I do not mean to suggest that material possessions of themselves are bad, or that some given level of wealth is too much for anyone to rightly enjoy. The *materialism* with which I have been concerned is a technical item, an abstract theory of reality offered in response to various long-standing problems of philosophy. There is, of course, another use of the term, one both current and common, that refers, not to theories of metaphysics, but instead, and in more practical terms, to an unhealthy preoccupation with the material condition of one's own life. I have not dealt explicitly in this book with the issue of materialism as it concerns personal lifestyle, but the conclusions reached in this book may have some implications in that regard.

Material reality is part of human experience. In our present condition, there is no such thing as doing without it and no reason to suppose that we must choose a life that is poor in its material enjoyments. The development of new technologies makes life a better and more dignified thing than it might be otherwise, and the giving of material objects and enjoyments is one of the ways that human beings are able to express their affection for one another. Indeed, our spirituality itself, I must think, finds its expression (in charity, in sacrifice, in sexuality, in participation in the arts, among others) through the medium of material events. For this reason I wish to avoid any wholesale condemnation of material pleasure of the kind that has appeared, on occasion, in the history of human expression. Nor do I imagine that all persons should have the same standard of living. The state that aims at any such distribution of wealth runs afoul of the precept (morally sound, I believe) that ambition should be rewarded and that the individual who works harder ought to have more.

No doubt some people live and consume far beyond their needs and are overly concerned with the project of their own material advancement. But that is not the main point of my interest. The thrust of this discussion is not the condemnation of wealth; rather it is the inquiry into what is valuable in accord with the conclusions reached to this point. I have said that we understand life best when we understand it as a spiritual event. Seen in such terms, the material world is a passing theater in which life's material conditions are but the setting for something far more important, namely, the ascent of the soul. Given this basic outlook, one can hardly imagine a more foolish choice of life plan than that of material acquisition (which is to say, the acquisition of wealth, comfort, prestige, reputation, and the like) at the expense of one's inward condition.

Life is filled with intimations of this truth. There is danger, writes Barrett, in holding on to the "aesthetic," or pleasure-seeking, stage of life when we feel ourselves growing beyond it. Kierkegaard, he notes, explores this attitude with sympathy, but insists in the end that it must collapse into despair. It is the destiny of the soul to progress beyond the stage of pleasure seeking and to advance to the moral, and beyond that to the religious. The soul that refuses this progress can only meet with despair—with boredom, and in time, with depression, and finally even suicide. That part of Greek life that sings in praise of sunlight and enjoyment, says Barrett, is always haunted by a sadness: In the poems of the Epicureans "there is a grinning skull behind the flowers." The aesthetic attitude can thus be only "a partial, never a complete attitude toward life."[28]

That is not to say that the aesthetic attitude is discarded along life's way, but only that it must be integrated within the more integrated and total attitude that must supplant it "as we become more seriously involved with ourselves and our life." Thus these stages, Barrett explains, are not like the floors of a building—I do not leave one stage behind when rising to another. Rather each attitude is a stage "on the way from the periphery to the center of the self."[29]

The paradox of this claim is that our real fulfillment comes in opening outward. It is in growing beyond the egocentric mode of life, in transcending this condition of self-preoccupation, that we find at last our real good. The rise from the aesthetic to the ethical is not a logical one. We make it without guarantee and with a sense of risk. Therefore, according to Barrett, we begin to exist at this higher level by an act of courage. But once making it, we learn that we exist more fully, not less, when we dare the venture. Herein we begin to understand, as well, our real nature and destiny.

This refrain, I realize, is familiar. It may even be a bit hackneyed. But perhaps we should ask why things of this kind are said, after all, by people whom we respect most highly and by a great many of us ourselves, for that matter, in our more serious moments. There is a broad agreement among the world's religious traditions that material enjoyment is a false end, and that it fails to speak to our own deepest nature. One instance of this claim, conspicuously reminiscent of Barrett's discussion, is discussed by Huston Smith in his earlier-cited work, *The World's Religions.*

Classical Indian society, explains Smith,[30] recognized four basic stages in the spiritual condition of a human being. These were *kama* (pleasure), *artha* (success), *dharma* (duty), and *moksha* (liberation). At the first of these stages, life's ultimate good is seen as pleasure, broadly construed as comfort, entertainment, and the like, for oneself. At the second the ultimate good is success, in terms of such outward forms of accomplishment as wealth, fame, and power. The focus of these first two stages is oneself, that is, one's lesser self, that limited and egoistic entity that is the end of selfish striving. Beyond these stages (together termed the Path of Desire) is the stage of duty, wherein it dawns upon an individual that there is a reason to act that transcends one's own immediate good, and that other persons are (if one may here borrow Kant's terminology) ends in themselves. Yet beyond this stage of life (these latter two constituting the Path of Liberation) comes enlightenment, or the transcending of limit altogether in final bliss and freedom.

These are stages, it might be added, not of personal development within any given lifetime, but of spiritual growth over the course of what may be many rounds of existence. It may be that an individual remains fixed, for the most part, in the mode of pleasure seeking for an entire lifetime. But his destiny, his ultimate fulfillment, lies beyond this level. It is a destiny that he must ultimately pursue, if not in this lifetime, then another.

I am not prepared, at this moment, to affirm or deny certain elements of doctrine (that, for example, of reincarnation) historically bound up with this tradition. But I wish to suggest that such a tradition represents, in broad outline, a reasonable extension of much that is contained within ordinary human experience. Consider, for example, the attitude we take toward an individual who remains stubbornly at the level of material self-interest. In various ways we tell this individual to broaden, to mature, to grow up, to gain a better sense of his proper place in relation to others. In telling him to do this, we mean to say, not merely that his present attitude is disagreeable to us, but also that it is fundamentally dishonest. His attitude must expand, it must grow to meet the truth of who he is and what he must do in order to fulfill his own destiny. The unduly selfish man is not true to himself, to what he really is in the depths of his own true nature. There is more to him than can be contained in the lesser mode of life, and he will not find rest until he admits the fact to himself.

How curious it all looks from the outside. How odd, how contradictory, when one takes a step back and observes. What do we really believe about ourselves and about the world in which we live? It is as if we straddle two whole worlds without quite taking stock of the fact.

Some years ago I picked up a current treatise of epistemology from the philosophy section of a major bookstore. Its thesis, as outlined in the introduction, was that human beings have ultimately no reason to believe any of the things that they ordinarily believe about reality, whether about themselves or about events of any kind transpiring in the world around them. Toward the end of this discussion, this earnestly skeptical author paused to extend his heartfelt thanks to all of those friends and colleagues who had helped him to arrive at his conclusions! Apparently this skepticism did not extend to his personal life.

If philosophy is to proceed in good faith, I believe, it will have to pay closer attention to the connection between its theoretical activity and the lives that its theorists actually live. It will also have to acknowledge the fact that philosophers begin their activities from radically different vantage points, and that philosophy is indeed a product not only of the intellect but also of each philosopher's own substance and sensibility. For this reason philosophy is not likely to find solutions to its problems in the way that mathematics, for example, may find them. My own references, throughout this book, to the immaterial and supernatural may seem to some readers rather far removed from reality. If so, these references will seem likewise to be removed from a realistic philosophy of life. But again, I think, there is nothing unduly odd or esoteric in the outlook that I have tried to develop. This outlook is consistent, I feel, with the things that most of us, skeptics included, believe and take for granted in the course of daily experience.

Consider, for one, the example of a professional philosopher who assigns to his seminar a difficult essay extolling the merits of hard determinism. Perhaps he himself thinks the essay to be correct in its conclusion. But think, now, of his reaction to the various students who receive this assignment. One student fails to read the material. He tries, perhaps, to obscure this fact by writing an unclear paper or by plagiarizing some other work. Not only does such a student receive a poor grade for the course, but he arouses the instructor's resentment as well. This attitude on the part of the instructor reveals, I think, a very different view of things from the one that he espouses in the classroom. For why *resent* a course of action that is but an integral part of the material course from all of time?

Think, too, of this instructor's attitude toward the forthright and ambitious student who confronts the assignment head-on. Such a student receives not only the better grade but also the instructor's admiration for the effort ("noble," it will be said) that he has expended. I doubt that there is a student or an instructor alive who does not recognize, in some version, the situation that I am describing. And yet how can such attitudes as these just noted be justified if the hard deterministic thesis is correct?

Consider, once more as well, the issue of material lifestyle. Whatever our philosophical views, we are apt to say of some given individual, on occasion, that he is materialistic, meaning that he is excessively concerned with the material condition of his life—to the neglect, presumably, of other, more important, characteristics. Whereas, that other individual—say, a Mother Teresa,[31] who embarks on a moral career and abandons the materialistic concern altogether—fills us with admiration. Would that we were like her, we may think at certain moments, were we strong enough. Why strong? If there is nothing to life ultimately but the collisions of particles, what difference does it make? We may say that this woman has a different style of life from ourselves, but in what sense is it more admirable? We can say, perhaps, that she has a strong will, but not, I think, that she wills herself in any positive direction. Indeed, if all reality is ultimately material, then what we call her strength is nothing more than the fixed and inevitable outcome of minute events that she herself neither creates nor comprehends.

It is only if we view life in spiritual terms that we can make sense of those common, yet deep and powerful, convictions that we have concerning the worth of certain individuals. We wish, after all, to say not merely that these persons differ from most others, but that they are willfully and heroically different, not merely unusual, but more fully developed, more attuned to the truth, than is the bulk of humanity.

Our growth involves in every respect a movement away from the material world. All that we deem as progress, as advancement, seems to lead us in some way beyond the world of nature. It is an innate tendency of the mind, thinks William Temple, to transcend the material world in the course of its upward development. He writes:

> It detaches itself from the course of the natural process and enters upon a realm of its own, where its conduct is determined, not by the impulsion of force, but by the apparent good. The mind of a human being increasingly organizes itself and its own world apart from the processes which, for the most part, control the body within which, and . . . as a function of which, the mind has come into being. As mind increasingly takes control of the organism, so it becomes increasingly independent of the organism as physiologically conceived.[32]

An example of this phenomenon is the way in which an individual absorbed in thought may become relatively immune to the pain that he might feel otherwise. Our concern with obligation is another. For obligation, Temple observes, "is not a calculation of the interests of the organism and of the way to serve these; it is an appreciation of value so distinct as to demand the sacrifice of all other interests for its sake. The mind which has achieved that is detached from 'the whole might of nature.'"[33]

In sum, the entire impetus of life—what we value, what we admire, what we sense, in the end, is our duty and our destiny—heads us beyond the material world and into the realm of the spiritual. Were we true to this apprehension, were we to bring it into rational accord with our view of life as a whole, our notions of success and failure would be altered. In some respects they would be reversed, in fact, from the ones that we tend to carry with us from habit. All that tends toward wealth, power, pleasure, self-indulgence, or outward appearance, as ends in themselves, would be placed to the side as being incidental to life's real good. All, in contrast, that tends toward decency, fairness, compassion, and justice—this, and only this, would be prized as valuable beyond estimate.

No harm, says Socrates,[34] can come to a good man, either in this life or in the life to come. What he means by this, I believe, is not that such a man can never suffer pain or material loss of one kind or another. He means instead that no accident of material fortune can ever diminish oneself. No outward loss can ever make oneself less or detract from one's own spiritual progress. Success is entirely in a person's own hands, regardless of what material conditions may surround him; life, as seen in such terms, cannot be judged in terms of its outward success or failure, nor can it be analyzed as a mere accident of matter in motion. It must be understood instead as being a pilgrimage toward a higher and better place, as the free and self-determining refinement of our own characters toward that same end.

Granted, once again, we may dismiss this end and all that is connected with it as being an illusion—a mere accident in some way of the material forces out of which, on the materialist account, our consciousness has arisen. But in so doing, I think, we must be prepared to dismiss our own deepest aspirations as being essentially worthless. Need we feel that there is some intellectual advantage in making this concession?

"It *feels*," says James,[35] "like a real fight," as if the world is an arena wherein real and important choices are made, where claims are made upon our wills that merit our absolute commitment. It feels as if life is a moral drama, the importance of which transcends whatever fleeting material facts or conditions that may attend it. We have no theoretical guarantee that this picture of life is the correct one. We have no such guarantee otherwise. But if it seems to us as if this is the case and if this general view of life conflicts with neither rationality nor empirical fact, then it is hard to imagine what reason we have to deny it. I thus submit that the best outlook upon life is one that makes of reality far more than what the materialist would make of it, one that entails our freedom and our spirituality, and thereby the prospect of a greater destiny as well.

Notes

Introduction

1. Bertrand Russell, "A Free Man's Worship." This essay is reprinted in Russell's *Why I Am Not a Christian* (New York: Simon and Schuster, 1957).

2. William Wordsworth, "Ode on Intimations of Immortality from Recollections of Early Childhood."

3. Thomas à Kempis, *The Imitation of Christ.*

4. *Katha Upanishad* 2.6.7–8.

5. Miguel de Unamuno, *The Tragic Sense of Life* (New York: Dover Publications, 1954), p. 39.

6. It is for this reason that Unamuno, for one, insists that philosophy is a product of the humanity of each philosopher (ibid., p. 28).

7. Kant introduces this notion in a criticism of traditional theology in his *Critique of Pure Reason.* He develops it at length in his subsequent *Critique of Practical Reason.*

8. See, for example, Swinburne's discussion, as noted in the concluding portion of Chapter 1.

9. A brief discussion of these views, in their relationship to ancient theories of materialism, is contained in Terence Irwin's *Classical Thought* (Oxford: Oxford University Press, 1988).

10. See, for example, Rudolph Carnap, "Psychology in Physical Language," contained in A. J. Ayer, ed., *Logical Positivism* (New York: Macmillan, 1959).

11. Robert C. Coburn, *The Strangeness of the Ordinary* (Savage, Md.: Rowman and Littlefield, 1990), p. 39.

12. It will suffice to say, he adds, that "the objects postulated by current theories of the atom, the nucleus, and the elementary particles, as well as their scientific successors, together with all the objects or stuffs solely composed of such things—presumably, water, carbon, alcohol, gold, proteins, cellulose, bone, blood, and so forth" count as such things.

Chapter One

1. See related discussion in Chapter 2.

2. Keith Campbell, *Body and Mind* (Notre Dame: University of Notre Dame Press, 1970).

3. A number of excellent books on early Greek philosophy have become available in the past several years. Among them are Merrill Ring's *Beginning with the Pre-*

Socratics (Mt. View, Calif.: Mayfield, 1987) and Richard McKirahan Jr.'s *Philosophy Before Socrates* (Indianapolis: Hackett, 1994).

4. Terence Irwin, *Classical Thought* (New York: Oxford University Press, 1989), p. 51.

5. See, for example, E. R. Dodds, *The Greeks and the Irrational* (Berkeley: University of California Press, 1951).

6. Homer's conception of the afterlife seems to be one involving a dark and diminished existence with none of the joys of life in this world. Achilles, the central figure of the *Iliad*, tells Odysseus (*Odyssey* 11.488 ff.) that he would sooner be the hireling of a landless man than ruler of all the underworld.

7. The classic illustration is found in *Meno* 82b ff., in which Socrates elicits from an untutored slave boy the answer to a question involving squares and the relative length of their sides.

8. A number of relevant passages and arguments are found throughout the *Phaedo*, a highly dramatic dialogue depicting Socrates' last hours prior to his execution for allegedly having corrupted the youth of Athens.

9. See, for example, *De Anima* 412b ff.

10. See, for example, his *City of God* 21.12, 15. It is a logical consequence of God's perfect foreknowledge, thinks Augustine, that the soul's destiny must precede its creation, though he argues (e.g., 5.9–10) that God's knowledge of this eventuality does not preclude an individual's free choice with respect to his own salvation.

11. The soul, writes Bonaventure, cannot be united with corporeal nature except by the conditions of moisture, air, and warmth. In like fashion, God does not preserve the soul and become united with it "unless it be *moist* with tears of compunction and filial love, *made spiritual* by contempt of earthly possessions, and *enkindled* with the desire of its heavenly home and its own Beloved." *Retracing the Arts to Theology* (Healy translation).

12. *Summa Theologia* 1.76.1. By the same token, the souls of man and animal are of basically different kinds, for although God has (Genesis 1.24) let the earth bring forth the living soul of the animal, he has (2.7) Himself breathed the breath of life into man (*Summa Theologia* 1.75.6).

13. For example, Origen (185–254).

14. "Even though," writes Descartes, "there may be a deceiver of some sort, very powerful and very tricky, who bends all his efforts to keep me perpetually deceived, there can be no slightest doubt that I exist, since he deceives me; and let him deceive me as much as he will, he can never make me nothing as long as I think that I am something." *Meditation II*, trans. Laurence J. Lafleur (Indianapolis: Bobbs-Merrill, 1964), p. 82.

15. "I am not," explains Descartes, again in *Meditation II*, "this assemblage of members which is called a human body; I am not a rarefied and penetrating air spread throughout all these members; I am not a wind . . . a breath, a vapor, or anything at all that I can imagine and picture to myself—since I have supposed that all that was nothing, and since, without abandoning this supposition, I find that I do not cease to be certain that I am something" (p. 84).

16. A detailed discussion of Hobbes's philosophy of human nature and its relation to the times is contained in vol. 3 of W. T. Jones's *A History of Western Philosophy* (Fort Worth: Harcourt Brace Jovanovich, 1980).

17. *Three Dialogues Between Hylas and Philonous* (Second Dialogue). This work is available in several editions and is contained in its entirety in Joel Feinberg, ed., *Reason and Responsibility* (Belmont, Calif.: Wadsworth, 1978), pp. 150–193.

18. Ibid., p. 179.

19. Thus he observes in the *Treatise*, "*all our reasonings concerning causes and effects are deriv'd from nothing but custom; and that belief is more properly an act of the sensitive, than of the cogitative part of our natures.*" David Hume, *A Treatise of Human Nature* (Oxford: Clarendon Press, 1951), p. 183. Perhaps the best general account of Hume's philosophy is Barry Stroud's *Hume* (London: Routledge & Kegan Paul, 1977).

20. Hume, *Treatise*, p. 252.

21. See especially the "Transcendental Analytic" section of his *Critique of Pure Reason*. One of the best discussions of Kant's philosophy is W. H. Walsh's *Kant's Criticism of Metaphysics* (Chicago: University of Chicago Press, 1975).

22. Gilbert Ryle, *The Concept of Mind* (New York: Barnes and Noble, 1949). Although critical of Descartes, the book contains a lucid discussion of his view of the problem.

23. See, for example, U. T. Place, "Is Consciousness a Brain Process?" reprinted in Antony Flew, ed., *Body, Mind and Death* (New York: Macmillan, 1969).

24. John Hick, *Death and Eternal Life* (Louisville: Westminster/John Knox, 1994). See especially chap. 6, "Mind and Body."

25. John Searle, *Minds, Brains and Science* (Cambridge, Mass.: Harvard University Press, 1984). See especially chap. 1, "The Mind-Body Problem."

26. Ibid., p. 16.

27. A good introduction to Sartre is his popular essay "Existentialism Is a Humanism." The essay is contained in Walter Kaufmann's *Existentialism from Dostoevsky to Sartre* (New York: New American Library, 1975).

28. Zeno Vendler ascribes this to Feng-hsiung Hsu, 1990. Zeno Vendler, "The Ineffable Soul," in Richard Warner and Tadeusz Szubka, eds. *The Mind-Body Problem* (Cambridge, Mass.: Basil Blackwell, 1994), p. 318.

29. Richard Swinburne, "Body and Soul," in Warner and Szubka, *The Mind-Body Problem*.

30. Ibid., p. 312.

31. Ibid., p. 313.

32. Ibid., p. 314.

Chapter Two

1. Curt Ducasse, "Is a Life After Death Possible?" reprinted in Peyton Richter and Walter Fogg, eds., *Philosophy Looks to the Future* (Prospect Heights, Ill.: Waveland Press, 1978), p. 422.

2. Ibid. A related point concerning the behaviorist thesis is made by Hywel Lewis, *The Self and Immortality* (New York: Seabury Press, 1973). He observes that "a moment's reflection . . . assures us that working or writing involves more at the time than the movements of my fingers and other bodily changes." This more, he explains, "is mainly the occurrent mental life through which I have been passing, my actual flow of thoughts, feelings, etc., together with the close integration of these with the

bodily effects I intend and the causal conditions of my mental processes in states of my body as well as in their own proper development" (p. 58). To leave out the mental content of this description, and to speak only of dispositions, he writes, "is to give us 'Hamlet' without the Prince" (p. 59).

3. This problem turns upon the distinction between so-called primary and secondary qualities, the former of which presumably exist on their own in the material world, whereas the latter seem to depend upon consciousness for their reality. This distinction, and its impact on the modern worldview, is noted in Chapter 5.

4. J. J. C. Smart, "Sensations and Brain Processes," in Paul Edwards and Arthur Pap, eds., *A Modern Introduction to Philosophy* (New York: Free Press, 1973), p. 242.

5. Ducasse, "Is a Life After Death Possible?"

6. Ibid., p. 426.

7. Frankl, *The Doctor and the Soul: From Psychotherapy to Logotherapy* (New York: Alfred A. Knopf, 1965). A relevant portion of the book is reprinted in Richter and Fogg, *Philosophy Looks to the Future,* pp. 222–230 (quotation on p. 224).

8. Richter and Fogg, *Philosophy Looks to the Future,* p. 224.

9. See, for example, Russell's "Do We Survive Death?" in *Why I Am Not a Christian* (New York: Simon and Schuster, 1957).

10. William James, "Human Immortality: Two Supposed Objections to the Doctrine," in *Human Immortality and the Will to Believe and Other Essays in Popular Philosophy* (New York: Dover, 1956), pp. 7–8.

11. Ibid., pp. 12–13.

12. Ibid., p. 15.

13. Ibid.

14. The passage (ibid., p. 16) is taken from Shelley's *Adonais.* This poem is an ode to the poet John Keats and is of course reprinted in many places. See, for example, G. B. Harrison, ed., *A Book of English Poetry* (London: Penguin Books, 1950).

15. James, "Human Immortality," p. 15.

16. C. D. Broad, *The Mind and Its Place in Nature* (New York: Harcourt, Brace and Co., 1925), p. 97.

17. Ibid., p. 98.

18. Ducasse, "Is a Life After Death Possible?" p. 425.

19. Huston Smith, *The World's Religions* (San Francisco: HarperCollins, 1991), p. 30.

20. Ibid.

21. *Phaedo* 94c ff. Grube translation.

22. Ibid.

23. J. B. S. Haldane, *The Inequality of Man* (Harmondsworth: Penguin Books, 1937), p. 209.

24. A. C. Ewing, *The Fundamental Questions of Philosophy* (New York: Macmillan, 1953), p. 231.

25. Ibid.

26. See chap. 6, "Mind and Body," of John Hick, *Death and Eternal Life* (Louisville: Westminster/John Knox, 1994).

27. Ibid., 119.

28. Paul Badham, *Christian Beliefs About Life After Death* (London: Macmillan, 1976), p. 99.

29. Ibid.
30. Ibid.

Chapter Three

1. See vol. 1 of Jones, *A History of Western Philosophy* (Fort Worth: Harcourt Brace Jovanovich, 1980).

2. Ibid., p. 6.

3. William Barrett, *Irrational Man* (New York: Doubleday, 1958). See chap. 4, "Hebraism and Hellenism."

4. Ibid., p. 73.

5. Ibid., pp. 77–78.

6. "Man," claims the sophist Protagoras, "is the measure of all things," thus maintaining, in effect, that reality varies with the experience of each perceiving individual. What is the case for truth in general, thinks Protagoras, is also the case with respect to good and evil, where a supposedly good man might be thought to be the opposite elsewhere. See, for example, Plato's *Protagoras* at 327c and following. Protagoras and other sophists are treated at length in vol. 2 of W. K. C. Guthrie's *A History of Greek Philosophy* (London: Cambridge University Press, 1969).

7. Ibid., vol. 1, p. 68.

8. *Euthyphro* 5d ff.

9. *Republic* 517b–c (Bloom translation).

10. This issue of virtue and its relation to self-interest is discussed in Plato's *Gorgias*. It is also the principal theme of the *Republic*.

11. Aristotle raises a number of objections to Plato's view of the forms in his works; see, for example, *Metaphysics* 1.9.

12. Jones, *A History of Western Philosophy*, vol. 1, chap. 7.

13. This admiration for the active intellect leads Aristotle to suggest that it is something "immortal" and "eternal" and hence, on some interpretations, at least, to be immortal in much the way that Plato imagined (*De Anima* 430a).

14. *Nicomachean Ethics* 1094a.

15. A succinct discussion of virtue ethics and its revival in recent years is contained in chap. 12 of James Rachels, *The Elements of Moral Philosophy* (New York: McGraw-Hill, 1993).

16. The essence of Epicurus's philosophy of life is contained in his surviving "Letter to Menoecus." The letter is reprinted in Peyton Richter and Walter Fogg, eds., *Philosophy Looks to the Future* (Prospect Heights, Ill.: Waveland Press, 1978). Portions of this letter and other materials are reprinted with commentary in Sheldon Peterfreund and Theodore Denise, eds., *Great Traditions in Ethics* (Belmont, Calif.: Wadsworth, 1992).

17. Epicurus wrote in "Letter to Menoecus": "The statements of the many about the gods are not conceptions derived from sensation, but false suppositions, according to which the greatest misfortunes befall the wicked and the greatest blessings the good by the gift of the gods" (Bailey translation, in Peterfreund and Denise, *Great Traditions*, p. 57).

18. *City of God* 19.25 (Dods translation).

19. *Summa Contra Gentiles* 3.25.

20. Rachels, *The Elements of Moral Philosophy*, chap. 4.

21. Alasdair MacIntyre, *A Short History of Ethics* (New York: Macmillan, 1966), p. 118.

22. The two principal formulations of this rule are given in Kant's *Fundamental Principles of the Metaphysics of Morals*. One, as noted above, is that an individual should act only in the way that he would have the rest of the human race act. The other, which Kant takes to be equivalent, is that one should act so as to treat humanity as an end itself and never solely as a means.

23. *Critique of Practical Reason*, pt. 2, "Methodology of Pure Practical Reason." The former observation, he continues, "annihilates, as it were, my importance as an animal creature, which after it has been for a short time provided with vital power, one knows not how, must again give back the matter of which it was formed to the planet it inhabits (a mere speck in the universe)." The second, on the contrary, "infinitely elevates my worth as an intelligence by my personality, in which the moral law reveals to me a life independent on animality and even on the whole sensible world."

24. "The creed," writes Mill, "which accepts as the foundation of morals Utility, or the Greatest Happiness Principle, holds that actions are right in proportion as they tend to promote happiness, wrong as they tend to produce the reverse of happiness." Taking some liberty with this phraseology, I have taken 'right' and 'wrong', respectively, to mean 'good' and 'bad'. For the latter two designations admit (as Mill, I believe, intends) of degrees, whereas the former do not.

25. Perhaps the best introduction to this style of philosophy is A. J. Ayer, ed., *Logical Positivism* (New York: Free Press, 1959). The volume contains several essays on ethics and social philosophy.

26. This rather famous statement is made in Book 3 of Hume's *Treatise of Human Nature*, ed. L. A. Selby-Bigge (Oxford: Clarendon Press, 1951), pp. 468–469. A related discussion is contained in the opening section of his *Enquiry Concerning the Principles of Morals*.

27. A. J. Ayer, *Language, Truth and Logic* (New York: Dover, 1952). See chap. 6, "Critique of Ethics and Theology."

28. See Russell's "Science and Ethics," chap. 9 in *Religion and Science* (New York: Oxford University Press, 1961).

29. Alexander Sutherland, *The Origin and Growth of the Moral Instinct* (London: Longmans, Green, 1898), vol. 2, p. 44.

30. Ibid., p. 49.

31. Russell, "Science and Ethics."

32. Ruth Benedict, "Anthropology and the Abnormal," in Arthur J. Minton and Thomas A. Shipka, eds., *Philosophy: Paradox and Discovery* (New York: McGraw-Hill, 1982).

33. Paul Ree, *Die Illusion der Willensfreiheit* (Berlin, 1885). The relevant portions are reprinted in translation in Paul Edwards and Arthur Pap, eds., *A Modern Introduction to Philosophy* (New York: Free Press, 1973).

34. Charles Brenner, *An Elementary Textbook of Psychoanalysis* (New York: Anchor, 1974), p. 2.

35. John Hospers, "What Means This Freedom?" in Sidney Hook, ed., *Free Will and Determinism* (Washington Square: New York University Press, 1965).

36. Ibid., p. 119.

37. Ibid.

38. Ibid.

Chapter Four

1. *Iliad* 19 ff.

2. Solomon Asch, *Social Psychology*. The relevant portions of this book are reprinted in Arthur J. Minton and Thomas A. Shipka, eds. *Philosophy: Paradox and Discovery* (New York: McGraw-Hill, 1982).

3. Ibid., p. 237.

4. To cite one instance, the so-called problem of the continuum. Not all infinite sets are considered to be of the same size, since not all can be put into one-to-one correspondence with one another. Thus the set of real numbers, for example, is "larger" than the set of rationals. But what is the next larger set above the rationals? Is it the set of reals (i.e., the continuum) or is it some other in between? Neither the answer itself nor the proper method of solution seems to be obvious at the present time.

5. For a related discussion see James Rachels, *The Elements of Moral Philosophy* (New York: McGraw-Hill, 1993), chap. 2, "The Challenge of Cultural Relativism."

6. William Barrett, *Irrational Man* (New York: Doubleday, 1958), pp. 169–170.

7. Hastings Rashdall, *The Theory of Good and Evil* (Oxford: Oxford University Press, 1907). 2 vols.

8. Ibid., vol. 2, pp. 206–207.

9. Ibid., p. 207.

10. Ibid., pp. 210–211.

11. Ibid., p. 211.

12. John Hick, ed., *Classical and Contemporary Readings in the Philosophy of Religion* (Englewood Cliffs, N.J.: Prentice-Hall, 1964). This passage is taken from Hick's appendix 4, "The Moral Argument," pp. 531–532.

13. Ibid., p. 532.

14. Lao Tzu, *Tao Te Ching*, 1. For text and commentary see Arthur Waley, *The Way and Its Power* (New York: Grove Weidenfeld, 1958).

15. C. S. Lewis, *The Abolition of Man* (New York: Macmillan, 1955), pp. 27–28.

16. Ibid., p. 28.

17. Ibid.

18. Rudolph Otto, *The Idea of the Holy* (Oxford: Oxford University Press, 1958), p. 112.

19. William James, "The Dilemma of Determinism"; in *Human Immortality and the Will to Believe and Other Essays in Popular Philosophy* (New York: Dover, 1956), p. 156.

20. This general line of argument was proposed by Kant in his *Critique of Practical Reason*.

Chapter Five

1. William James, *The Varieties of Religious Experience* (New York: Penguin, 1982), Lecture 2, p. 34.

2. Ibid., Lecture 3, p. 53.

3. William James, "The Will to Believe," in *Human Immortality and the Will to Believe and Other Essays in Popular Philosophy* (New York: Dover, 1956), p. 25.

4. James, *Varieties of Religious Experience*, p. 61.

5. Julian of Norwich, *Revelations of Divine Love* (London: Burns and Oates, 1961), p. 92.

6. B. R. Tilghman, *An Introduction to the Philosophy of Religion* (Cambridge, Mass.: Blackwell, 1994).

7. This fragment is translated by John Burnet and is contained in his *Early Greek Philosophy* (London: Adam and Charles Black, 1948), p. 119.

8. Lucretius, *On the Nature of Things,* trans. C. Bailey (Oxford: Clarendon Press, 1924).

9. Galileo, *Opere Complete Galileo Galilei,* vol. 4, cited in chap. 3 of Edwin Burtt, *The Metaphysical Foundations of Modern Science* (New York: Humanities Press, 1951).

10. Tilghman, *Philosophy of Religion,* p. 141.

11. Barrett, *Irrational Man* (New York: Doubleday, 1958), p. 111.

12. Galileo, *Dialogues Concerning the Two Great Systems of the World,* cited in Burtt, *Metaphysical Foundations,* p. 68.

13. Ibid., p. 79.

14. Richard Tarnas, *The Passion of the Western Mind* (New York: Ballantine, 1991), p. 282.

15. See, for example, Auguste Comte, *Introduction to Positive Philosophy,* trans. Frederick Ferre (Indianapolis: Hackett, 1988).

16. "The abolition," writes Marx, "of religion as the *illusory* happiness of men, is a demand for their *real* happiness. The call to abandon their illusions about their condition is a *call to abandon a condition which requires illusions.* The criticism of religion is, therefore, *the embryonic criticism of this vale of tears* of which religion is the halo." "Contribution to the Critique of Hegel's Philosophy of Right," in *Marx's Early Writings,* trans. T. B. Bottomore (London: C. A. Watts, 1963).

17. Anthony M. Alioto, *A History of Western Science* (Englewood Cliffs, N.J.: Prentice-Hall, 1993), p. 301.

18. Ibid.

19. W. T. Jones, *A History of Western Philosophy* (Fort Worth: Harcourt Brace Jovanovich, 1980), vol. 4, chap. 5.

20. Thomas Robert Malthus (1776–1834), an English philosopher and economist, had maintained that life is naturally a struggle owing to the fact that the tendency of human populations, if not checked, is to multiply far beyond their means of subsistence.

21. Jones, *History of Western Philosophy,* vol. 4, p. 196.

22. Ernst Haeckel, *The Riddle of the Universe* (New York: Harper and Row, 1900).

23. Hans Driesch, *The History and Theory of Vitalism,* trans. C. K. Ogden (London: Macmillan, 1914).

24. Sigmund Freud, *The Future of an Illusion* (New York: W. W. Norton, 1989), p. 23.

25. Ibid., pp. 26–27.

26. Ibid., 30.

27. Ibid., p. 38.

28. Ibid., p. 42.

29. Bertrand Russell, "Grounds of Conflict," *Religion and Science* (London: Oxford University Press, 1961), p. 8.

30. Ibid., p. 14.

31. As expressed, for example, in his earlier-cited essay, "A Free Man's Worship," in *Why I Am Not a Christian* (New York: Simon and Schuster, 1957).

32. Ayer, *Language, Truth and Logic* (New York: Dover, 1952), chap. 6.

33. D. Z. Phillips, *Death and Immortality* (New York: St. Martin's, 1970).

34. See Hartshorne's "Time, Death and Everlasting Life," in *The Logic of Perfection* (La Salle, Ill.: Open Court, 1962).

35. Antony Flew, "Theology and Falsification," in John Hick, ed., *The Existence of God* (New York: Macmillan, 1964).

36. Hare's response to Flew, as well as a variety of others, are contained in Basil Mitchell, ed., *Faith and Logic* (London: Allen and Unwin, 1957).

37. It appears as a chapter, "Theology and Verification," in Hick's *The Existence of God*.

38. Robert Jastrow, *God and the Astronomers* (New York: Reader's Library, 1978). The relevant portions of this book are reprinted in Janelle Rohr, ed., *Science and Religion—Opposing Viewpoints* (San Diego: Greenhaven Press, 1988).

39. Rohr, *Science and Religion*, p. 135.

40. Isaac Asimov, "Do Scientists Believe in God?" Originally published in *Gallery* magazine and reprinted in Rohr, *Science and Religion*.

41. Ibid., pp. 140–141.

42. Thomas Gurley, *American Atheist*, October 1980 (reprinted in ibid.).

Chapter Six

1. Joshua 10:12–14.

2. Genesis 19:26.

3. See, for example, Stace, *Religion and the Modern Mind* (Philadelphia: Lippincott, 1960).

4. Originally published in the *Atlantic Monthly*, September 1948; reprinted in Steven Sanders and David R. Cheney, eds., *The Meaning of Life* (Englewood Cliffs, N.J.: Prentice-Hall, 1980).

5. Ibid., p. 38.

6. Ibid., p. 39.

7. Ibid., p. 40.

8. A basic tenet of Islam—for discussion see Alford T. Welch, "Islam," in John R. Hinnells, ed., *A Handbook of Living Religions* (Middlesex, UK: Penguin, 1991).

9. Krishna is portrayed in the *Bhagavad-Gita* as an *avatar*, or incarnation, of Vishnu. His revelation to the protagonist Arjuna comes in Book 11: "Of a thousand suns in the sky, if suddenly should burst forth, the light, it would be like, unto the light of that exalted one" (11.12, Edgerton translation).

10. Though not biblical, Mary's postmortem ascension, body and soul, into heaven is a traditional part of Roman Catholic belief.

11. Norman Malcolm, "The Groundlessness of Belief," in Stuart C. Brown, ed., *Reason and Religion* (Ithaca: Cornell University Press, 1977).

12. See Moore's "Proof of an External World," in *Philosophical Papers* (New York: Collier, 1966).

13. G. H. Von Wright, *Wittgenstein* (Minneapolis: University of Minnesota Press, 1966), p. 171.

14. Ibid., pp. 172–173.

15. Ibid., p. 175.

16. *On Certainty,* #167.

17. Malcolm, "Groundlessness of Belief," p. 146.

18. Ibid.

19. William James, *The Varieties of Religious Experience* (New York: Penguin, 1982), pp. 66–67.

20. Ibid., p. 71.

21. Ibid., pp. 70–71.

22. Reprinted in Paul Edwards and Arthur Pap, eds., *A Modern Introduction to Philosophy* (New York: Free Press, 1973).

23. Ibid., p. 256.

24. Norman Vincent Peale, *The Power of Positive Thinking* (New York: Prentice-Hall, 1952), p. 259.

25. See David Swenson, "The Transforming Power of Otherworldliness," in E. D. Klemke, ed., *The Meaning of Life* (New York: Oxford University Press, 1981).

26. James, *Varieties,* p. 4.

27. Ibid., p. 10.

28. Ibid., p. 13.

29. Ibid., p. 14. The reader may notice that this discussion is reminiscent of that in James's "Human Immortality," wherein the survival hypothesis is examined in relation to medical data.

30. James, *Varieties,* pp. 17–18.

31. Ibid., p. 18.

32. Richard Swinburne, *The Existence of God* (New York: Oxford University Press, 1979).

33. Ibid., p. 252.

34. Ibid., p. 254.

35. Though again, recalling James's discussion, one might ask if Swinburne isn't actually more conservative than necessary on this point. Suppose, for example, that an individual, after ingesting a certain drug, has an uncharacteristic experience, wherein he is told that this drug is itself destructive and that he ought not to continue taking it. Does the material condition of this experience (i.e., the altered chemistry of his brain-state at the time) require us to discount its veracity?

36. Swinburne, *Existence of God,* p. 266.

37. See, for example, Hick's *Essays in Religious Pluralism* (New York: St. Martin's, 1985). The essence of Hick's theory is presented in essay #3, "A Philosophy of Religious Pluralism." A related collection of material is his *God Has Many Names* (Philadelphia: Westminster Press, 1982).

38. The *sunyata,* or void, is a condition (Hick, *Essays,* p. 69) "in whose emptiness of ego the world of time and change is found again as fullness of 'wondrous being.'"

39. The *nirguna Brahman,* or Brahman without qualities, is the Ultimate Reality of certain schools of Vedic Indian philosophy.

40. John Hick, "Mystical Experience as Cognition," in Richard Woods, ed., *Understanding Mysticism* (New York: Image Books, 1980), p. 434.

41. Ibid., pp. 434–435.

Chapter Seven

1. This story is reprinted in Walter Kaufmann's *Existentialism from Dostoevsky to Sartre* (New York: New American Library, 1975), pp. 281–299.

2. Ibid., p. 287.

3. Ibid., p. 285.

4. Ibid., pp. 295–296.

5. Thomas Nagel, "The Absurd," reprinted in Steven Sanders and David Cheney, eds., *The Meaning of Life* (Englewood Cliffs, N.J.: Prentice-Hall, 1980), p. 158.

6. Ibid.

7. Ibid., p. 161.

8. Ibid., p. 163.

9. See Chapter 3.

10. The best discussion of this subject available is contained in John Hick's *Evil and the God of Love* (New York: Harper and Row, 1966). See especially his account of the "soul-making" theodicy.

11. Leo Tolstoy, *My Confession*, trans. Leo Wiener (London: J. M. Dent, 1905).

12. See, for example, Augustine's *City of God* 19.3. This view is reiterated in Aquinas's *Summa Theologia* 1.75.4, where Aquinas deals with Paul's statement (2 Corinthians 4:16) that "though our outward man is corrupted, yet the inward man is renewed day by day."

13. Carol Gilligan, *In a Different Voice* (Cambridge, Mass.: Harvard University Press, 1993).

14. Peter Van Inwagen, *Metaphysics* (Boulder, Colo.: Westview Press, 1993), p. 200.

15. See, for example, Victor Weisskopf, *Knowledge and Wonder* (Cambridge, Mass.: MIT Press, 1979). "Atoms," writes Weisskopf, "do not make sense when compared with our descriptions of ordinary particles and our expectations of how they should behave" (p. 89). In our ordinary way of looking at things, an electron must be either a particle or a wave; "it cannot be both at the same time" (p. 119). But our understanding of subatomic phenomena seems to require a freedom from restrictions that apply elsewhere. "Atomic phenomena," says Weisskopf, "present us with a much richer reality than we are accustomed to meeting" at the level of ordinary observation (p. 124).

16. Michael Lemonick, "Glimpses of the Mind," *Time* 146, no. 3 (July 17, 1995).

17. It is worth adding that the author of the *Time* article seems to have some instinctive sense of the unlikelihood that empirical investigation of the kind discussed will ever provide an understanding of the nature of consciousness. It may be, the article concludes, folly to suppose that the mind itself can ever fully comprehend the mind, and scientists may be verging upon a reality that is beyond their ken—"something that might be described as the soul."

18. Chapter 2.

19. Genesis 1:26.

20. *Confessions* 1.1.

21. A splendid discussion of the principal *Upanishads* is contained in chapter 3 of Swami Prabhavananda's *The Spiritual Heritage of India* (Hollywood: Vedanta Press, 1979).

22. William Barrett, *The Death of the Soul* (New York: Doubleday, 1986), p. 94.

23. Ibid.

24. Hywel Lewis, *The Elusive Self* (Philadelphia: Westminster Press, 1982), p. 3.

25. It may be objected at this point that I have failed to take stock of the difference between "constitutive" and "eliminative" versions of materialistic reduction, the former of which (see the Introduction) is less severe in its implications. But the same problem arises, I believe, on either view. For the claim that one material state of affairs is objectively *better* than another implies that there exists, over and above material reality, some further principle with which the claim is in accord. But that means, once more, that reality is not exhausted by an inventory of its material components.

26. Kant, *Critique of Practical Reason,* trans. T. K. Abbott (Amherst, N.Y.: Prometheus Books, 1996).See especially bk. 2, chap. 2, pt. 4, "The Immortality of the Soul as a Postulate of Pure Practical Reason." This attainment of a perfect will, writes Kant, is possible "only under the presupposition of an infinitely enduring existence and personality of the same rational being" (Beck translation).

27. See the lecture "The Value of Saintliness," in William James, *The Varieties of Religious Experience* (New York: Macmillan, 1961).

28. William Barrett, *Irrational Man* (New York: Doubleday, 1958), chap. 7.

29. Ibid., p. 164.

30. Huston Smith, *The World's Religions* (San Francisco: HarperCollins, 1991), chap. 2.

31. For an interesting glimpse of this woman and her moral philosophy, see Malcolm Muggeridge, *Something Beautiful for God* (San Francisco: Harper and Row, 1971).

32. William Temple, *Nature, Man and God* (London: Macmillan, 1934). See Lecture 18, "Moral and Religious Conditions of Eternal Life." This volume comprises Temple's Gifford Lectures at the University of Glasgow in the academic years of 1932–1933 and 1933–1934.

33. Ibid.

34. *Apology* 41c-d.

35. William James, "Is Life Worth Living?" in *Human Immortality and the Will to Believe and Other Essays in Popular Philosophy* (New York: Dover, 1956).

Selected Bibliography

Alioto, Anthony M. *A History of Western Science*. Englewood Cliffs, N.J.: Prentice-Hall (1993).

Aristotle. *De Anima* (On the soul). Trans. Hugh Lawson-Tancred. London: Penguin (1986).

_____. *Nicomachean Ethics*. Trans. David Ross. New York: Oxford University Press (1992).

Augustine. *City of God*. Trans. Marcus Dods. Edinburgh: T. & T. Clark (1892).

Ayer, A. J. *Language, Truth and Logic*. New York: Dover (1952).

Ayer, A. J., ed. *Logical Positivism*. New York: Free Press (1959).

Badham, Paul. *Christian Beliefs About Life After Death*. London: Macmillan (1976).

Barrett, William. *Irrational Man*. New York: Doubleday (1958).

_____. *The Death of the Soul*. New York: Doubleday (1986).

Bhagavad-Gita. Trans. Franklin Edgerton. Cambridge, Mass.: Harvard University Press (1981).

Brenner, Charles. *An Elementary Textbook of Psychoanalysis*. New York: Anchor (1974).

Broad, C. D. *The Mind and Its Place in Nature*. New York: Harcourt, Brace (1925).

Brown, Stuart C., ed. *Reason and Religion*. Ithaca: Cornell University Press (1977).

Burnet, J. *Early Greek Philosophy*. London: Black (1920).

Burtt, Edwin. *The Metaphysical Foundations of Modern Science*. New York: Humanities Press (1951).

Campbell, Keith. *Body and Mind*. Notre Dame: University of Notre Dame Press (1970).

Comte, August. *Introduction to Positive Philosophy*. Trans. Frederick Ferre. Indianapolis: Hackett (1988).

Dodds, E. R. *The Greeks and the Irrational*. Berkeley: University of California Press (1951).

Driesch, Hans. *The History and Theory of Vitalism*. Trans. C. K. Ogden. London: Macmillan (1914).

Edward, Paul, and Pap, Arthur, eds. *A Modern Introduction to Philosophy*. New York: Free Press (1973).

Ewing, A. C. *The Fundamental Questions of Philosophy*. New York: Macmillan (1953).

Feinberg, Joel, ed. *Reason and Responsibility*. Belmont, Calif.: Wadsworth (1978).

Flew, Antony, ed. *Body, Mind and Death*. New York: Macmillan (1969).

Frankl, Viktor. *The Doctor and the Soul: From Psychotherapy to Logotherapy*. New York: Alfred A. Knopf (1965).

Freud, Sigmund. *The Future of an Illusion*. New York: W. W. Norton (1989).

Friedrick, Carl J., ed. *The Philosophy of Kant*. New York: Modern Library (1993).

Gilligan, Carol. *In a Different Voice*. Cambridge, Mass.: Harvard University Press (1993).

Guthrie, W. K. C. *A History of Greek Philosophy*. London: Cambridge University Press (1969). 6 vols.

Haeckel, Ernst. *The Riddle of the Universe*. New York: Harper (1900).

Hamilton, Edith, and Cairns, Huntington, eds. *The Collected Dialogues of Plato*. Princeton, N.J.: Princeton University Press (1973).

Harrison, G. B., ed. *A Book of English Poetry*. London: Penguin Books (1950).

Hartshorne, Charles. *The Logic of Perfection*. La Salle, Ill.: Open Court (1962).

Hick, John. *Evil and the God of Love*. New York: Harper and Row (1966).

_____. *God Has Many Names*. Philadelphia: Westminster Press (1982).

_____. *Essays in Religious Pluralism*. New York: St. Martin's (1985).

_____. *Death and Eternal Life*. Louisville: Westminster/John Knox (1994).

Hick, John, ed. *Classical and Contemporary Readings in the Philosophy of Religion*. Englewood Cliffs, N.J.: Prentice-Hall (1964).

_____. *The Existence of God*. New York: Macmillan (1964).

Hinnells, John R., ed. *A Handbook of Living Religions*. Middlesex, UK: Penguin (1991).

Homer. *The Iliad*. Trans. Richard Lattimore. Chicago: University of Chicago Press (1951).

_____. *The Odyssey*. Trans. Richard Lattimore. New York: Harper Perennial (1991).

Hook, Sydney, ed. *Determinism and Free Will in the Age of Modern Science*. Washington Square: New York University Press (1965).

Hume, David. *A Treatise of Human Nature*. L. A. Selby-Bigge, ed. Oxford: Clarendon Press (1951).

Irwin, Terence. *Classical Thought*. Oxford: Oxford University Press (1988).

James, William. *Human Immortality and the Will to Believe and Other Essays in Popular Philosophy*. New York: Dover (1956).

_____. *The Varieties of Religious Experience*. New York: Penguin (1982).

Jastrow, Robert. *God and the Astronomers*. New York: Reader's Library (1978).

Jones, W. T. *A History of Western Philosophy*. Fort Worth: Harcourt Brace Jovanovich (1980). 5 vols.

Julian of Norwich. *Revelations of Divine Love*. London: Burns and Oates (1961).

Kant, Immanuel. *Critique of Practical Reason*. Trans. T. K. Abbott. Amherst, N.Y.: Prometheus Books (1996).

_____. *Critique of Pure Reason*. Trans. Norman Kemp Smith. New York: St. Martin's Press (1965).

Kaufmann, Walter. *Existentialism from Dostoevsky to Sartre*. New York: New American Library (1975).

Klemke, E. D., ed. *The Meaning of Life*. New York: Oxford University Press (1981).

Lewis, C. S. *The Abolition of Man*. New York: Macmillan (1955).

Lewis, Hywel. *The Self and Immortality*. New York: Seabury Press (1973).

_____. *The Elusive Self*. Philadelphia: Westminster Press (1982).

Lucretius. *On the Nature of Things*. Trans. C. Bailey. Oxford: Clarendon Press (1924).

MacIntyre, Alasdair. *A Short History of Ethics*. New York: Macmillan (1966).

Minton, Arthur J., and Shipka, Thomas A., eds. *Philosophy: Paradox and Discovery*. New York: McGraw-Hill (1982).

Mitchell, Basil, ed. *Faith and Logic*. London: Allen and Unwin (1957).

Moore, G. E. *Philosophical Papers*. New York: Collier (1966).

Muggeridge, Malcolm. *Something Beautiful for God*. San Francisco: Harper and Row (1971).

Otto, Rudolph. *The Idea of the Holy*. Trans. John W. Harvey. Oxford: Oxford University Press (1958).

Peale, Norman Vincent. *The Power of Positive Thinking*. New York: Prentice-Hall (1952).

Pegis, Anton C., ed. *Introduction to St. Thomas Aquinas*. Toronto: Random House (1948).

Peterfreund, Sheldon, and Denise, Theodore, eds. *Great Traditions in Ethics*. Belmont, Calif.: Wadsworth (1992).

Phillips, D. Z. *Death and Immortality*. New York: St. Martin's (1970).

Popper, Karl. *The Open Universe: An Argument for Indeterminism*. Totowa, N.J.: Rowman and Littlefield (1982).

Prabhavananda, Swami. *The Spiritual Heritage of India*. Hollywood: Vedanta Press (1979).

Rachels, James. *The Elements of Moral Philosophy*. New York: McGraw-Hill (1993).

Radhakrishnan, S., ed. *The Principal Upanishads*. London: Allen and Unwin (1953).

Rashdall, Hastings. *The Theory of Good and Evil*. Oxford: Oxford University Press (1907). 2 vols.

Richter, Peyton, and Fogg, Walter, eds. *Philosophy Looks to the Future*. Prospect Heights, Ill.: Waveland Press (1978).

Ring, Merrill. *Beginning with the Pre-Socratics*. Mt. View, Calif.: Mayfield (1987).

Rohr, Janelle, ed. *Science and Religion—Opposing Viewpoints*. San Diego: Greenhaven Press (1988).

Russell, Bertrand. *Why I Am Not a Christian*. New York: Simon and Schuster (1957).

_____. *Religion and Science*. New York: Oxford University Press (1961).

Ryle, Gilbert. *The Concept of Mind*. New York: Barnes and Noble (1949).

Sanders, Steven, and Cheney, David R., eds. *The Meaning of Life*. Englewood Cliffs, N.J.: Prentice-Hall (1980).

Searle, John. *Minds, Brains and Science*. Cambridge, Mass.: Harvard University Press (1984).

Smith, Huston. *The World's Religions*. San Francisco: HarperCollins (1991).

Stace, W. T. *Religion and the Modern Mind*. Philadelphia: Lippincott (1960).

Sutherland, Alexander. *The Origin and Growth of the Moral Instinct*. London: Longmans, Green (1898). 2 vols.

Swinburne, Richard. *The Existence of God*. New York: Oxford University Press (1979).

Tarnas, Richard. *The Passion of the Western Mind*. New York: Ballantine (1991).

Temple, William. *Nature, Man and God*. London: Macmillan (1934).

Tilghman, B. R. *An Introduction to the Philosophy of Religion*. Cambridge, Mass.: Blackwell (1994).

Tolstoy, Leo. *My Confession*. Trans. Leo Wiener. London: J. M. Dent and Sons (1905).

Unamuno, Miguel de. *The Tragic Sense of Life*. Trans. J. E. Crawford Flitch. New York: Dover Publications (1954).

Van Inwagen, Peter. *Metaphysics*. Boulder, Colo.: Westview Press (1993).

Von Wright, G. H. *Wittgenstein*. Minneapolis: University of Minnesota Press (1966).

Walsh, W. H. *Kant's Criticism of Metaphysics*. Chicago: University of Chicago Press (1975).

Waley, Arthur. *The Way and Its Power*. New York: Grove Weidenfeld (1958).

Warner, Richard, and Szubka, Tadeusz, eds. *The Mind-Body Problem*. Cambridge, Mass.: Basil Blackwell (1994).

Weisskopf, Victor. *Knowledge and Wonder*. Cambridge, Mass.: MIT Press (1979).

Woods, Richard, ed. *Understanding Mysticism*. New York: Image Books (1980).

About the Book and Author

There are certain questions that lie at the heart of our existence: Who are we? What is this life in which we find ourselves engaged? Is "reality" what we see before our eyes, or is it something more and beyond? Philosophers have, in response to these questions, tended to favor one of two antithetical approaches: an understanding of the material world through the lens of science or a model based on the existence of a spiritual realm, a world beyond the senses.

Although Kelly Nicholson does not claim to disprove the materialist account of reality, he argues that our allegiance to certain common-sense assumptions about ourselves and the world—that, for example, we are rational and purposive creatures; that some courses of action are truly better than others; that human experience, on the whole, is basically trustworthy—involves us implicitly in a worldview that is spiritual and nonmaterialistic in its basis.

Nicholson's book is a philosophically astute exploration into the nature of human existence. In presenting the topic, he examines at length issues in ethics, philosophy of the mind, metaphysics, and the philosophy of religion. He introduces students of philosophy and religion to such concepts as mind-body dualism, moral relativism, logical positivism, naturalism, and reductionism as well as to the key thinkers in these debates, from the ancient Greek philosophers to Hume, Ayer, Searle, and Swinburne.

Kelly Nicholson has taught extensively over the past twenty years in the United States as well as in China and the Slovak Republic.

Index